THE *feel* OF SILENCE

IN THE SERIES

Health, Society, and Policy

EDITED BY
Sheryl Ruzek and Irving Kenneth Zola

THE *feel* OF SILENCE

Bonnie Poitras Tucker

TEMPLE UNIVERSITY PRESS

Philadelphia

Temple University Press, Philadelphia 19122
Copyright © 1995 by Bonnie Poitras Tucker, except the Foreword, which is
© Temple University
All rights reserved
Published 1995
Printed in the United States of America

⊗ The paper used in this book meets the requirements of the American National
Standard for Information Sciences—Permanence of Paper for Printed Library
Materials, ANSI Z39.48-1984

Text design by Tracy Baldwin

Library of Congress Cataloging-in-Publication Data

Tucker, Bonnie P., 1939–
    The feel of silence / Bonnie Poitras Tucker : foreword by Fred Hafferty.
        p.   cm.—(Health, society, and policy)
    ISBN 1-56639-351-5 (alk. paper).—ISBN 1-56639-352-3 (pbk.)
    1. Tucker, Bonnie P., 1939–   .   2. Deaf lawyers—United States—
Biography.   I. Title.   II. Series.
KF373.T83A3   1995
340'.092—dc20
    [B]   95-7684

To my family, with love: my parents, Thelma and James Poitras; my children, Kevin, Ronale, and Scott; my daughter-in-law, Heidi; my grandchildren, Aubreigh, Amber, Austin, and Ashlyn; my brothers, Jim and Richard; my sister-in-law, Joyce. You make it all worthwhile.

Thanks to the many friends who read portions of this book and offered advice and encouragement. Special thanks to Don McGee, Vicki Lewis, Rosanne Keller, Maxine Turnbull, and Henry Kisor. And thanks to Melanie Bishop for her input.

There are those among us who live in rooms
of experience that you and I can never enter.
—JOHN STEINBECK

Contents

The second life

The third life

foreword FRED HAFFERTY

All deaf people are not alike, and all deaf experience is not similar. Some deaf people choose to live and interact primarily with and among other deaf people. Others, like Bonnie Tucker, choose to live predominantly within the hearing society. Still others elect to navigate across both worlds. As is quite evident in the case of 1995's Miss America, Heather Whitestone, the choices made, particularly in terms of a preferred mode of communication (oralism versus sign), can be very controversial.

It is not easy to identify a person who is deaf. There is no wheelchair or white cane to announce their presence. Modern technology has banished the "hearing horn" or even the need to wear a large amplifier and microphone on one's chest (assuming that there is enough residual hearing to warrant amplification). The miracles of miniaturization have made it possible to place a complete hearing aid within the ear canal itself, making it that much more difficult to casually notice when someone is "wired for sound."

At the same time, this very invisibility, while minimizing stigma based on appearance, generates other problems and barriers. Our daily routines, including communicating with others, are governed by a large set of taken-for-granted assumptions about the way things are (or should be). When we speak to someone, we assume that we will be both heard (acknowledged) and understood. Social interaction would grind to a halt were this not the case.

For the most part we are unaware of these expectations—until they are violated. Thus, when we speak or call out to someone and they respond inappropriately or fail to answer altogether, a common reaction on the part of the speaker is to feel slighted or perhaps even embarrassed. Concurrently we might think the other person is boorish, rude, or even stuck-up. The possibility that what we said simply did not exist for the other person usually is not a first-order interpretation. Social convention dictates that apologies are due more *to* the speaker ("Oh, I'm sorry. I didn't hear you") than *from* the speaker ("Please forgive me. I didn't speak loudly enough").

In short, our inconvenience or loss of face is more important than their absence of hearing.

I share both differences and similarities with Bonnie Tucker. I am not totally deaf, I attended public schools without too many incidents (I think), and I never have desired to be a lawyer. On the other hand, I have found myself on the receiving end of some of the same negative stereotypes and expectations. Like Bonnie, I do not feel that I have a "problem," but I am aware of how hard it is at times for others to communicate with me. I know (mostly by conjecture) that I "ignore" (and thus offend) people regularly. I also know that I cannot go through life looking over my shoulder figuratively—or even literally—in an effort to minimize the possibility of such occurrences in the future. Nonetheless, I also know I will be the one who will experience another level of loss as you decide not to talk to me again, not to be my friend, or not to employ me because you find me rude or distant.

In spite of the fact that most hearing-impaired people share in the experience of marginalization, important differences exist among them. Some prefer the label "deaf," others "Deaf," and still others "hearing impaired" or "hard-of-hearing." To outsiders, this plethora of preferences may appear bewildering or even silly. Matters become more complicated still when labels considered patently offensive (e.g., "cripple") come into vogue among insiders who promote the politics of confrontation.

Even the factors that underscore these distinctions may not be obvious. The rather commonsensical expectation that differences in labels simply reflect one's degree of audiological loss (e.g., "deaf" for total hearing loss, "hearing impaired" for serious loss, and "hard-of-hearing" for lesser degrees of loss) turns out not to be the case. Instead, labels reflect matters of social identity and identification. For example, although the label "Deaf" has been claimed by those who *may* be totally (audiologically) deaf, the more important bond comes from the sharing of a common language— American Sign Language (ASL)—along with common values and life experiences. Another difference that divides the deaf community is whether an individual was born deaf or became deaf after normal language development had taken place. In these ways, even profoundly deaf individuals might be considered "deaf" or "hard of hearing" but not "Deaf" by those who identify themselves as members of the Deaf community. ASL has come to reflect (and legitimize) these distinctions with different signs for "deaf," "Deaf," and "hearing impaired." There is even an insulting sign that is used among deaf insiders to indicate a person who is audiologically deaf but who lacks Deaf pride or a Deaf identity. Deaf insiders circumvent the tedious task of having to repeatedly finger spell the individual letters of their own name by having a single "deafsign," a name that by custom cannot be assumed but rather must be given by another Deaf person. In short, the Deaf community, like any other community, is internally stratified, with its own set of norms, customs, and stereotypes, all buttressed by a common language.

Bonnie Tucker has chosen not to be a part of this Deaf community. Her story, therefore, is written from a different perspective. She does not purport to speak for all deaf people. Similarly, the myriad identities, differences, and alliances between and among deaf people preclude me or any one person from speaking for this book or attempting to interpret its multitude of wonderfully textured messages. I can tell you that reading this book made me smile, cry, empathize, and object. I suspect that it will touch readers across a similar range of emotions. At the same time, I am a sociologist, and it would be almost impossible for me not to draw the reader's attention to some of the broader social issues embedded in these pages.

One such issue involves the role of sign language in contrast to oralism in educating deaf children. This controversy is far from new, but no less volatile for its extensive history. During most of the 1800s, the preferred instructional approach was the gesture-based and hand-oriented language of sign, or what became known in this country as ASL. In the late 1800s and early 1900s this practice was challenged by no less famous a person than Alexander Graham Bell. Bell favored teaching based on the written, spoken, and lip-read word. In a series of debates and confrontations, Bell was challenged by Laurent Clerc and later Edward Gallaudet in a struggle over the future of a deaf community and culture in this country.

This conflict is worth capsulizing because it illustrates some of the more fundamental ways that deafness and deaf people are thought about in the United States, both historically and today. For Bell and his supporters, deafness was a tragedy and a privation. Their solution was to normalize the deaf, by "correcting God's blunders" and "improving on nature" through technology (hearing aids and telephones) and genetic engineering. They supported legislation restricting marriage among the "socially unfit" and called for genetic counseling before marriage to dissuade deaf people from having children. They also sought to banish sign language, to disperse the deaf, and to discourage publishing, organizing, and even socializing among the deaf. Bell campaigned to have deaf children educated exclusively in the majority language. He feared that a "deaf variety of the human race" was being created. For Bell, deafness was a physical handicap. It could not be cured, but it could be alleviated by teaching deaf people to speak and lipread and thus to pass as hearing.

In contrast, Laurent Clerc, the major figure in the history of sign and deaf education in the United States, saw deafness as a social condition. For Clerc, the basic problem for the deaf was not their impairment but the hearing majority. Deafness was something that could be alleviated only when the hearing majority came to accept deaf culture and language. For Clerc the goal of education was personal fulfillment; for Bell it was integration with the hearing majority. Clerc saw the deaf as representing one aspect of the "natural range" of human nature; Bell saw the deaf as representing deviance. Where Clerc found strength in human variety, Bell found weakness and danger.

Current debates over sign versus oralism or mainstreaming versus separate educational environments appear more moderate. Calls for sterilization or legislatively based steps to discourage marriages among deaf people are largely absent. Nonetheless, oralists continue to argue strongly that deaf children need to be given the maximum opportunity to develop their oral skills so that they can integrate into the larger hearing society as much as they choose to do so as adults. For some this means the banning of sign, since learning ASL is viewed as interfering with learning to speak. With expanding technology such as cochlear implants and improved hearing aids, oralists advocate training deaf children to use their residual hearing to the maximum extent possible.

Members of the Deaf culture are less enamored of the goal of maximum integration and the pursuit of improved technologies. They prefer that all deaf children be taught ASL as a first language with English appearing in a supportive or backup role. Some within Deaf culture argue that even this is too assimilative and that all face-to-face communication should be visual, with English relegated to reading and writing. The intent is for deaf children to take pride in their deafness and to be full members of the Deaf culture. Why struggle with speech, they ask, when the best that most deaf people can hope for is to be inferior hearing people? Why be outcasts in hearing society when we can live happily in our own community? they ask.

Members of the Deaf culture view calls for assimilation and inclusiveness by health professionals or the hearing majority with suspicion and reservations, sometimes with good reason. They view the broader hearing society, not necessarily as sinister, but as self-servingly naive. Public opinion polls may record a tolerant, supportive, and inclusive public, but social action records the presence of a profound ambivalence about disability issues and persons with disability on the part the nondisabled majority.

The Americans with Disabilities Act may have been passed with expectations of inclusiveness and equality but one does not need to tunnel too deeply into how matters of disability are depicted in the media to understand that this society prefers images of disability that minimize the presence of deficiencies while maximizing the notions of compensation and achievement. As a society, we are fascinated with depictions of what Irving Kenneth Zola has termed the "supercrip." Newspapers, magazines, and television are rife with stories about individuals who have "triumphed over adversity," who "have proven their doctors wrong," who are "an in-spiration to us all," and who have "risen above" *their* "limitations" (note the locus of disabilities here). We shower accolades on those who strive to compete on *our* playing field. At the same time we murmur prayers of grat-itude that we have been spared the call to perform on theirs.

The line between inspiration and expectation is both narrow and treacherous. News coverage of the recent death of Wilma Rudolph re-minded us not only of her Olympic triumphs but also of how she "over-came" polio and how, as a child, her parents refused to treat her as "handi-capped." The intent of these reports may have been inspirational, but other messages were conveyed as well. However laudatory the headlines, readers encounter depictions of "defects" that reside within individuals and not within the surrounding physical or social environment. In this way, the pub-lic is socialized to think of people as disabled rather than of settings or cir-cumstances as disabling. In turn, we uncritically assume that the most ap-propriate—and admirable—response to these "tragedies" is implemented at the personal-individual rather than the societal level. We cheer when the lame run marathons, marvel when a deaf person becomes a professional mu-sician, and gasp with possessive pride when a blind person becomes a noted photographer (all real examples). Meanwhile, our praises along with our pleasures radiate into the disability community accompanied by the mes-sage that we expect them to rival these accomplishments . . . or at least to attempt to do so. In short, we ask those we find threatening to amaze and reassure us by demonstrating how little their handicap matters and there-fore how normal they can appear to themselves—and to us.

But what about those who fail to make the grade, those who are un-able to "rise above" *their* "plight"? Both we—and they—are left with the lurking (if distasteful) suspicion that what they lack is more a matter of per-sonal resolve, will power, or commitment than of physical "shortcomings." People like Marlee Matlin (deaf Oscar winner for *Children of a Lesser God*) and the recent Miss America Heather Whitestone appear to travel com-fortably in the public eye. Their deafness hasn't kept them from achiev-ing great things. So what *is* the problem? Perhaps most deaf people just don't try hard enough? If all of this feels too insensitive, then we can redi-rect our misgivings and ambivalence onto the parents who "probably" failed to push the child hard enough, who treated the child as if he or she were handicapped, or who neglected to insist that the child do everything normal kids do, all acts and actions allegedly scorned by the parents of our transcendent cultural icons. In short, we anoint with praise those who please us while showering with suspicion and blame those who menace our security.

All of this is a rather protracted way of asking readers to recognize this remarkable autobiography for what it is . . . and what it is not. This is a story of an exceptional person, of unusual achievements, of agonizing defeats, and of a buoyant spirit. It is a story of personal insights, deep convictions, and an ongoing hope for the future. It is a story about love, forgiveness, family stress, and family commitment. It is not a prescription for success nor does the author intend her story to be read as such.

Instead, read it to laugh, read it to cry, but most of all read it to think. As with all good books, there is much more here than meets the ear.

THE *feel* OF
SILENCE

Please, what do you hear? They say the ocean soars and roars. What does it sound like to soar and roar? They say that bacon sizzles while popcorn pops. Are those sounds the same, yet of different lengths? When bacon sizzles, does it make a series of tiny pops—pop, pop, pop? What does a pop sound like? What does it mean when someone says, "I hear the water boiling on the stove"? How can tiny bubbles make noise?

They tell me that when you hit a tennis ball properly, it "sounds right." And when you don't turn properly on your skis, the scraping noise (whatever that is) that the skis make on the hard-packed snow or ice "sounds wrong." What are they talking about, really?

And tell me about music. They say that country sounds different from western, and mellow sounds different from elevator or classical. And rock sounds different from everything else. It's all so confusing. Can you explain it in words I can understand, without using words like *ripple* and *rumble* and *easy listening?* Because I, who cannot hear, don't understand *ripple* and *rumble* and *easy listening.*

I spin the roll of toilet paper—hard—and the paper unwinds to the floor. Does it make a noise as it unfurls? As it hits the floor? When ice cream melts and drips on my sleeve does it make a noise? Or will it only make a noise if it drips onto a hard surface, like the ground, rather than on my soft sleeve? When I squeeze the toothpaste tube, does it make a noise? What if the tube is empty when I squeeze? They tell me that escaping air makes a sound. How? When?

When I accidentally scraped my fingernail across the blackboard as I wrote on the board during my law school class, the students protested. The sound must have been very faint. How could they have possibly heard it from so far away?

Tell me, in words that have meaning to me, what you hear. But first, I'll tell you about the feel of silence.

introduction

Describe yourself—go ahead, don't be shy. Tell me who and what you are. Did you say you were a mother, a father, a businessperson, a secretary, a lawyer, a teacher, a doctor, a homemaker? Did you identify your race, your sex, your age, the color of your hair? I'll bet your description didn't include the word *hearing*. Why should it? Hearing, for you, is a given.

I, however, cannot accurately describe myself without using the word *deaf*. Because deafness means so much more than the simple inability to hear. A deaf person is defined by his or her deafness. I am a mother, a grandmother, a lawyer, a law professor, a skier, a tennis player, a lover of books and the outdoors, and deaf. This book is about the last part—about being deaf.

When all is said and done, and however much I hate it, my deafness is not a simple state of being. It's a state of feeling, of thinking, of experiencing that is unknown to one who is not deaf. This story is about those thoughts, feelings, and experiences that are unique to a deaf person; this is a story about what for you, if you are hearing, may have been unfathomable.

This book is intended to give you a peek through the doors of my experience.

I speak of deafness from the perspective of a profoundly deaf person, unable to wear hearing aids, who has always lived in the larger, hearing, world. My goal has been to follow what I sometimes jokingly refer to as the Seven Commandments for myself as a deaf person (I trust God will forgive my plagiarisms):

O N E: Don't create false images. Deafness should be kept in perspective—certainly a major part of my life, but not the be-all and end-all of my existence. The image I create of myself will be the image others see. I want to be viewed as a person who happens to be deaf, rather than as a deaf person. At the same time, however, I'd like you to understand my deafness.

T w o: Take part in the world at large—don't unnecessarily eliminate options. Ninety-nine percent of the world's population can hear and speak. I don't want to cut myself off from those people and limit myself to living among a much smaller community of deaf people. I want to live my life to the fullest in the midst of *all* kinds of people.

T h r e e: Accept responsibility for the ramifications of deafness. I'm the first to agree with those who say it's not my fault I'm deaf, or it's not fair to expect you to work harder or do more just because I am deaf. Those statements are true. It's not my fault and it's not fair. But it's not anyone else's fault I'm deaf, either. So there's a limit to how much I can expect others to do for me because I'm deaf. While I should request—even demand—*reasonable* accommodations, I cannot request or expect *excessive* accommodations, because the real world simply doesn't work that way. The initial responsibility, to do all I can do to overcome the physical limitations posed by the inability to hear, is mine.

F o u r: Have patience. As this story will show, life is one never-ending frustration for someone who is deaf. Deaf people have two choices. We can work ourselves into a constant frenzy of impatience, or we can learn to be patient. Unfortunately I haven't learned yet. But I keep trying.

F i v e: View deafness with a sense of humor. The trick is to laugh at the constant annoyances rather than let them bog me down. I do better at this one.

S i x: Maximize all possible communication skills. I'm lucky. I was able to learn to speak very well, and I'm an expert lip-reader. Not all deaf people are so lucky, particularly others who have been unable to wear hearing aids (although modern technology has made it possible for most deaf children today to learn to use their residual hearing and to learn to speak—albeit with differing degrees of clarity). Whatever our communication abilities are, however, we deaf people can never take them for granted. I have to constantly think about my communication skills. As a lawyer I've learned that my biggest communication problems arise when I don't plan in advance what I can and should do to ensure that communication will be effective in particular settings. The trick lies in the planning.

S e v e n: Know when to cry uncle. All of us have to decide, in every given situation, what our limit is. Deafness often makes the decision about when to cry uncle more complex. I don't want to give in to my deafness too soon, but at the same time I don't want to push beyond my limits. I'm not always sure what my limits are! I struggle to define them, and to accept myself once I've made the choice to scream . . . Enough.

These are pretty simple commandments, actually. But they are fraught with controversy today, when "Deaf culture" advocates are becoming so vocal.

"Deaf is dandy," proclaim the leaders of the Deaf subculture in vivid, expressive sign language. Members of this growing subculture, who capitalize the word *Deaf* to show their affiliation with this unique segment of our society (and to distinguish themselves from those deaf people, like myself, who have chosen to assimilate into the larger hearing society), seek to popularize this catchy slogan in much the same manner that black people popularized the slogan "Black is beautiful."

What does it mean to say that "Deaf is dandy"? According to the leaders of the National Association of the Deaf (NAD), it means being glad that one is unable to hear or that one's children are unable to hear; it means feeling fortunate to be one of a privileged few. Because "Deaf is dandy," doctors should not advocate speech and audiological training for deaf babies or children; because "Deaf is dandy," doctors and parents should not try to "fix" deaf children. Instead, doctors and parents should recognize deaf children as simply being "visually oriented" and should expend their energies in ensuring that these special children are Deaf. Indeed, some prominent members of the Deaf subculture have described the growing practice of placing cochlear implants in profoundly deaf children as "assault by zapping the auditory nerve tissue, electrically," and have analogized cochlear implants to the Iraqi invasion of Kuwait and to the beating of a blind man to induce him to see stars.*

Most "Deaf is dandy" followers strongly oppose the use of speech by deaf persons, believing instead that deaf people should speak in their "natural" language of signs. These people, for example, strongly object that Marlee Matlin, the deaf actress on the TV show *Reasonable Doubts*, sometimes speaks on the show. More recently some of them objected when Miss America 1995, who is deaf, spoke rather than signed during the Miss America pageant.

Adhering to their strong belief that "Deaf is dandy," some Deaf expectant parents have told me wistfully, but very sincerely, "We pray every night that our baby will be Deaf." Still other believers that "Deaf is dandy" advocate taking deaf babies from the homes of their hearing parents, who are not immersed in the Deaf subculture, and requiring such children to be raised by Deaf families.

I am viewed as a traitor to my heritage because I would gladly grab any opportunity to fix my deafness. Deaf people lack one of the five critical senses, plain and simple. That lack is something to be repaired, to the ex-

---

NAD Broadcaster, vol. 13, no. 1 (January 1991), p. 3.

tent that reparation is possible. Thus, deaf is *not* dandy, and spelling *Deaf* with a capital D doesn't change anything.

But that is not to say that I am opposed to sign language. I have not learned to sign for a very practical reason—I have no one to sign with. My life is spent primarily among hearing people who do not know how to sign. When I am with deaf people who sign I make a valiant attempt to learn some signs. Unfortunately, by the time I have the opportunity to sign again I've forgotten the signs I previously learned. Needless to say, my sign language skills have hardly progressed. For some deaf people, however, sign language is the preferred—and very viable—means of communication. It's the word *preferred* that is significant.

Free choice is the paramount consideration. Every deaf person should have the right to choose what mode of communication to use. To exercise that right, however, a real choice must be possible. A deaf person who has never been taught to speak, but only to sign, has no choice about how to communicate. Sign language is the only possibility, and thus it is not an option but a necessity. I believe strongly in the need to teach deaf children to speak, so that ultimately they can make this very important choice for themselves. (It is universally recognized that in most cases it is not possible to teach a deaf person to talk later in life—speech must be acquired during childhood.) If a deaf teenager or adult later chooses to live within a Deaf community and reject speech as the primary mode of communication, however, that choice must be respected. Each of us, after all, has the right to choose our own destiny.

Nor am I so unreasonable, or unrealistic, as to expect all deaf people to be superachievers. One of the legitimate complaints made today by people with disabilities is that society expects us to be supermen or superwomen, *supercrips* (derived from *supercripples*). People with disabilities are tired of being told, "Look at Joe Smith; despite being a paraplegic he has climbed Mount Everest—you can do the same." Not everyone, whether disabled or not, wants to climb Mount Everest or has the ability to do so.

People who are deaf, like all people, have the right to live ordinary lives in an ordinary fashion without having to be supercrips. I am frequently asked to speak to parents of deaf children about my experiences as an attorney and law professor who is also deaf—to let them see what is possible for their deaf children. I am always uncomfortable in that role and make sure to begin and end my talks with a caveat: "Your child doesn't have to be a supercrip to be successful and happy."

I guess maybe this book is written in a supercrip mode, since, by choice, I've tended to be an overachiever. But my portrayal of deafness is real, and the book focuses on real problems and frustrations. In a nutshell, deafness ain't fun. But for many of us it's there—a fact—something to cope with. Each of us has to choose how best to cope. My way of coping might not be your way, or someone else's way. But that's okay.

The first life

CHILD AND STUDENT

Chapter ONE

Two women are hanging out clothes on adjacent clotheslines. It is 1941, late fall in Massachusetts, and in the air there's still the promise of warmth. A little girl runs back and forth between the two walls of sheets and towels; she likes the bright white, the way the sun bounces off it, the damp coolness of the fabric. She presses it between her hands, to her face. She plants a corner of a towel in her mouth. The taste is cold and clean.

"Bonnie, stop that," her mother says. The women continue their conversation.

Bonnie holds her hands high, runs for one sheet flapping like a sail in the wind. She pushes through, feeling the cotton against her palms, then on her face, and as she reaches the world on the other side the damp sheet rushes over her head. She does this again, taking off her wool hat so she can feel the coolness in her dark curls.

"Bonnie, be still, please?" Her mother gives the neighbor an apologetic look.

"I have three," the neighbor says. "Teenagers now. I've been through it all."

Bonnie continues charging toward the sheets, running under them, hands held high.

"Bonnie Poitras! I said stop this instant!"

The neighbor watches as Bonnie runs under her laundry, this time grabbing a towel and tugging hard. The towel falls to the ground, and Bonnie with it. The ground at her face is cold and hard, but she doesn't cry.

"That's enough," her mother says. "You see what you've done? This was clean and now you've gotten it all dirty, and it's not even ours."

Bonnie looks surprised, like she has only just now been reminded that there was anyone else present. And what has made her mother so mad?

"It's no problem," the woman says.

"I'm sorry," the mother says. "It's the terrible twos. She just won't listen." She leans down, her face close to Bonnie's. "Now you sit down right here and just wait until I'm finished."

Bonnie sits.

"And put your hat back on, you'll catch a cold."

Bonnie does.

When Thelma Poitras hangs up the last sock, she gathers her basket and the remaining clothespins and calls out to her daughter, "Okay, honey, let's go inside."

Bonnie is looking at the clouds. One of them looks to her like a poodle she saw once. She likes the way you can see them move if you watch for a long time.

"Bonnie," her mother says louder. "Let's go in and make some lunch." The neighbor cannot help noticing the child's face—it registers nothing.

"Honestly," Thelma says, shaking her head. "She will not mind." She walks over to where Bonnie sits looking up at the sky.

"You know, I don't think she hears you," the neighbor says.

"What?"

"Her face. It looks like she's not hearing what you say."

Thelma pulls Bonnie up by the arm, brushes off the back of her coat.

"Oh she hears me alright, don't you, Bonnie?" Again, she squats in front of the child. "How old is Bonnie?" she says. Bonnie holds up her right hand, two fingers. "That's right. Two. Can you say terrible twos?" Her mother repeats this, smiling. "Terrible twos. Say it."

"Tewwible twos," Bonnie says.

The neighbor laughs. "She speaks well for her age," she says.

Inside, Thelma cannot stop thinking about what Helen said: I don't think she hears you. Bonnie's willfulness was intermittent; at times she could be very obedient. She puts Bonnie in the high chair, gives her a spoon, tapping it on the wooden tray. "Play the drum for me," she says. Bonnie smiles and beats with the spoon three times. Thelma stands back a ways, still facing her daughter. "Play the drums," she says. Bonnie hits her tray three times and laughs. Thelma goes to the stove, stirs the spaghetti sauce, and says loudly, "Play the drums for mommy." Her back is to the child. Bonnie doesn't play.

She repeats this. "Bonnie, honey, play the drums." She hears nothing, then turns to face her daughter, who waits patiently for lunch, the empty spoon planted firmly in her mouth.

Facing her, Thelma says, "Play the drums?" Bonnie pulls the spoon from her mouth, bangs it repeatedly on the tray, laughing. She does it again and again, while her mother watches. She can't understand why her mother won't smile.

THE FEEL OF SILENCE

Immediately upon discovering that I had a profound hearing loss, my parents decided that my only chance at normality lay in playing games. Word games.

Thus, rather than calling me deaf, which I clearly was (and am), they called me hard-of-hearing. Someone who was deaf was not permitted to attend a school for hearing children. Someone who was merely hard-of-hearing, however, did not have to be relegated to the segregated world of the deaf. (Back then schools rarely tested for hearing, and so my parents' word was accepted at face value.)

The word "deaf" was almost never spoken in my home. Nor, if I could avoid it, did I deliberately tell anyone that I was deaf until I was in my midthirties.

Some people call that denying my deafness. I prefer to call it facing reality, for I learned at an early age that to live freely and easily in this hearing world, to be treated as an equal, I had to fake hearing. Something happened to people who learned I was deaf before they really knew me. Equal treatment became impossible. I learned that whenever I was introduced as "Bonnie Poitras, who is deaf," the chances were ninety-nine out of a hundred that I would be treated like a retarded child.

Still, at some point in my adulthood I got tired of playing word games. Yes, I am deaf. And I make no bones about it. I am very profoundly deaf, and no medical procedure, no hearing aid, has yet been invented that can cure my profound deafness. But there is nothing wrong with my brain. I'm as smart as most of the people I know, and smarter than some. And there's nothing wrong with my vocal chords, either (contrary to the derogatory terms *deaf and dumb* and *deaf mute*).

Now, instead of demanding equality by faking an ability to hear, I simply demand equality, period.

Chapter
TWO

It's not so surprising that my mother didn't realize I was deaf until I was two. She and my father, Jim, were both nineteen when I was born. A striking couple, they were physical opposites. My very pretty mother had blond hair, blue eyes, and a fair complexion and was five feet one inches short. My handsome father had dark hair and eyes and a dark complexion and was six feet two inches tall. When I was born, they'd been married six days short of a year and were still happily playing house. My mother was ecstatic to be a mommy and played with me all day long, as if I were a little doll. For hours, she'd read to me, talk to me. Sitting on her lap, watching her lips, I followed most of what she said.

I was very lucky. Lipreading came easy to me, and I was a natural mimic. As far as I knew, everyone understood each other by watching each other's lips and faces. Instinctively I moved my lips the same way my mother moved hers. As I sat on her lap for literally hours each day I could *feel* her talk. And as I tried to repeat the words she said over and over and over to me, "Ma-ma," "Da-da," I made my chest and neck feel the same way hers felt. Just as she blew air when she moved her lips, I blew air when I moved my lips. Had my mother known I was deaf, she could not have worked more effectively or more diligently with me. And I suspect, although no one knows, that I had quite a bit of hearing as an infant and had memory of sound to fall back on. So when my parents learned that I was deaf, I had a reasonable vocabulary for a two year old. Certainly my two-year-old speech did not provide a clue to my deafness.

By the time I was three, my mother had so successfully taught me certain rhymes that I'd be called upon to perform for company. It must've been entertaining. So small, and so young, I'd recite sayings memorized by rote on command. The one I remember still went like this:

Multiplication is vexation.
Division is as bad.
The rule of three perplexes me.
And practice drives me mad.

I said it, they tell me, as perfectly as any hearing child could. And they all clapped for me, and how could I not like that? Early on I learned how to please.

I don't know how my parents reacted to the fact that their first child was deaf. But they had both faced adversity in their lives and had developed an inner strength. My mother's father died when she was a young girl. Her mother, unable to cope with her two youngest children while working full-time, sent my mother and her brother Jackie to live on a farm in a sort of quasi foster child arrangement, where they were expected to work hard for their keep. Between the ages of ten and thirteen my mother lived on that farm. She hated it. And she was desperately grateful when her sister Vivienne, ten years older and on her own, sent for her. At thirteen my mother returned to New York City to live with her sister and mother, eventually working almost full-time and attending high school part-time. To my mother, this was a life of bliss. She felt fortunate to be home.

My father's background was very different. Born in Montreal of French Canadian parents, my father was raised in a bilingual household. The middle of three children of a gentle, religious mother and a forceful, domineering father, he spent most of his school years in Jesuit boarding schools, where the regime was strict. His father was a financier of sorts, who at one point was a self-made millionaire. When my father was in his early teens his family moved to Roslyn, New York, where their estate included butler, chauffeur, and maids. A few years later my grandfather made some disastrous business decisions, and the family was forced to leave their home in Roslyn in the middle of the night to avoid creditors. Henceforth, my grandfather supported his family as an insurance salesman. Despite numerous grandiose schemes, he was never again able to do more than eke out a modest living. Thus, my father, like my mother, worked during his high school years to help the family. Making money, rather than spending it to attend college, was the necessary goal for both of my parents.

That their firstborn was deaf may have been viewed by my parents as just another of life's unpredictable whims. To this day, we've not discussed the matter. I do know that my father's brother, my uncle Maurice, concluded that my deafness must be purely psychological. Working toward becoming a navy pediatrician, he theorized that I would hear as soon as I got over whatever emotional trauma I was suffering. Some other family members agreed with Uncle Maurice's unlearned, but well-intentioned, opinion, and the matter was infrequently discussed in my parents' presence.

Whether they were more distressed about the fact that I was deaf or the possibility that I might have a psychological problem that they may have inadvertently caused is a question you'd have to ask my parents. But I remember, a few years later, my mother's distress when she was unable to respond to innuendos concerning the terrible shame that my psychological troubles hadn't straightened out. And I remember my own vague guilt, my ill-defined worries about what I had done—or was doing—to keep myself from hearing.

My parents didn't have long to focus on my deafness. In 1944 my father was drafted and sent to fight as a private in the Second World War. My parents were devastated. By then I had a baby brother, Jimmy; he was two and I was four. My father closed the small perfume business he'd started in Springfield, and my mother moved with Jimmy and me to New York City, where my father's parents lived, and where my parents would be able to see each other when my father was on leave from basic training.

It was almost impossible to find affordable housing in New York City at that time. My mother considered herself lucky when, after much finagling, she convinced two elderly sisters to rent her an apartment vacated by a recently deceased third sister, whose obituary my mother had read in the newspaper. No matter that the apartment—on 146th Street between Broadway and Riverside Drive—was in a shaky neighborhood. We were lucky to have a roof over our heads.

We rented the third floor of the brownstone belonging to these two old ladies. One was deaf, one was blind, and both were somewhat senile. Neither could remember from one day to the next that we lived in their house.

One evening a week my mother volunteered at the Red Cross, doing her part for the war effort. A young friend of hers babysat for Jimmy and me. Always at dusk, the little old ladies chained the door. I would watch from an upstairs window on those nights as my mother returned home, cold and shivering on the stoop. She rang and rang the bell. But it was a long time before Mother came upstairs. As she later told me, the scenario went like this: When Mother rang the bell, the sister who could hear would locate the sister who could see and together they'd go to the door.

"Yes?" The woman spoke to my mother through the chained gap. Neither of the women made a move to open the door.

"Hello," Mother said. "It's me, Thelma." She'd muster up a smile.

The sisters would ponder together quizzically and come to no conclusion.

"I'm sorry," the sighted sister said, as she'd begin to close the door, reducing the already narrow gap that connected our mother to us.

"Please, wait!" my mother said. "Don't you remember? I'm Thelma, the one you rented the third floor to. My children are upstairs with the sitter."

Again they'd seek from each other some confirmation of the obvious that neither was capable of.

"I don't know a Thelma," the hearing sister would say, "do you?" The deaf one would look confused.

"Sure you do," my mother would say. "I'm the tenant, Thelma . . . my kids are upstairs."

The women would shake their heads. "I'm sorry," they said. "Good-night, now." And they'd shut the door.

My mother would ring the bell again and wait for the whole thing to start over. Sometimes it took twenty minutes of persuasion before the old sisters let my mother in. This was a long winter. I don't think that apartment ever really felt like home to Mother.

In desperation, she searched for another apartment, but there was none to be had. Even if one had opened up, superintendents were getting hundreds of dollars in payoffs to rent apartments to people. Mother could barely keep up with expenses on my father's private's wages and her own small salary from working at my aunt Vivienne's shop. She'd never be able to accumulate the kind of money necessary to secure a better place. It seemed we were destined to remain strangers in our own home.

One afternoon in early spring the super from the apartment building across the street approached us. We were walking back from buying groceries. He'd witnessed for eight months Mother's pleading with the land-ladies to let us in.

"I have a place opening up," he said. "In a week."

Mother was speechless with hope.

"It's yours if you want it."

Though she was holding a bag of groceries in one arm, and Jimmy in the other, she seemed to lighten all of a sudden, to stand a little taller.

"You are wonderful," she said to the man, her face brighter than I'd seen it for a long time. This lightness was contagious, and I, too, felt sud-denly buoyant, began jumping up and down.

"Bonnie, honey, careful, you'll break the eggs," Mother said, and then she reached down and hugged me, and it was me and her and Jimmy all pressed together, and her perfume, and his baby smell, and except for hav-ing my father home again I imagine we felt about as whole as a family can.

THE FEEL OF SILENCE

"Hear the wind blow, dear; hear the wind blow," goes the popular refrain. I ponder this—it's incomprehensible. What is there to hear?

Some say that the wind sounds different when it comes from different directions. Can that be true? It boggles the mind.

I know that the rain makes noise: the heavier the rain the louder the noise. I know that because many people have told me so. But no one has told me when—or how—the rain makes noise. Is it the fall of rain itself that carries sound, or does the sound come only when the rain hits something, such as the ground or the windowpane?

Does snow also make noise? I always thought the expression "softly falling snow" referred to the tempo of the snowfall; a way, for example, of distinguishing between a blizzard and a light flurry. Am I mistaken? Does the word "softly" refer to the soft sound the snow makes as it hits the ground?

Do falling snowflakes sound one way when they land on a frozen snowbank, another way when they land on grass, and still another way when they land on a mound of soft, fluffy, powdery snow? How bizarre!

I understand how rustling paper makes noise. I can feel it. The paper is crisp; when I crunch it in my hands it crinkles. It seems logical that the crunching and crinkling would make a noise. What I don't understand is how rustling clothing makes a noise. Clothing is soft and pliant; when I crumple it, it moves easily—it doesn't fight back like paper does. No, it's not logical that the rustling of clothing makes noise. It's not logical at all. Yet they assure me it does. But what kind of noise? Surely rustling clothing doesn't sound like rustling paper. It must make a much more peaceful noise—sort of a silky sound.

On the TV game show *Jeopardy*, a recent answer was "Sounds like the noise spilled soup makes when it hits the floor." Before my mind could stop whirling, Alex announced that the correct question was "What is a splat?" My imagination fails me. Soup seems to me to be a quiet liquid. Is nothing quiet, then? "Listen," I hear one person say to another. "Listen carefully." I can only imagine.

I read the other day that in the movie *E.T.* the sound of E.T. walking was made by a woman squishing Jell-O in her hands. Now I know that everything we read in the newspapers isn't true, but isn't this going a bit far, even for a newspaper? Jell-O making a noise? Some things are too far-fetched to be believed. But then, they tell me people make noises with their armpits. They are joking, aren't they? Even I am not that gullible.

Chapter THREE

The railroad flat was to be our home for over five years, until I was ten and a half years old. (They called them railroad flats because one room led into the other. To get to the second bedroom one had to walk through the first bedroom, and so forth. Just like railroad cars.) I don't know how my mother survived those early years. A good chunk of Mother's small salary went to pay the nursery where Jimmy and I spent our weekdays. I hated that nursery. I don't know if the nursery owners knew I was deaf, but I vividly recall that much of the time I didn't understand what was happening as the people who worked there did not always take pains to face me when they spoke. I was too young to articulate those concerns to Mother, however, and in any event she had little choice. The nursery was essential.

Mother would get up at dawn, dress us, and lead us on the five-minute walk, twenty-minute subway ride, and ten-minute walk again that took us to the nursery. Then she would take another subway to work. Jimmy and I were given a breakfast of cereal and a good hot lunch at the nursery. For dinner, since we'd had our hot meals for lunch, Mother made inexpensive soup or peanut butter sandwiches. Every Saturday without fail we had macaroni and cheese, cheap, plentiful, and filling. Mother skipped breakfast and ate as little as possible for lunch, sometimes skipping it altogether in order to save subway fares for the trip to Grandma and Papa's on Sundays. Sunday dinner at their apartment was the best meal of the week.

Typical children, Jimmy and I were blissfully unconcerned about, and unaware of, our mother's daily financial and emotional struggles. On the weekends, and during summer evenings, we played for hours on the fire escape of our apartment, which I recall fondly. My two closest friends on our street were two little black girls, Fifi and Charlene, who never seemed to notice that I couldn't hear or to think me any different from themselves. Except for Tommy, the son of the janitor across the street (who lived in a basement full of pipes), and Peter Mamacos, who lived upstairs from us, Jimmy and I were the only white kids on the block. I don't think we ever noticed.

While I may have been oblivious to my mother's struggles, I was only too aware of my own. Since Mother had to work full time, she had less time to read and talk to me. Every evening, however, no matter how tired she was and no matter how much I objected, Mother worked with me on my speech. For at least an hour, sometimes more, we worked. Speech drills, recitation, getting the sounds just right.

Mother was a perfectionist, insisting, with threats of dire consequences (primarily loss of reading privileges, which I viewed as catastrophic), that I practice in front of a mirror the lesson we'd worked on each night. I hated it. But I worked hard, faithfully following her instructions, because when I was finished to her satisfaction, I was allowed to read. And it was when I was reading that I was happiest. As early as the age of four I loved books and spent as much time with them as possible. What stood between me and them were these lessons.

"Just do as I say," my mother said as she tried to teach me how to whisper. "Use your voice, just as you do when you talk, but make it softer, easier, breathier." I tried. I alternated between making no sound at all and making sounds that were too loud—not a whisper.

"A whisper comes from the throat, not the stomach," exclaimed my mother. "Try and speak from the throat."

"How does sound come from the throat?" I silently mouthed to myself. But I tried again, many times. I really wanted to whisper. Over and over I tried to force sounds from my throat instead of my stomach. My throat rebelled; it would not cooperate. "Are you *sure* no sound is coming out?" I wailed. "I'm sure," my mother responded.

Sometimes my brother, Jimmy, chimed in, more humiliating because he was younger. What could he possibly have to teach me?

"Just do as I do," he said, as he tried to teach me how to whistle. "Pucker your lips and blow." I puckered; I blew. No sound occurred. "Try again," Jimmy urged. "Force the sound through your lips." "What sound?" I muttered under my breath. But I tried again, many times. Over and over I puckered and blew. Over and over Jimmy demonstrated. To no avail.

Though I never mastered whistling or whispering, I am still reaping the dividends from most of those nightly trials. Later, Mother enrolled me in formal speech and lip-reading training at the New York League for the Hard of Hearing. Mrs. Ronei was my teacher; I loved her. Twice weekly, my mother and I took the long subway ride to and from the League, where Mother waited patiently for me to complete an hour of therapy. But it didn't take long at all for Mrs. Ronei to conclude that I was already as good a lip-reader as was possible. My mother's persistence, in conjunction with what seemed to be a real talent on my part, had paid off.

Another trial I remember from our railroad-flat days reaped no dividends, however. I will never forget the nightly blackouts we had in New

York City during the war. I lived in terror of the dark, in which I was both blind and deaf. During the first few weeks of the black outs, I spent a good portion of my days dreading the nights. How many more hours did I have to enjoy the daylight before I'd have to sit in darkness and silence? How would I know when the bombs started to fall if I couldn't even tell when someone was talking? Eventually we obtained blackout curtains, which enabled us to keep some lights on in the apartment during blackouts. I began to breathe freely again.

During that period of early childhood, if I thought about my deafness at all it was to puzzle over just how I was different. I found my deafness something of an enigma.

I was puzzled about other things as well. Two particular memories stand out. In the first:

I was five or six years old. We were riding in someone's car. I was sitting in the back seat with Mother and my brother, Jimmy. We were all talking and laughing. The day was ending, and the sun finally dropped, marking the onset of dusk. I could no longer see Mother's or Jimmy's lips. I stopped talking (as I usually do to this day in the dark). But—wait! I was leaning against Mother, and I could *feel* that she was still talking. "That's strange," I thought. "How can she talk in the dark?" I moved sideways to lean against Jimmy. Amazingly, I could feel him talking too! "What am I doing wrong?" I wondered. "How can they talk in the dark while I can't?"

But I didn't ask this question, afraid they'd find out how stupid I was.

In the other memory:

I watched my mother as she opened the door to our apartment and greeted a visitor. Several times I watched. Every time she opened that door someone was at the doorstep. Great! I loved visitors. So I tried. Reaching on tiptoes I opened the door. No one was there. I shut the door, puzzled. Later I tried again. Still no one there. Then, without warning, my mother would suddenly walk to the same door and open it. Always, someone was there. I was truly vexed. Did Mother have magic powers to make visitors appear?

I don't remember how old I was before I realized that my mother opened the door in response to a knock or a bell.

Being deaf led to a few special worries, as well. I remember Christmas, especially. Santa Claus was coming to town. Again. With snowy white beard and mustache that completely enwrapped his face (and covered his lips). Again. Oh how I envied the children who sat on Santa's lap and talked to him so freely. With fierce concentration I scrutinized Santa as he chatted with the kids in line ahead of our family. No, it was hopeless. I couldn't do it. Once more I'd have to sit on Santa's lap like a dunce, unresponsive to his invisible questions. How long would Santa continue to bring presents to such a stupid little girl? Would this be the year he'd give up on me?

My deafness was something to be hidden as much as possible. *Deaf* was a four-letter word better left unmentioned in polite company. I first "heard" the word spoken when I was about six years old. Mother had taken me to the doctor for some childhood ailment or other. During the visit Mother expressed her concern about something I wasn't doing that she thought I should be doing. While I didn't catch Mother's complaint, I did lip-read the doctor's reply. "After all, Mrs. Poitras," the doctor responded, "you must remember that Bonnie is deaf."

When we left his office I asked Mother. "The doctor said I'm deaf. What does that mean?"

"Oh," said Mother with a shrug, "don't pay any attention to that. You are just a little hard-of-hearing."

Mother made every effort to ensure that I had a normal childhood. On the weekends, and sometimes in the summertime in the evening, she would take Jimmy and me to Riverside Drive to play with the children of her friends whose neighborhood she thought was more respectable. To Mother's despair, I didn't get along well with those children. They simply didn't like me, no matter how hard I tried.

It never occurred to me (or apparently to any of the mothers) that one reason the children didn't like me was that I simply couldn't keep up with their games. More than half the time I didn't know what was going on. Like most children, they never stood still. Hard as I tried, my eyes could not keep pace with their mouths. I'd catch a word here and there, but I missed the gist. And my responses were often inappropriate. I remember particularly one game called war. I never did learn the rules of that game. I couldn't figure out who was the enemy, who was on whose side, or what we were supposed to be doing. Whatever it was, I never seemed to do it right.

Another game we played was kick the can. One person was "it," counting to sixty while everyone else scattered to find hiding places. The object was for the person who was "it" to guard a tin can placed in the middle of the wide sidewalk on Riverside Drive, while also trying to find all the other players. "I see Brian in the bushes by the fence!" If he was right, Brian would have to come forth and sit on the curb, a prisoner. "I see Stacey under the park bench!" And so on. Sometimes finding people involved leaving the can unattended while you went to look. It was during these times that a player who'd not been discovered yet could make the truly heroic move of running out and kicking the can, setting all the prisoners free. They'd hide again and the poor person who was "it" would start all over. The only way to avoid having all your prisoners freed was to hear the person running toward the can, to get there before that person, and to plant your foot firmly on the can. If you were there, not only could this player not be a hero, but he'd have to join the others on the curb, a lowly prisoner.

Kick the can was a game I learned to detest. Initially I didn't understand how the game worked. It was never explained; you were just supposed to get it. Then, once I finally gleaned the rules, understood the role of the can, I couldn't hear it being kicked. Nor could I hear the accompanying shouts of the kids, their hoots and laughter as they were freed.

So I did what I always did—I faked it. I could mimic the other kids to a point, running to hide when I saw them do that. I followed one girl to a row of bushes between two fences, but she shooed me away. It was more strategic to hide alone; no one wanted anyone else to make a noise or a move that might give them away. I'd played hide-and-seek before—this seemed to be what we were doing. I found myself a good spot.

Once hidden away, I was cut off from the game, from the world. But I was used to this feeling. Accustomed to spending a lot of time alone, I was content in my ditch at the foot of the river path. Dusk came and went. Mosquitoes ate at me hungrily at first, then less as darkness set in. Henry was "it"; I waited for him to come find me.

For all the time that passed, I thought I must be playing this game very well. Maybe I would even be the winner.

Loser was more accurate. The game had long since ended when my mother, not Henry, found me. She was worried sick. They'd all been looking for me; why didn't I ever come out when the can was kicked? My mother hugged me, brushed the dirt off me. The kids, all but Jimmy, stared, like my getting out of that ditch was a spectacle.

On the way home it was Mother who cried. My heart was broken too, but I refused to show it. I knew it was my fault that those children didn't like me, but I didn't know what to do about it. I felt guilty; I must be an awful person to be so unlikable.

THE   FEEL   OF   SILENCE

I use my eyes when you use your ears. What you hear I lip-read. I've always been a very good lip-reader. But lipreading is not a perfect science. For the most part it only works in one-to-one situations, in bright light, with a person who has neither a mustache nor an overbite that covers his lips nor a foreign accent that distorts the lip movements that the lip-reader has been trained to recognize. And it doesn't work with mumblers or with anyone who is in and out of your line of vision.

The best guesstimate is that only 30 percent of speech sounds are independently lip-readable. The sounds b, p, and m, for example, look identical on the lips, so that the words "bat," "pat," and "mat" are indistinguishable when spoken by themselves. But in context, I can understand which word has been said: "I hit the ball with the bat" is clear. I can eliminate "pat" and "mat," as they are nonsensical within that sentence. If I'm on your wave length, I can lip-read everything you say—in context. With some words, however, such as proper names, there is no frame of reference. Those words are not lip-readable.

Suppose you were a sculptor, a very good one. Yet no one else in your society knew anything about sculpture. Thus, to your peers your magnificent sculptures looked merely like a more advanced form of the simple clay pots they learned to make at the local parks and recreation center. Or suppose you were an extremely talented painter. Yet the people of your society knew nothing of art. Thus, those who viewed your masterpieces saw them as simply a more advanced form of the crayon drawings they made in grade school. How would you react to the ignorance of those around you? Would you feel cheated and frustrated?

Lipreading, like sculpting or painting, is an art. Yet our society has little understanding or appreciation of that art. Sometimes that is very frustrating to those of us who are talented lip-readers. For the most part, however, we have learned to swallow that frustration and to take pleasure in our own abilities. Thus, when someone says that as a lip-reader I can't possibly comprehend more than 30 or 40 percent of what is said, I shrug it off. I know that in most situations I understand 100 percent of what is said, and I know that usually when I don't understand all of what was said I am fully aware of what I have missed and can remedy the situation if I choose to do so. And my knowledge is enough—I don't need the knowledge or understanding of others. But . . . sometimes . . . I lose it. I let childish, self-defeating emotions take over.

I answered a phone call (via an interpreter) at my office one day from an FBI agent, asking that I fly to Miami for a week to take part in a surveillance operation. The FBI wanted me to lip-read the public conversations of some people who were under investigation in a large case. I was intrigued—it would be challenging to lip-read from the side and from a distance, especially when the people speaking did not *want* to be understood. But, unfortunately, I could not be available on the applicable days. The FBI agent told me he would contact other lip-readers and call me back the next day to let me know what had developed.

Sure enough, the next morning the agent called to tell me he'd arranged for two lip-readers to do the job. When I heard their names, I was astonished. One was my friend, a hearing interpreter. "I think there's been a mistake," I offered. "Mr. X is an interpreter, he is not a lip-reader." "Oh, but he assured us that he is a lip-reader," stated the FBI agent. Sure that a dreadful misunderstanding had occurred that could have serious repercussions, I called my hearing friend. Laughing as I talked, I said, "The FBI seems to be under the mistaken impression that you are a lip-reader." "But I *am* a lip-reader," my friend replied. "I told the FBI that I'm not as good as you are; I told them that I only lip-read 50 percent as well as you do. But I *am* a lip-reader."

My friend would not call himself an artist or a sculptor, yet he had no qualms about calling himself a lip-reader. I let those childish, self-defeating emotions take over that time. Can anyone but an expert lip-reader understand what an expert lip-reader can do?

Chapter
FOUR

When the time came for me to go to school, one of Mother's friends suggested that she enroll me in the state school for the deaf. Mother was horrified. "She's not deaf like that!" Watching her say this, I wondered how many different ways there were to be deaf. Which kind of deaf was I?

Mother mentioned the comment to Mrs. Ronei. Surprisingly, Mrs. Ronei agreed with my mother. "Bonnie does too well to be placed in the deaf world," she said. "Why make her Deaf, with a capital D?" I would go to a regular school, just like everyone else.

When we walked to the neighborhood school to register me for first grade, I watched as Mother explained to the lady that I was "hard-of-hearing." My eyes watered when the lady responded that if I had a hearing problem it was out of the question for me to attend that school. They simply had too many children to worry about one who had a problem. But there were no tears for my mother. She gave the lady a withering look and said, "That's no loss on our part; after seeing this school I wouldn't send a dog here." And off we marched. I was miserable. Was I not to go to school, then?

Oh yes, I was to go to school. My enterprising mother was not about to give up. Since the regular public school wouldn't accept me, and we lacked the funds for me to attend a full-fledged private school, even a parochial school, Mother found something in-between. Somehow she learned of a Lutheran church that was just starting a school. Having no facility in which to house the school, however, the church was setting up classes in an abandoned grocery store. And so my first years of school were spent in the back rooms of a grocery store, being taught the three Rs by teachers who taught two grades at a time. First and second grades shared one teacher, third and fourth grades shared another, and so on. Mother thought the program so successful that, two years later, she enrolled Jimmy in the same school.

The food that had been stored in these back rooms was taken out before classes were held there. But mouth-watering smells remained. Depending on where you were seated, you might smell spices, or the buttery smell of a big wheel of cheese, or the salt smell of a slab of cured bacon.

Sometimes it was the thick, slow smell of overripe fruit, like a syrup that might intoxicate you into sleep. Or did I only imagine these smells out of boredom? Imagining, for instance, one of the meaner boys being seated where onions and garlic had been, permanently branded with their odor. I imagined it was him the other kids avoided, pointing, giggling, holding their noses.

Instead it was me, not because of how I smelled, but because of how I didn't hear.

I hated school, both for its cruelty and for its boredom. For the most part I couldn't understand the teachers, who walked around the classroom (out of my line of lip-reading vision), spoke while facing the blackboard (instead of me), or responded to questions and comments made by non-lip-readable children sitting behind or to the side of me. There was no way to stay abreast of what was being said. Since I absorbed very little in the classroom, I had to work at home to keep up. The eight hours of every school day were an exercise in endurance.

I tried a few times to read but learned the hard way that reading during school hours, even a textbook, was strictly verboten.

"Bonnie, you *must* pay attention. Give me the book." Sometimes it was a week before the precious book was returned to me.

What was I to pay attention to? The teacher's back at the board? An oral math game I couldn't follow? Questions and answers spoken by lips I could not see? I learned to focus, discreetly, on the clock, the passage of time. How many more hours, minutes, seconds, till I was free?

The clock above the wall calendar ticked off the seconds—there were sixty in a minute. I found it took one split second to make a dot with my pencil on the page in front of me. It took five seconds then, to make four dots forming a square, and one dot, held prisoner, in the center. Twelve such squares made up a minute. Sixty minutes, or 720 squares, marked off an hour, of which there were eight in a day. It became obsessive, this dot-making, time-keeping, and at the end of a day, what I had to show for eight hours in school were pages and pages of carefully placed dots, squares with that one dot caught in the middle of each. Though it passed the time in a way that never got me in trouble, there wasn't one second of the school day that I wasn't painfully aware of.

Worse than the boredom were the inevitable embarrassing incidents. Even simple things like roll call made me anxious. Waiting for the last name *Poitras*, toward the end of the alphabet, I would focus my eyes on the teacher (who was often moving around) and pray that I would recognize my name. Sometimes I missed it altogether, but worse was when I said "Here" in response to someone else's name. With proper names there is no frame of reference, no context. So I watched the teacher carefully, and when she said a name that looked like *Bonnie Poitras*, I said "Here."

You don't have to hear to know when people are laughing at you. Faces swell and distort, redden, grow monstrous, when you're the object of humor for a room full of children. The teacher never came to my rescue.

"Oh, so we have two Monica Potters in this class. What's the matter, Miss Poitras, have you forgotten who you are?" More laughter, as thick, as all-encompassing, as the smells in those back rooms.

No, I hadn't forgotten who I was. I was Bonnie Poitras who couldn't hear. Had I wanted to forget it, I couldn't have. For the teasing of the other children continued long after the initial incident. Children tend to gnaw on one bone until another comes along to distract them. It seemed to me that the distraction from one incident usually involved another incident in which my embarrassment was even greater.

To compensate I developed an imaginary existence. For several hours every school day, in my mind, I became "Sally." I had long blond hair (unlike Bonnie's mousy brown tresses), I did not wear glasses, and—best of all—I could hear!

All through those miserable years I daydreamed about Sally's life as a hearing person. In my head I carried on long conversations with people— often in groups. I was always surrounded by others, always the center of conversation. When I was in class Bonnie occupied the classroom chair, but Sally was elsewhere: sometimes in another class hearing what the teacher and students were saying, but more often at recess playing and talking with lots of children. It was only by being Sally part of the time that I could cope with being Bonnie the rest.

But I wasn't crazy. I didn't have multiple personalities. I knew too well that Sally was a fantasy. And as hard as I tried to turn into her, I never could.

At the end of 1945, my father returned from the war. The day we were to meet his train, my mother put on her best dress and was putting on earrings when one rolled under the bed. Her bedroom was dark, windowless, in the very center of our "train" of rooms. Jimmy and I got down on hands and knees to help her find the earring, but it was too dark to see. My mother, nervous, excited, in a hurry, squatted down so as not to kneel on the wood floor and snag her nylons. While we put faces to the floor, she lit a match and held it under the bed so we could see. Just as I saw the earring and reached for it, the mattress ignited. It took no time at all to spread. Mother made us leave the room, and we watched from the doorway as she beat at the flames with a blanket, then poured two kettles of water where the flame had been. There was a bad smell, like none I'd smelled before, and little ashes, like tiny leaves, floated in the air. The marital bed was both charred and wet, not what my mother would've planned for their reunion.

My father was overjoyed to be home, but as he entered the flat he'd never seen, he was appalled less by the smell of a recently burning bed than by the reality of the apartment, the neighborhood we were living in. He determined at that moment to get us out of there, never dreaming it would take him three years.

It's not that he didn't try. He tried hard. But with thousands of servicemen returning from the war, jobs were scarce, especially for unskilled high school graduates. For three long years my father worked two jobs. During the day he sold insurance and anything else that was salable; at night he worked in a bakery or at one of a variety of similar jobs. We rarely saw him, although we saw much more of Mother, because my father was determined that she would stay home and raise the family properly. He'd have worked three jobs if that was what it took, and at least one Christmas season he did just that to buy us all presents.

During those years Jimmy and I remained at St. Matthew's Lutheran School, sharing one teacher between two grades. When I was ten years old and Jimmy seven and a half, our brother, Richard, was born. One year later our family was finally able to leave New York City for the suburbs. Mr. Levitt had just completed his now famous low-cost housing tracts, primarily for veterans. When my father's name came to the top of the list, we moved to Levittown, Long Island. I was ten and a half years old, and just finishing the fifth grade.

I don't recall anything memorable about our life in suburbia. Jimmy and I, like many siblings, fought, and fought, and fought some more. After Jimmy threw my clothes out the bedroom window one day, my parents, unable to stand it any longer, decided we must be separated. So I was given my very own bedroom in our two-bedroom Levitt Cape Cod, while Jimmy and Richard shared the other bedroom and my parents moved to a sleeper sofa in the living room. In retrospect, I don't know why they just didn't strangle us.

Our first summer after moving, my parents sent me alone to visit Grandma and Papa, who had left New York City and returned to Montreal when the war ended. I was enormously excited. I loved my grandparents, and they loved me. Grandma was a wonderful person, the kindest I have ever known. My mother once said that in all the years she knew my grandmother she never heard her say an unkind word about anyone. Quite a tribute from a daughter-in-law.

Grandma was quiet and gentle. My grandfather, by contrast, was loud, opinionated, and domineering. Only someone as inherently sweet as my grandmother could have lived with Papa for fifty-plus years. He smoked one cigar after another; to this day when I smell cigar smoke I recall Papa. And, like my father, Papa alternated between wearing a mustache and shaving it off. All through my childhood I never knew from one day to the next if it would be easy to lip-read them.

You can get a feel for Papa by learning what he ate for breakfast. Every morning he broke two raw eggs into a bowl with three pieces of bread and almost a quart of milk. He ate that extraordinary mixture while drinking a glass containing the juice of three fresh lemons, which he expected to see at his breakfast plate in winter as well as summer. This daily breakfast, he assured me, would make him live to a ripe old age. It was a ritual that was not to be tampered with, and I well remember the one time I saw someone do so.

I was married and had two children when Papa visited us at our home in Scottsdale, Arizona. Since Papa was an avid fisherman we took him for a weekend to Kohl's Ranch, a famous Old West type of place in northern Arizona well-known for its trout fishing. Upon entering the local coffee shop for breakfast on Sunday morning, Papa ordered his usual. He was informed that, regrettably, they had no fresh lemons. Papa went into a rage. "What do you mean, you have no fresh lemons?" he screamed. "This is Arizona, for Christ's sake; I get fresh lemons in Canada!" He was not to be pacified. I wanted to crawl under the table. My husband almost did.

Papa always spoke his mind (a trait I have not so fortunately inherited). Another time when he visited my husband and me and our children, we took Papa to Rocky Point, Mexico, to do some deep-sea fishing. When in Mexico our policy was to purchase one bottle of liquor for every adult over the age of eighteen to bring over the border to Arizona. Liquor is much cheaper in Mexico, so this practice is common among Arizonans. And the law allows importation of only one bottle per adult. If you have more than your limit, the liquor is confiscated and you may be fined. On this trip we followed our usual practice. Since we were three adults and three children we purchased three bottles of liquor. As we drove through the immigration check point, the officer asked the standard question. "Are you bringing any liquor or drugs into the United States?"

My husband replied, "Yes, we have three bottles of liquor; one for each adult."

Immediately Papa jumped in. "No, no," Papa said. "I, myself, do not drink liquor. One bottle is not for me."

"Papa," we implored, "we know you do not drink liquor; you are just bringing a bottle in for the party we are having next week."

Our efforts were in vain. No amount of persuasion could convince Papa to import a bottle of liquor that he was not going to drink. We stood in silence as the customs official apologetically emptied the contents of the bottle into a sink.

So much for saving money.

My grandparents were bilingual, speaking French at home and English outside the home. They believed that the way to learn a second language was immersion in that language. My lengthy visit was the perfect opportunity to immerse me in French. Ordinarily that would be good strategy. But those were not ordinary circumstances. Language acquisition has much to do with hearing that language spoken. I could not.

Used to lip-reading English, I could not adapt to lip-reading French. French words are pronounced differently. The rolling r's alone are impossible for the non-French—unused to them—to lip-read. Most of the time I had no frame of reference from which to begin reading the French words that poured off my grandparents' lips so rapidly. In short, I was lost. My grandparents couldn't understand it. What was wrong with me that I couldn't pick up simple French words on the lips when I had no trouble at all lip-reading their English?

"Just say what you see," Grandma gently urged, while Papa threw up his hands in despair and paced the room. I tried to make sense of their French words and repeat them. For the most part, I failed miserably. I just didn't have the familiarity with the lip movements that lip-reading requires. I got so I could lip-read the simple phrases that every adult visiting my grandparents asked me (such as "How old are you?"—in French, "Quel âge avez-vous?") and could respond in kind ("J'ai dix ans"—"I am ten years old"). And I learned to lip-read and speak the simple phrases that one used at the table ("Passe-moi le beurre, s'il vous plaît"; "Passe-moi le sel, s'il vous plaît"). But that was as far as I got. I'm afraid I was a terrible disappointment to my grandparents in that respect.

I disappointed Grandma in another way. A devout Catholic, she took me several times that summer to St. Joseph's shrine, a famous Montreal landmark claimed to be the site of numerous healings, miracles.

Outside, three hundred steps led to the shrine. The tradition is to climb those steps on your knees, saying a prayer on each step, a sort of architectural rosary. The steps were dotted with people doing this; my grandmother did it; my father remembers doing it as a child. On each of our visits to the shrine, Grandma prayed vigorously for my hearing to be restored. I could feel her expectation as we entered the part of the shrine devoted to miracles. This entire room was filled with crutches, wheelchairs, and canes left by people who purportedly had been cured of diseases, deformities, paralysis. The room had a dusty smell, stale, the smell of shredded disability. My deafness, were I cured, would become a part of this smell, left here like some old crutch. My grandmother believed it would happen; I never had the remotest hope. But if it made her happy to visit the room of miracles, I was happy to go.

As we left the shrine after each visit Grandma would test my hearing over and over, speaking to me while she had me shut my eyes so I couldn't lip-read. I'd shake my head. I heard only silence, smelled only that dusty smell. What I tasted was her disappointment.

When the summer was over I returned to American suburbia, where as usual I retired to my room and my books. I spent most of my time in grades five through eight reading. While I sometimes played with a few neighborhood children who were younger than I, I lived for the hours I could spend in my room with my books. Jimmy, to the contrary, was an outgoing, personable fellow and had a multitude of friends who wandered in and out of the house all day long. They ignored me completely. I was envious but tried hard not to show it.

It was during that period that my family acquired a television. I remember the night my father brought it home, the way we all sat around as he took it out of the box, placed it carefully on an old trunk. Jimmy plugged it in, while my father adjusted the antennas. The big moment was supposed to be when we turned it on; everyone sat and waited as the picture appeared, first as a dot in the center, then grew to full size. That first night we sat transfixed by the miracle. Baby Richard thought the people were inside the set and kept looking behind the television, under it, for where they'd gotten in, where they were hiding. My father kept saying, "No, son, it's a broadcast," words that meant nothing to my baby brother.

The television itself meant little to me. Once the novelty of the screen had worn off, the novelty of the controls, I saw no point to it. All I saw was a bunch of meaningless pictures. I couldn't understand any of the dialogue, since for the most part lipreading—without *any* sound—is not possible on television. The characters are too small and too far away, their lips basically invisible. Usually the speakers face not the TV viewers but the characters to whom they are speaking. And much of the time the cameras focus on the character the speaker is talking to rather than on the speaker herself. So this whole TV thing was quite boring, I thought.

But I was the only one who felt this way. In the evenings my parents and brothers were glued in front of the screen. They'd rush through dinner to watch Milton Berle or Ed Sullivan. What was the big deal? When they watched, they were mesmerized; they wouldn't respond if I said something to them. It took repeating myself before they'd return to the room, to reality. Wasn't this silly? What did they see in the TV that I didn't? Surely it would grow old for them soon. Unable to understand what was going on, I retreated as usual to my room and my books.

Books are my one true love. Certainly they have been the most influential force—the centrifugal force—of my life. Books for a deaf person mean language, understanding of the world, being a part of that world. Hearing people pick up language as a matter of course, from overhearing other people talk, from the radio, from television, from hearing someone sing on a tape—in short, just from being. Language acquisition for a hearing person is as instinctive as breathing. It happens naturally, without concentration, even if you don't want it to. Language acquisition doesn't happen naturally for a deaf person, unless you count language acquired from reading books as natural acquisition. I do.

I could read before I went to school. At four and five I devoured the Bobbsey Twin books; I wept when I had read them all and there were no more to look forward to. By first grade I had progressed to the Nancy Drew mysteries, which I read as fast as I could get my hands on them. I lived for our family's weekly treks to the library and was so frustrated with the library's policy of allowing each person to check out only four books a week that I threw a temper tantrum. Four measly books—I could read those in two days; for the remaining five days of the week I had nothing to read. Try as I might, I could not ration my reading. To this day I prefer to read an entire book at one sitting.

I read everything—biographies, autobiographies, historical novels, the classics. I read Ayn Rand's *Fountainhead;* the fatter the book the better. While other kids were busy socializing, I was devouring the works of authors such as Taylor Caldwell, Irving Stone, John Steinbeck, and William Faulkner.

Some educators claim that one cannot read unless one first understands the words one is reading. I disagree. Even as a child I learned words as I read, from their contexts. With the advent of television, children stopped reading as much as they used to. Now they sit for hours in front of the TV screen—a misfortune for all children, but for deaf children a calamity. Books teach deaf children not only correct language but contemporary slang and popular expressions. That's how books draw deaf children into the mainstream world.

My books also provided the friends I lacked. The Bobbsey twins; Nancy Drew; Amy, Beth, Meg, and Jo in *Little Women.* Except for those characters, I spent much of my childhood alone.

Jailers threaten prisoners with solitary confinement. The fear of being kept from human companionship is strong. But being alone is not the worst fate that can befall a person. To be in the midst of a group of happy, smiling people, yet be unable to understand or participate in their conversation, is worse. Even as a child I preferred being by myself. Being alone in a group is *real* solitary confinement.

THE FEEL OF SILENCE

Unless deaf people have come across them in a book or article, many commonly used phrases remain mysteries. We deaf people simply don't catch anything on the fly. So I'd as soon be without my legs or arms as be without my books.

When I was in law school, a deaf man asked me for some free advice about getting a divorce from his wife. He gave a lengthy explanation about how his wife had slept with this man and that man and another man. I tried to cut the conversation short. "I understand," I said, "You want a divorce because your wife sleeps around." He stared at me, puzzled. "What, what?" he asked. "What do you mean she sleeps around? How does someone sleep around, like in a circle? You mean on a round bed?"

A well-educated deaf woman, who had graduated from and worked for Gallaudet University for the Deaf, once asked me to meet some people for lunch while I was in Washington, D.C. When giving directions to the restaurant she said that the hearing person who'd told her where the restaurant was had said that it was "catty-corner" to a certain building. "I don't know what that means, do you?" the deaf woman asked.

Recently I was surprised when an intelligent deaf friend did not know the meaning of the term "pomp and circumstance," or what the word "wry" referred to. And when I asked for an emery board she had no idea what I meant. "Oh, that's a paper nail file," she concluded after I'd explained.

And sometimes reading doesn't do the job, either. The first time I saw someone flippantly use the term "fifty-seven varieties," while clearly indicating that I should know what he was talking about, I was stymied. And when one of my children first asked, "Do you dig it, Mom?" I was at a loss. It's no wonder, really, that a deaf friend didn't know what the term "hangnail" referred to, or what in God's name I'd meant when I'd said, "Don't sweat it." You don't generally find expressions like those in books or articles.

Chapter
FIVE

Most people point to high school as a difficult time in their lives. And for most, the common denominator is onset of puberty. Puberty, let me tell you, was nothing compared to deafness. Awkward stage? My whole life had felt like one. Girls getting "the curse"? I'd lived with my curse since I could remember. Bodily changes? So what?

At this age I recognized that speech was my nemesis. Deaf people can never take speech for granted. No matter how well we learn to speak in a manner that satisfies the Great Hearing God, we have to keep working at it. And when we stop, our speech begins to slip, to become less intelligible.

I was in my first year of high school when my parents decided to send me for more speech therapy. I had not been practicing, and my parents were concerned that I was no longer saying the letters *r*, *s*, and *l* properly. So they looked around for a place to send me, someplace that would not break the family's budget. They found a clinic where one therapist worked with two to four clients at a time.

I was assigned to a group consisting of just one other person, a teenage boy who, like me, had trouble with the letters *r*, *l*, and *s*. For this reason we would work together. In addition to being deaf, Ethan had cerebral palsy, which made it impossible for him to control his mouth movements. I do not know what Ethan's voice sounded like, but his speech looked distorted, even grotesque. I did not want any part of this. I particularly did not want to be paired in a class with that boy. I refused to practice. Maybe if I returned to every class with the same poor speech, the teacher would tire of me or switch me to another group. For a while, she was patient with my lack of improvement.

Ethan apparently worked diligently to improve his speech, though his mouth was still something I chose not to look at. On one particular day, he must've made a breakthrough. The therapist's face lit up.

"Wonderful!" she said, delighted with his progress. "I'm so proud of you, Ethan, you're doing great." Ethan beamed.

Then it was my turn. "Bonnie," she said, "let's hear what you've done for today." I spit out my drills without enthusiasm, without trying. I had not practiced, as I'd promised myself I wouldn't.

The speech therapist looked at me, as disgusted as she'd been pleased with him. "That is really terrible," she said.

"My God," I thought, "if *his* grotesque speech is good, and mine is terrible, what must I sound like when I talk?" So began one year during which I refused to speak in public at all.

For a while, no one cared or noticed that I wasn't speaking. I already had a reputation as strange. I was a loner by necessity, the only deaf student in a hearing high school, with glasses to boot; I was fair game for everyone. But I'd developed a pretty tough hide.

Until the slam book.

Slam books were disguised as regular school notebooks, so they could be passed around a class without being confiscated by a teacher. I'd seen people writing in them, passing them back and forth. On the top of each page was the name of a student, one page for every student in the ninth grade. Then, all over the page, people wrote comments about the person, anonymously. The idea was that you could slam someone without their knowing who'd written the bad remark. The pages of the popular people made the term *slam book* a misnomer: "Cute and sweet," "A great friend," "What a bod!" and so on. But other people bore the brunt of this fad, and I know I was not the first to be hurt by it.

I'd been trying to sneak read *A Tree Grows in Brooklyn* during English class. Class ended, something I knew not because I heard a bell but because I saw everyone else respond to it, a mass exodus. Finishing the page I was on made me the last to leave. As I entered the hallway, the speech teacher, Mrs. Fletcher, who was also the faculty advisor to the Hi-Y Club, was passing by.

"Could you come into my room for a minute, Bonnie?" she said. "I'd like to talk to you." Mrs. Fletcher was cute and always nice to everyone, more like one of us than a teacher. I nodded.

"Wait here," she said, "while I run to the rest room." And as she left, she pointed to one of the desks, where there was a notebook. "Uh-oh," she said, "looks like somebody left something." I walked over to pick it up.

I opened the notebook to look for the name of the person who'd left it and immediately recognized it as a slam book. The names were arranged alphabetically. I read a few pages and kept turning them. I could feel my throat tighten.

There it was: *Bonnie Poitras*—a whole page for me. Written there, in all different handwritings, for all the world to see, was the same phrase, over and over: "Deaf, dumb, and blind."

I ran out of the building, not meaning to run out on Mrs. Fletcher, but there was no way I could turn back.

While the students may not have noticed that I wasn't speaking, the teachers did, because I refused to answer questions. Soon my parents were informed. They were frantic. Since I didn't share with them my childish misconceptions about my terrible speech, they didn't know what the problem was. This was par for the course for me, as I almost never discussed issues relating to my deafness with my family. In fact, I still don't. People have asked why that is so, and I cannot really answer the question. I don't know whether my reticence follows from my parents' implied attitude that I should deal with my deafness on my own and not bitch about it, or my own self-imposed attitude to the same effect. And frankly I don't think it matters. The fact is, for whatever reason, I did not discuss issues relating to my deafness with my family.

Although they didn't know the reason for the problem, my parents were now aware of the problem itself and sought to correct it. Since my speech had not improved as a result of the group speech therapy, they thought a possible solution might be private speech lessons. They sent me to a therapist named Joel Stark. On three separate occasions during my high school years I spent several sessions with Joel, and each time he quickly remedied whatever speech difficulties I was having at the moment. He was great. He knew just what to do, and, more importantly, he knew how to do it *fast*, because my patience for speech therapy was minimal.

But for all I appreciated Joel Stark, it was Mrs. Fletcher, not speech therapy, who finally pulled me back into the mainstream.

If there was a teacher at Hicksville High who was the opposite of Mrs. Fletcher, it was "Miss Smith," the dreaded physical education teacher. No one was exempt from her wrath, and there was plenty of it. She started the class out screaming, scolding, demoralizing someone, and she never stopped. Just knowing I had phys ed next hour was enough to make me queasy. In retrospect, I think Miss Smith hated herself more than anyone. She was unattractive and overweight, had a dour personality, and never smiled. I suspect she had few friends.

Though Miss Smith terrorized many girls, some of us were bound to get it more often. The weaker you were, the more sickly, the less athletic, the more abuse you would get. Every class period with her began with her dictating exercises to us. It wasn't a set routine I could memorize; she changed the order of the torture daily. Inevitably, we were told to touch our toes. I had to keep my head up in order to see her face, to see what she would tell us to do next.

"The correct position, Poitras, is with your head down," she would say. I'd lower it momentarily, then look back up to follow her next order.

"Keep your eyes on the floor!" her lips screamed at me. "How many times do I have to tell you?" I'd hold my head down a little longer this time, then peek up again. Soon she took to marching over to me, pushing my head down and holding it there.

I had other reasons to hate phys ed, such as always being the last chosen for teams, and being no good at anything but reading, which is generally not considered a team sport. The class was reminiscent of those confusing games I'd tried to follow as a child. War. Kick the can. I had trouble taking it seriously.

One afternoon, I was placed in the outfield for softball. I walked way out, where I hoped no balls would come. Once out there, the game in progress, it was easy to let my mind wander. The last class of the day—after this torture, I was free. I stopped paying attention.

Our team had not been up to bat, and class was almost over; the other side was beating us badly. Suddenly, a fly ball soared so close to my head it almost hit me. I saw it way too late to catch it. Guiltily, I ran to retrieve it where it still rolled through the field. When I turned around, class had been dismissed and girls were filing back into the locker rooms. But Miss Smith was headed straight for me.

"What is it with you?" she yelled, her expression incredulous. She pushed on my shoulder till I was forced to sit on the ground. She lowered her face into mine. I could smell something sour on her breath.

"Are you stupid as well as uncoordinated?" She stared. "Answer me, Poitras." I was true to my vow of silence.

"No wonder you're always the last to be chosen!" she screamed.

Out of the corner of my eye, I saw Mrs. Fletcher approaching. Her classroom was in earshot of the phys ed field.

"You have no right to speak to her that way," she said. There was a color in her cheeks I'd never seen before. She'd never been mad that I knew of. "She's just a young girl."

She took my arm. "Come on, Bonnie," she said, and we moved away from Miss Smith, leaving her fading in the distance.

The best person in the world had just joined my team, and the way she made me feel I would've done just about anything for Kay Fletcher.

After much gentle persuasion (and even a little bribery), Mrs. Fletcher eventually convinced me to sign up for her public speaking class. She promised that I would not have to speak in class until I felt I was ready, and she kept that promise. After a summer of rest and recuperation, and after observing some of the mediocre speeches given by my classmates in Mrs. Fletcher's class, I told her I was ready. My first speech was no worse than anyone else's and may have been better than some.

After ensuring that I had rejoined the speaking world, Mrs. Fletcher turned to other matters. With her encouragement I signed up for the yearbook staff and eventually became editor-in-chief (by default—no one else wanted the thankless job). I joined the Hi-Y club and the Leaders Club. I even became a junior varsity cheerleader. Not bad for someone who wouldn't even speak in school for a year.

The more I participated in the hearing world, the more I wanted to. From the day she learned of my deafness my mother—unconsciously at first, and later consciously—focused on raising me to be as independent as possible. Wanting no part in the raising of a dependent "handicapped" child, my mother went to the opposite extreme. I was encouraged, even required, to do things for myself. Can't make a phone call? Tough. Learn to write letters or walk to accomplish the necessary communication. Can't understand what's going on? Tough. Figure out another way to get the information or learn to live without it. I never complained to my parents about problems relating to my deafness. I always felt (rightly or wrongly) that complaints would be unacceptable. My mother simply didn't want to hear any whining, and my father was so busy working that it would never have occurred to me to complain to him. To this day I think they did me a favor, for I learned to depend on *myself*.

No one in my family ever said I couldn't do *anything* because I was deaf, with one exception. From riding my bike in the street (where I couldn't hear the cars whiz by) to getting a driver's license and a rickety old car at the age of seventeen, I did it all—except babysitting. Every girl my age had been earning money this way since about seventh grade. I liked kids, especially babies, and had helped a little with my youngest brother; I was anxious to put my independence to work in some money-making enterprise.

When it came to this, Mother put her foot down. The first time a neighbor woman asked me to babysit, my mother made up some reason why I couldn't. I protested. She let me do everything else, why not this? The second time she answered the phone to a babysitting request, I saw her say to the woman, "Bonnie does not babysit." I knew my mother well enough to know when a decision was firm, but that didn't stop me from arguing with her.

"What if there's an emergency," she said, "and you don't hear it? We're talking about a child's life, Bonnie. The case is closed."

Her adamant stand did more than frustrate me, it scared me. I'd never thought of myself as a dangerous person. Because babysitting was the first and only thing she'd ever prevented me from doing, the restriction seemed that much more significant. I began to wonder if I would ever have children of my own, or would that be selfish and irresponsible of me? Would I be endangering their lives? I didn't then, and don't now, take well to limitation. When someone believes I'm incapable of something, especially if they see my inability as a product of my deafness, I feel that much more motivated to do whatever it is and determined to do it better than most. Mother's refusal to allow me to babysit planted a seed in me. When I did have children, I would prove that I could be trusted with this responsibility. As with everything else, I would find ways to compensate. I would prove that a hearing person could do nothing that I couldn't. Merging seamlessly with the hearing world was a goal underlying every other. Always has been. Always will be.

Another activity every teenager was involved in was music. The radio. Top forty. Forty-fives of all the latest hits. Obviously, listening to radio or records would've been a useless pastime for me.

On the last class day before Easter break, one of my teachers let us play charades, as a prevacation treat. We were assigned partners. Each of us acted out the title to a song, television show or movie, which our assigned partner had to guess. I paid close attention, as I'd learned to whenever games came up; to this day, for me the word *game* does not connote fun.

I was third to play, and I'd watched the two boys before me guess *Ozzie and Harriet* and *The Wizard of Oz*. I hadn't heard of *Ozzie and Harriet,* but I'd read the book that *The Wizard of Oz* had been made from. I figured I had an even chance of being able to do this, until my partner put his hand to his mouth, like a megaphone, a gesture that indicated he was about to act out the title to a song. I could feel my heart drop down to my gut. I pasted the fake smile on my face.

Gerry Franklin, my teammate, started swaying his hips in a way that embarrassed me; the class exploded in laughter. I laughed along, not sure what was funny. He was pretending to hold a microphone; he kept running his hand through his hair and mouthing the words of this song I didn't know. I continued to smile. I might've been able to lip-read what he said and take a stab at the title, but he continued to hold his hand in front of his mouth. Once, when he took his hand away to slick back his hair, I saw the word "love" on his lips, and then the word "be." Love be what? I felt myself growing hotter, as the class grew impatient. People started rolling their eyes, making looks at each other that meant How stupid could I be? Then the teacher intervened. "Bonnie, how about just saying the name of the musician?" They all looked at me for an answer. When I hesitated, someone said, "Oh, come *on!*" I was still silent. Thirty seconds seemed as long as my life thus far. The other kids' faces were incredulous. The smile began to tremble, my mask to fall apart. Finally the teacher said "Class?" and they all crooned, in unison, "Elvis!" I had no idea who that was but was now fairly sure I had read the lyrics of the song on Gerry's lips. Desperate to save face, I blurted out, "Love Be Tender!" and I could see and feel and taste and touch the roar in that room. I felt myself shrink, like Alice in Wonderland, and dreamed of a tiny trapdoor I could escape through, never to return. The correct title was "Love *Me* Tender," of course, and every human being on earth knew this except me.

I didn't watch the rest of that game but sat amidst my own hot embarrassment and tried to think of a way out.

After school that day, I marched directly to the nearest music store for some self-help books. We had a piano in our basement, old and dusty and probably out of tune. But what did I care?

At first I looked for books that would teach me how to be a pianist. But those books were too complicated. I figured it would take my entire time in high school to master the art of piano playing and put that knowledge to any practical purpose. So I compromised. I bought a very elementary pamphlet explaining how to play right-hand notes on the piano. I bought another elementary pamphlet explaining how to make up chords with the left hand. Then I bought sheet music for each of the popular songs of the day, which the store clerk patiently selected for me. Not piano music, but guitar. Piano music was too hard, and it had both right- and left-hand notes. Guitar music had only simple right-hand notes and a single mark above those notes telling the reader what chord to play with the left hand.

Our piano was an old ugly upright with peeling paint. It had a deep tone that I could feel. I felt a certain kinship with this instrument, discarded in our basement. Just as I was not to be dismissed, neither would I let this piano be. So what if it wasn't pretty or new? The newer ones were too high pitched, making it impossible to feel the resonance. I had tried them out at the music store, and it wasn't the same. I couldn't feel the music on any piano but mine.

For hours every day I banged on my old piano. I discovered that if I played the right-hand notes—the melody—on the very base chord of my old piano, I could actually *feel* the vibrant sounds. I would count up or down the "ladder" on the sheet music to see how many notes to raise or lower my voice between sounds and sing along as I played. If I really liked the song I was working on, I learned to play chords with my left hand to accompany the melody and my voice. After a few hundred—maybe even a thousand—renditions of one song I got so I could play and even sing that song in a credible fashion. As you might guess, the first one I mastered was "Love Me Tender."

Pretty soon, it was a love affair between me and that piano. To me, it moved and it breathed as it taught me these songs. A bridge to the hearing world. My family grew to hate it. As I spent every waking moment learning new tunes, they suffered through what must've been some discordant sounds.

"If you're this serious about it," my father said once, "let's look into a new one. We could rent one until we can afford to buy."

"I don't want a new one," I said.

"Some of the stores allow the rent to go towards owning it eventually," my mother said.

Obviously they weren't listening to me. It wasn't a question of money. I liked *this* piano.

"This weekend," my father said, "we'll see what we can find."

"I like the one I've got," I shouted.

My parents just looked at each other. They were used to me being willful, but this was something they couldn't understand. They gave up.

By that Christmas I'd learned many of the popular songs of the day, most of the Christmas carols, and a lot of what I call the must-know songs. You know, companionship songs, such as "You Are My Sunshine" and "I've Been Working on the Railroad." If there had been enough hours in my weeks I would have tackled even more.

My old piano became my best friend. I was happiest when I was figuring out new songs or singing over and over the ones I'd mastered. "Ricochet Romance." "Three Coins in a Fountain." And a favorite, "Que Sera, Sera"—"Whatever will be, will be, / The future's not ours to see, / Que sera, sera."

Even now, each year as I sing Christmas carols with everyone else, I remember the melodies that I felt on my piano. And in my heart I feel the wonderful sounds of Christmas as loudly as everyone else hears them.

THE FEEL OF SILENCE

My world is not really silent. I hear voices in my head. I assign voices to people. You sound the way I see you. I can't be swayed by a sweet, cajoling voice. I watch your eyes, the muscles in your cheek, the quiver of your lower lip, the tenseness in your shoulders, the way you hold your neck. I see more than others hear. And the voice I assign to you is the one that fits the real you. I sometimes talk about sweet, soft-spoken Mary, only to have a hearing person tell me that Mary really has a deep, loud voice. Why is it that people's real voices often bear so little relationship to their real personalities?

What do I sound like? Do I have a pleasant voice? An unpleasant voice? A high-pitched voice or a low-pitched voice? Do I ever sound sexy? Seductive? Breathy? Husky? What does sexy sound like?

Can you hear the laughter or the sadness in my voice? The anger?

They tell me that when I get upset or excited my voice gets shrill. What is "shrill," anyway? And how do I keep my voice from reaching that apparently annoying pitch?

When I went to give a lengthy presentation before seven hundred people, I tried out the microphone ahead of time. I placed people at the front and back of the huge room and asked them to help me set the microphone properly and show me how to best position myself in front of the mike to achieve optimum acoustic conditions. Someone got a bright idea. "Let's ask the technician to put more bass in the mike—it will make your voice sound nicer." So we asked. And the technician obliged. Everyone agreed that my voice did, indeed, sound "nicer." How? Why? I've always assumed that men have deeper voices than women, which means they have more bass in their voices, doesn't it? Do men, then, sound "nicer" than women?

You who can hear have an advantage. Hearing your voice, you can disguise it at whim to hide your feelings. My voice, however, generally reflects my true feelings, whether I wish it to do so or not. "Why are you using that tone of voice?" someone will ask. Oh God, I've done it again.

My voice is not a part of *me*. It is a disembodied concept that floats independent of me. Don't judge me by that voice, please. It's activated by forces outside my control. And I can't escape it. It follows me wherever I go.

I once met a hard-of-hearing man who chose to live in the world of Deaf people. But on occasion he crossed over from one world to the other. When it came to sex, however, he didn't like crossing over. "I prefer to make love with Deaf women," he told me. "Hearing women make noises in bed and sound like frogs."

Is he putting me on?

$Chapter$
SIX

My last two years of high school were unmemorable. Outside of school, I remained a loner. I had few friends and never dated. On our senior trip to D.C., I sat alone on the long train ride. Although I decorated the gym for both junior and senior proms, I attended neither. One unsuspecting boy did ask me to the prom, a quiet fellow no more popular than I. Later, when he broke the date, I heard that someone had warned the guy, "Hey, you don't want to take her to the prom. She can't hear right and she's *strange.*"

My parents, neither of whom had gone to college, programmed all three of us kids to think that we had no choice but to go. It never occurred to me to that I wouldn't. After high school came college. It was one of the unspoken rules. But before college came the New York State Regents' Exams, tests you had to score well on if you expected to get into a decent school. Between the dreaded Regents' exams and certain classes I despised, high school became more of an obstacle than ever before.

Most of my grades were good, because after school I could read the textbooks and teach myself what I was missing in class. But one class, biology, was impossible. The teacher's main method of both teaching and testing was to use a slide projector and slides. Naturally the room had to be dark, leaving me with an extra handicap—blindness. I could see the slides fine, but they were senseless without the running commentary the teacher was giving orally in the back, in the dark. All around me students took copious notes. I tried to catch up by reading and rereading the text, but the material in the slides was supplemental—not covered in the text.

I started to have bad dreams. In the dreams, I was in a class that seemed foreign to me, as though everyone else in the room had been attending all year but for some reason I hadn't, yet I was expected to catch on, catch up, without any help. My ignorance, or the fact that I hadn't even attended up to this point, was something to be kept secret, like my deafness. The teacher and the other students all possessed mouths that moved like rubber; their faces, like those in a fun-house mirror, stretched this way and that. Were they even speaking my language? I'd grope through every book on my desk, searching for a clue to the subject we were studying, finding nothing. The books were thick and heavy and the pages hard to turn, and before the dream ended I'd be dropping them all, picking them up, dropping them again, making a terrible disturbance. The dream always ended the same way. The teacher would take out a test, a quarter-inch packet of pages stapled together, enormous; we were to stay all day until we finished. My tongue would start to feel large, an obstruction in my mouth, as I tried to tell the instructor that I couldn't possibly take the test, I was unprepared. But what came out of my mouth was as indecipherable as the words their rubber mouths spoke. Inside me it felt more like an agonized groan than a coherent plea. All the flexible faces laughed in their rubbery, monstrous way, and I'd wake up in a cold sweat.

In my real-life biology class, when the slide test came around, I was lost. My grade in this class was the lowest I'd ever received except in French—a big fat C minus on the report card stared at me like an open laughing mouth.

A C minus in a science class would not get me into a good college. As much as I hated biology, I signed up to retake it in summer school. The teacher was able to give me the extra attention I needed, and I got the A I'd come to require of myself.

Once the traumas of Regents' and the biology class were over, it was time to choose a college. After poring over various catalogs and discussing the matter with Mother, I made the decision to go to Cornell. The application process went well. On the basis of my high school record I made it to the final interview conducted by a Cornell representative in New York City.

I'd gotten a new dress for the occasion. I waited in a long line of other hopeful applicants for my turn to speak to the representative. I could've died when I saw he had a thick mustache. Impossible to lip-read. He asked me the first question. A series of hidden movements under the mustache. I asked for a repeat and caught a word or two, enough to figure out he'd asked about a major.

"I plan to major in journalism," I said, sure of the major, if not of the question.

"Mumble mumble mumble?" he asked, and again I had to ask him to repeat. The question remained a mystery—one word only, it seemed, not much to grab onto. Perhaps, I thought, he'd asked me why.

"I've always been an avid reader," I said, "and good with writing. I was editor-in-chief of my high school yearbook."

"Mumble mumble grumble," he said. I could see by his expression he wasn't pleased.

I was silent; he said something again, indecipherable. I decided I had no choice but to confess. "I'm sorry, sir," I blurted, "I'm hard-of-hearing and I'm having trouble lip-reading you because of your mustache."

His face registered the information. I imagined what he was thinking behind that expression: blind, deaf, and dumb. "Well," he finally said, overenunciating, so that I understood. "This is a problem. Cornell would be much too difficult for you."

"Sir," I protested, "I've always done very well at school, despite my hearing loss. My grades are high. I've been very active. Have you seen my transcript?"

He shook his head. "I'm sorry," he said. I didn't need anyone to tell me that he'd made up his mind.

When the rejection letter arrived in the mail, I wasn't surprised, but I was angry. I wasn't being given a chance. I put the letter back into the official Cornell envelope and threw it in the trash. Even from there, it pulsated rejection. Blind, deaf, and dumb, it said, over and over, like an echo.

I ended up at Syracuse University, a school that would let me attend with a hearing impairment but wouldn't let me major in journalism. Journalism for a hard-of-hearing person? Unheard of! To be accepted at Syracuse I had to agree to major in home economics. But in a smooth move on my part, I arranged to have a dual major in journalism and home economics (Department of Child Development). Which, of course, meant that in addition to taking the journalism courses I was interested in, I had to spend four years taking child development and other home economics classes that I had no interest in. Until one miserable semester of Sewing 101, I thought it was a relatively small price to pay for the privilege of joining society.

B efore I could go to college, financing had to be arranged. Since money was still tight at our house, although getting looser (my father was by this time manager of a school bus company, and we had moved out of our small Levittown home into a split level house in Hicksville), my parents requested help from the state's vocational rehabilitation office.

The counselor my mother and I visited at that office was amazed at my lip-reading prowess. When he mentioned that he lived in Massapequa, I politely responded that Massapequa is a lovely town. "Didja see that?" he said. "She can lip-read 'Massapequa.' " "Hey, let's give it a try," he went on. "Can you tell the difference between 'Massapequa' and 'Mississippi'?"

"Massapequa."

"Massapequa."

"Mississippi."

"Mississippi."

Faithfully playing my part in this dog-and-pony show, I responded properly every time.

"How utterly absurd," I thought, as he raved about my "glorious talent," for "Massapequa" and "Mississippi" are probably two of the easiest words to lip-read. The more syllables a word has, the easier it is. It's the one-syllable words that are difficult. Moreover, "Massapequa" and "Mississippi" look nothing alike on the lips. But far be it from me to disillusion him. He didn't seem the type who would take correction well.

And I was wise to keep quiet. We got the vocational rehabilitation assistance, and I was financially ready for college. I was also ready intellectually and emotionally, or so I thought.

Actually, I entered Syracuse University in the fall of 1957 a very naive and unworldly freshman wearing the traditional orange beanie. No one could have been less prepared for the impervious tyranny of her peers.

My roommate, assigned to me via an impartial, random process, was from a small town in upstate New York. We immediately disliked one another. I didn't tell her I was deaf, so she talked to me in the dark, after all the lights were turned out for the night. She also talked to me while my back was turned. Naturally, I didn't respond. She thought, understandably, that I was rude, and she acted accordingly. I don't remember how we gradually came to adjust to one another, or how she came to discover I was deaf and not ignoring her. Eventually we became good friends, and we kept in touch for years after we graduated.

Adjusting to dorm life was trying. All those thousands of squealing girls racing up and down the 150 or so steps between Mount Olympus—as our dorm was appropriately labeled—and the rest of the campus, including the dining hall. Sorority rush week was even more trying. Endless socials, moving from sorority house to sorority house making ridiculous, trivial small talk with countless unidentifiable faces. Hundreds and hundreds of lips to read. Ripping open the sealed envelopes to see which sororities that I had bid to return to had also bid for me to return. Then the ultimate crowning: I was to be an honored member of Chi Omega.

Initiation took place in the dark; for part of the time we were blindfolded. As always, whenever blindness was added to my deafness, I was terrified; without being able to hear or see I was truly lost. To turn back, however, was impossible. Not to be a member of a good sorority was unthinkable. *Anything* was worth it.

Some of the initiation activities were just a nuisance; others left me cold with fear. One night they came for each of us, covered our heads with sheets, and walked us to a meeting. I imagined the other girls squealing in their temporary blindness. For me, inside that sheet, was a terror I hadn't known. Worse than the blackouts as a child, I began to feel not only deaf and blind but claustrophobic, imagining that soon I might stop breathing. This was fun?

Whatever happened that night, once they got us to the meeting, is a mystery to me. I was absolutely numb with fear and don't know to this day what took place.

I heard that in some sororities it was worse. One girl in my dorm told me that at her sorority initiation they were blindfolded and given things to eat. Some foods were recognizable—a grape, an olive, a dill pickle. Other menu items were inedible, concoctions the members had made themselves, and pledges gagged their way through whatever they were fed. One girl swore she was made to eat a Vicks Vaporub sandwich. Another girl was given a raw oyster with a string around it, told to swallow it and then pull it back up. In the process, she lost the whole buffet, vomiting so suddenly that the sister feeding her barely dodged the spray. (Justice, I thought.) We Chi Omega pledges had it a little easier. But whatever horrors were endured by other pledges, they were shared horrors. My horrors were mine alone.

For me, the worst part was the dark. So many of these initiation rites took place in blackness, in the basement. The night we were sworn in, top-secret sorority information was passed from member to member in a whisper. Girls cupped their hands around their mouths and spoke into each others ears. The secret went around the circle. As it came nearer to me, I froze. What would I do? I racked my brain for the type of information it might be, something I could make up that would suffice when it was my turn to pass it on. Nothing came to me. The secret was coming closer.

Between the dark and the cupped hands there was no way in this world I could've absorbed the message. When it was my turn to receive it, the secret arrived as hot air in my ear. A few short blasts of air. I needed time to think.

"What?" I tried to whisper back. Whispering isn't my forte. The whole group shushed me, and then the sister to my right blew it into my ear again.

I turned to the girl on my left; her open ear was waiting. I cupped my hands like everyone else. I invented a secret, like an oath: "Privacy, honesty, and loyalty," I whispered to the best of my ability. Though I imagine it was louder than it should've been, my hands formed a barrier that kept the whole room from hearing what I'd made up. There must've been a half dozen of those messages passed around that basement. For each one, I manufactured a statement about Chi Omega, and no one knew that the five girls who came after me never got the real message, but some quick comment I'd made up. So much for tradition. Because we'd all taken an oath not to ever mention the secrets revealed during initiation, it never came up, the discrepancy between what some of the sisters heard and what the others did—those so unfortunate as to be seated after me. Blind, deaf, and dumb.

None of this sorority nonsense was geared to deaf pledges, and you'd think I would've quit putting myself through this hell. But back then you didn't attend college as an individual. Every social scene was generated by the Greek system, and if you weren't associated with some sorority or fraternity, you might as well forget about having friends, or functions to go to. I kept thinking the bad parts of the whole ordeal were almost over, but the misery didn't end with initiation week. From there we progressed to chapter meetings, again top secret, again in the dark.

Every Monday night at 6:45 we Chi Omegas lined up for our weekly plunge into darkness and mystery. Silently, in single file, we marched to the basement of the sorority house and held chapter meetings by candlelight. I never did figure out what was talked about. It reminded me of that time in the car with my mother and brother, when I first realized that other people could communicate in the dark, that I was somehow deficient. Left out.

After I'd accepted that chapter meetings were something I'd attend but never understand, the annual sing-along appeared to taunt and haunt me. Each year every sorority and fraternity house at Syracuse participated in the intrafraternity sing-along. A very competitive event. Some musically talented member of each Greek house was assigned the unhappy task of drumming its members into shape to sing two thoughtfully chosen songs in perfect harmony at a scheduled time and place. The lucky winners won a nice trophy and lots of prestige. Make no mistake; this was serious business. We practiced nightly for about two months. *No* excuses were accepted, including deafness. So every night for two months I presented myself for harmony practice and vainly tried to harmonize.

You haven't lived until you've heard a deaf person's special brand of harmony; the sisters on either side of me rapidly came to hate me. They yelled; I defended myself—to no avail. No amount of arguing was sufficient to bend the fixed, rigid rules. Sing I must, even if I *could not* sing and my sorority sisters didn't *want* me to sing. Finally I sang—silently, moving my lips in perfect unison with those of my neighbors.

Compared to all this, classes were a relief. At least I was prepared for the problems of being deaf amidst hearing classmates and instructors. I'd had twelve years of experience at compensating. And I did well in all my courses, however much extra work that entailed.

Money was always a problem, as it was for most college students. While vocational rehabilitation paid for my college tuition (with the aid of some small scholarships) and my parents paid for my room and board, I was responsible for all other expenses—clothes, books, and entertainment. When school was in session I worked twenty hours a week at SU's education library. I was happiest there, surrounded by so many books. But that job would end with graduation, and I'd have to go out and find work like everyone else. All the potential employers I could think of would not likely want a deaf person as a permanent employee—how competent a secretary could I be if I couldn't hear phones ring? How capable a waitress when there were some customers I couldn't lip-read? I'd done both during summer breaks from college—but it was easy to fake it temporarily. I couldn't fake it forever. Just the thought was anxiety producing, and bad dreams began again.

And something happened to intensify those dreams. After work at the library one day, I entered the service elevator on the fourth floor of the education building, and the elevator went haywire. Up and down it went, up and down, between the basement and the fourth floor. The door never opened; the elevator never stopped, no matter what button I pressed. I pressed them all; I shouted. The constant motion began to make me sick, the fear to make me panic. Would I spend the night in here alone, with no air to breathe? Would I die? I had no idea if anyone heard my shouts.

It was at least an hour before maintenance personnel finally got me out. On top of a bad case of elevatorphobia, I was embarrassed to learn that the custodians had been trying to coach me for more than half the time I was trapped in that box. They could have saved their voices. A small crowd had formed as the men worked to regain control of this errant elevator. I had to wade through it, past curious faces, in order to exit the building. I hadn't cried the whole hour I was prisoner, and I held my head high as I cut through the spectators, but once outside, walking as fast as I could to my room at the sorority house, I couldn't stop the tears.

The next day I returned to work, stoic. I made myself enter the elevator, one more in a series of threats I'd learned to force myself through. But I was growing weary of the challenges, wondering if I would make it through college after all, or if I should surrender right now. More than anything, I was tired of being deaf.

The elevator performed as designed. The door closed and opened when it was supposed to. I entered the library and began shelving books in the reference section. I checked the call number on the first book, a catalog for Gallaudet University. A school for deaf people. On my high school's senior trip to D.C. we'd passed the campus. I remembered distinctly riding past the sign. When I'd asked the tour guide about the place, he'd told me it was "the nation's only college for people who can't hear." I'd looked carefully out the window. Everyone else had gone on chattering among themselves while I'd peered through the glass for some glimpse of the people who made up the place. But I'd seen only trees, walkways, buildings—if there were people, they were a blur. No clue to what a deaf world was like. Everybody relegated there because of a handicap, a weakness. What a thing to have in common, I thought. Like a disease. It had reminded me of a leper colony, and I'd shuddered and turned my face away.

Now, I opened the catalog, thumbed through it. The pictures showed people smiling, happy. You could not tell from the photographs that they were deaf. I knew the smiles were probably like my own, pasted there like an apology. I closed the book, shelving it quickly between two other fat volumes where it became just one in a long row. I went on to the next book and didn't look back.

THE FEEL OF SILENCE

I took my five-year-old granddaughter to the Washington, D.C., Children's Museum the other day. While a friendly employee was showing her how to make paper flowers, she wanted to tell me a secret. She kept trying to whisper in my ear, and I kept pulling back to look at her lips and reminding her I had to see her lips to understand.

What kind of a secret is that? Everyone knows that a *real* secret must be whispered in the ear with hands cupping the mouth. My own children told me that a million times.

In my dream the figure is blurry; it has no real shape. "Repeat after me: La, la, la, rah, rah, rah," it pleads. I sit at the table, eyes glued on the mirror. "La, la, la, rah, rah, rah," I repeat. The blurry figure frowns, looks sad. "Not quite," it says. "Place your tongue like this and try again."

"My tongue was placed like that before," I wail. To no avail. "Try again," the blurry figure instructs. I try. And try. And try. I always wake up before succeeding. The dream is always over too soon.

In my dreams I'm still deaf. So my dreams are full of the same gaps and silences as my reality. And of the same efforts.

Even in my dreams I stare at people with such concentration that I use up all my energy and I'm tired before I wake up.

Even in my dreams I miss the punch line of the joke and am unable to fill in the holes that I miss when the speaker turns his back or darkness strikes.

Even in my dreams I lack the freedom to talk with whom I choose. I must carefully scrutinize each potential friend or acquaintance to see if he or she is lip-readable before interaction is possible.

Even in my dreams I spend large periods of time with a fixed smile on my face. (How long does it take for a smile to look frozen and phony, I wonder?)

Even in my dreams I'm the last to know . . . everything.

Chapter SEVEN

The one thing that drove me in college, more than my desire to do well academically, was my desire to be a cheerleader. As a first-year student one couldn't be, but in the beginning of my sophomore year I would be eligible to try out. There were six female cheerleaders, and as many men. Even though I knew this was the goal of hundreds of other Syracuse women, I was undaunted. If I couldn't try out my first year, I'd spend the time preparing.

In the spring I tried out for the synchronized swim team. I wasn't that invested but figured it would be good competitive practice for the cheerleading tryouts I did care about. If by some miracle I made the team, all the better. I'd learned in high school that the best way to hide the fact that you're a misfit is by being involved in as many things as possible. Others have to admire you for that. And it's a good way to meet people.

It's no mystery why these tryouts proved a disaster for me—I had to take off my glasses to swim. I was virtually blind at a distance of further than two feet, and I couldn't lip-read at all without my glasses. We all lined up in the water facing the swim coach, who proceeded to tell us what to do.

"Turn to the left," she apparently said, and I followed the girl next to me, successfully.

"Do a scissor kick," the coach must have instructed. This was performed underwater, the legs kicking in a scissor motion up above. I almost pulled it off, but since I had to watch the girl next to me I was a step behind everyone else, making a mockery of synchrony.

"Now, somersault gracefully." I made a heroic effort to catch up, did my somersault, but the constant motion of everyone else, and my own dizziness, made this follow-the-leader game impossible. Have you ever tried to watch someone else while you were somersaulting? Flailing there underwater, trying to catch the next move, I was anything but graceful. I imagined I looked more like someone drowning.

At an unobtrusive moment between routines, I exited the pool as deftly as possible. Got my towel and wrapped it around me. I would rather have worn it over my head as I walked into the locker rooms. How stupid

I had been to think I could do this. How humiliating. I told myself it didn't matter. I didn't want to be on that team anyway. Cheerleading tryouts would be different. I'd practiced all year, hadn't I? And I had the JV experience from high school. I was determined to get what I wanted, and nothing, certainly not this synchronized charade, was going to stop me.

The tryouts were judged by the current cheerleaders, both males and females. We went through several processes of elimination. Each time, after we'd done the last cheer they'd asked for, they'd post a list of people who were still under consideration. Bonnie Poitras was always on that list. I felt sorry for those that were eliminated, but I was determined not to be one of them.

I did the third routine as well as I'd done the others. By now I'd practiced so much it was automatic. And I'd had lifelong practice at the pasted smile, so this came easily. When they posted the last list of finalists, mine was among the twelve names on it. I geared up for the final round. I practiced my kicks, turns, and jumps. I could do this stuff as well as anyone else, and better than most. If I became a cheerleader, what a ticket that would be! At Syracuse, I couldn't imagine a stronger link to the hearing population than this one. I was about to merge in the most important way.

For the final competition one additional judge was added: the dean of women. She didn't scare me. No one could stop me now. I was confident I would be chosen. And then it was my turn to perform. I counted slowly. One, two, three, four, five, six, seven, eight. My year of practice paid off. I performed this final cheer effortlessly, and no one could've smiled more convincingly.

When the final tryouts were over, I returned to my sorority house to await the results. I knew that the people who had been chosen would be visited by the current cheerleaders. I waited. And waited.

Two of the male cheerleaders, Gary and Chris, were houseboys at Chi O. I knew they'd be back to tell me what had happened. Finally they came. I could tell by their faces that it wasn't good news. Then Gary spoke. "Bonnie, this is off the record, but the dean of women voted against you."

Chris said, "She has the final say." My face must've been a big question. Both of theirs were sympathetic.

"Something about your file," Chris stammered, "a hearing problem?"

"None of us even realized," Gary said. "We think you were great, but she's firm. We're really sorry. Congratulations for making it to the last cut."

I was absolutely blinded by rage. I didn't say anything. The dean of women, proud defender of the honor of Syracuse University, had intervened. She knew about my deafness because I was receiving vocational rehab assistance. "Obviously," I later learned she had said, "a deaf girl would not make a good representative of our university."

I was devastated. Cheerleading was the epitome of everything I sought—acceptance, normalcy, to be as successful as a hearing girl could be. I wasn't the only one who didn't get chosen, of course. I saw the faces at each cut. The dejection, the disbelief. But my tears were for more than being cut from the cheerleading squad. My tears were for being cut because I was deaf. For years afterward, whenever I was tempted to tell a professor or employer I was deaf, I remembered that dean of women and held my tongue.

After the cheerleading fiasco I was numb for weeks, walking through my days, my classes, my job without any spirit. Things that might've made me feel better didn't. For instance, because my grades were so high, I was one of only a few sophomores in Chi Omega to be invited to live in the rather elegant sorority house. It was a huge improvement over the dorm, but nothing was going to improve my mood.

And living in the Chi O house presented some new problems. Because the bedrooms that we shared two or three to a room were very tiny (many contained no beds, at most, one), most of us actually slept in a large dormitory. To avoid having thirty alarm clocks going off at various intervals in the dormitory, sisters were assigned shifts as wake-up persons. The three sisters assigned to wake up the rest of the group each week would sleep in their small rooms, set their alarms, and wake up everyone on their shift (7:00, 8:00, or 9:00 A.M.). When it was time for me to be wake-up person, I "set" my head rather than an alarm. I dreaded it. I would be so worried that I would oversleep and be held responsible for at least fifteen people missing classes that I would inevitably wake up every hour on the hour all night long to see what time it was. By the time I had finally awakened all the girls on my shift, I was usually so exhausted that I'd sleep half the day. This was good training for life as a mother, and then as an attorney, because eventually I learned to set my head pretty well.

But some things I could not do, such as take a turn at the sorority house switchboard. I thought about the job I'd had the previous summer at an insurance company. I was to relieve each secretary for about two weeks when she went on vacation. Of course, when the phone rang at the desk of the secretary I happened to be relieving, I couldn't answer it. I wouldn't even be aware it had rung. But because I moved from desk to desk so frequently, it took the company almost two months to figure out that the phone was never being answered at whichever desk I happened to be sitting at. I, of course, had not told them I was deaf. By that time I had only one month to go, so I was able to persuade the company to let me finish out the summer. My faking paid off that time. I couldn't fake it at Chi O, however.

I broke the news to my sorority sisters en masse. I was "hard-of-hearing" (although I am sure many of them had figured that much out for themselves by then, and a few knew I was deaf). Instead of putting in time at the switchboard I chose to take over the sorority's correspondence.

There were mixed reactions among my sorority sisters. Most of them accepted my hearing loss or ignored it. Some were condescending and spoke to me in a sickeningly sweet manner, as though they were speaking to a poor relative to whom the rules of society demanded they be polite despite their superiority. But a few were unkind. It was not socially unacceptable in the late fifties and early sixties—at least in the Greek world— to openly denounce persons who were so uncouth as to possess some physical failing. The "Christian" Greek houses wouldn't accept blacks or Jews. Disabled people were out, as well. I knew of no other disabled member of a campus sorority while I was at SU (although I did know of one blind member of a fraternity—a great pianist who played the piano at many of the fraternity's parties).

Looking back, I'm ashamed of having been a part of that system.

Two of my sorority sisters were outspoken in their objection to me. A deaf person, permitted to soil the sanctity of the Chi Omega sorority house? "Missy" was the worse of the two and frequently let me know how she felt.

"People with handicaps should stay among their own kind," she'd say, "and not impose themselves upon the more fortunate." Though it wasn't always possible, I did my best to avoid those two women. I considered myself lucky that I wasn't thrown out.

For the most part, the majority of my sisters soon forgot about my deafness and reduced it to its proper perspective. Not once, however, did anyone speak up in my defense against my two antagonists. Perhaps they were unaware of the taunts and sarcasm aimed at me by those two women. Or perhaps they felt just as awkward and embarrassed as I did, and equally incapable of words.

Despite these problems, I made some good friends among my sorority sisters, some of whom I keep in touch with, thirty-three years later.

And books were a saving grace, still my most reliable means of enjoyment. I was enrolled in a sophomore lit class where we were reading American novelists. The more I liked the book we were reading, the more unbearable the class became for me. In the classes I didn't like, I felt no great loss when I couldn't tell what was going on. I'd become used to this. But I loved literature. I loved to read. And here was a group of people who felt similarly. The class was an elective, so the students were there because they wanted to be. I may not hear, but I'm observant enough to know when discussion is lively.

On the day we were to discuss *Look Homeward, Angel,* I especially wanted to participate. I'd read it in high school, and it was one of my favorites. Hungrily, I had read it again, staying up late at night to finish. People were so excited about the book they were gathered in the hall talking about it, analyzing it, before the bell even rang for class to begin. In class, the professor started off by reading her favorite passage. Hands went up. Interpretations volleyed back and forth. Everybody wanted to speak at once. Occasionally it got so rowdy, she had to calm them down. I had strong opinions about the importance of this book, what it said about America, what it said about the individual. But I couldn't possibly follow all the moving lips in the room. Anything I might say could have already been said or might sound irrelevant placed next to some other comment. I was dying to make my points but unsure where to fit them in. Much worse than biology class in high school, this was a different sort of frustration. Biology I didn't give a hoot about. These literary works were precious to me, and I longed to contribute.

A satisfying conversation, one-on-one, can be a gift. To be privy to a discussion in that classroom full of people, on something I care about—now that would be a luxury. I followed nothing that was said that day. As I left the room, I saw four people arrange to continue their talk in the cafeteria. While they ate lunch accompanied by a stimulating discussion, I would be dining on my envy. I could've asked to join them. Four would certainly be easier to follow than thirty. But I still would've missed much of the conversation. So, disappointed and defeated, I went home to my isolation.

The next day, at my job at the library, I went straight to the reference section. I'd shelved the book, and I knew where it was. I took it off the shelf and looked at it, this time in earnest. Gallaudet. A school for the deaf. Maybe it was worth looking into.

I took the bus from Syracuse to D.C. I lied and told our Chi O housemother that I was going to visit a friend. When I got to Gallaudet's admissions office, the woman in charge started speaking in sign language to me. "No," I told her, "I don't sign. Please just speak. I read lips." She looked shocked but finally began speaking somewhat haltingly. She was not deaf herself. But she insisted on continuing to sign as she spoke, even though the signs meant nothing to me. Actually, all that motion distracted me from reading her lips, and so our conversation was strained. She finally set me free to roam around the campus, telling me to be back in an hour, when she'd have a deaf student show me around.

This student turned out to be a handsome guy. Student body president and quarterback of the football team, Jack approached me with hands going a mile a minute. Oh, no, I thought, not this again. I made the only gesture I was familiar with, a common wave. He waved back, then proceeded to sign like crazy. "Wait," I interrupted. "Do you speak? Because I read lips."

He said he'd rather sign, but he agreed to move his lips while signing.

As we walked around campus, it became apparent that Jack was very popular—everyone greeted and spoke to him in sign language. Did no one at this university speak? Did no one ever try to teach them?

We were both thirsty, so we went to the student union for a Coke. "How long have you been deaf?" I asked Jack. I repeated it a couple of times, since lip-reading wasn't his medium. He held up ten fingers. "Since age ten?" I asked. He nodded, then began to sign—and mouth—an explanation. I gathered something about a bicycle accident, but eventually we had to write down what we were trying to communicate. Jack had full hearing until the age of ten, had a well-developed vocabulary and normal speech. Why, then, did he now refuse to talk? It was baffling. It would've been so easy for him to retain that ability, but he'd let it atrophy, he'd given in.

Jack didn't view it as giving in, however. He viewed it as a simple change of life-style. Back when he was hearing, he spoke. Now that he was deaf, he signed. It was self-evident. Why couldn't I understand it? He was happy and well adjusted in this world of Gallaudet, he explained. And he was, I could see it.

"But how do you operate outside of Gallaudet?" I asked him. "I don't," he mouthed, smiling. "Why should I? We have everything we need right here."

That hit me like a brick. This is *it*? I thought. This quarter of a square mile? This is all there is?

"What will you do when you graduate?" I asked.

"Work here, maybe, or work with deaf people someplace else," he replied, unconcerned.

I knew at that moment, without a single doubt, that I couldn't be happy with that. As difficult as my life was, I'd always been a part of the hearing world where everybody spoke, and where there were no fences, actual or figurative. I felt more alien in this segregated deaf environment than I did among the hearing. I'd gone to seek acceptance in a place that only made me feel more isolated. On the bus ride back to Syracuse, I had a lot of time to think. I concluded that while I may not fit perfectly in the hearing world, I didn't *want* to live in a small Deaf world. I couldn't live in an isolated conclave. I simply couldn't.

There was a big world out there. Problems or not, I wanted to be part of it.

THE FEEL OF SILENCE

Although I have not chosen to isolate myself from the hearing world and live within a segregated Deaf community, I empathize with those Deaf people who have chosen that path of least resistance. Oh, yes, I empathize.

We deaf people who choose to live in the larger, primarily hearing world pay a big price. We face frustrations every day that those who spend their lives primarily with and among other Deaf persons do not have to deal with on a regular basis. Indeed, a primary reason Deaf culture advocates choose to live in a Deaf world is that they don't *want* to deal daily with those frustrations. Who can blame them? Every now and then I think they've made the more intelligent choice.

When I consider the consequences, however, I change my mind. In my view the Deaf culture advocates pay an even higher price. They have narrowed their horizons by choosing to live in a self-created subculture that does not embrace society as a whole.

What's in a label? A lot, in my opinion. Take the terms *deaf, hard-of-hearing,* and *hearing impaired.* God, what a lot of flak there has been about their use.

Many proponents of oralism, which focuses on the use of auditory habilitation and lipreading, and of the auditory-verbal approach, which focuses on the use of residual hearing via technologically improved hearing aids or cochlear implants, support the use of the generic term *hearing impaired* for all individuals with hearing losses, however minor or severe. Degree of hearing loss plays only one part in determining an individual's ability to function in mainstream society. Other significant factors are the type of training the individual has received, the goals set for that individual, and the individual's personal preferences. Thus, the theory goes, it is inappropriate to label someone with a profound hearing loss as *deaf* when that person functions as hard-of-hearing, or vice versa. To avoid inappropriate labels a generic term is preferred.

Proponents of sign language and of the "Deaf is dandy" philosophy, to the converse, want to be defined as what they are: Deaf (or, in an appropriate case, hard-of-hearing). Members of that group strongly object to the term *hearing impaired* as focusing on broken or defective hearing rather than simply identifying the person as one who just happens to be deaf or who just happens to be hard-of-hearing.

I prefer to be called deaf rather than hearing impaired, but not for the same reason. I don't object to the implied reference to broken or defective hearing, because that, to me, is what deafness means. But I prefer to be called deaf because that's what I am. I have no hearing. And I can't wear hearing aids. I am as deaf as it is possible to be. To say that I am hearing impaired implies that I have a slight hearing problem. Since nothing can be further from the truth, I view calling myself hearing impaired as analogous to pretending to be something I am not. I did that for enough years; I don't want to do that anymore.

Members of the "Deaf society," however—those who prefer to sign rather than to speak and who live primarily in a Deaf world, call me hard-of-hearing. Despite the fact that many members of the Deaf society have considerable hearing—and some are audiologically only hard-of-hearing—to them I am not deaf because I do not sign and I live primarily in the hearing world. They view deafness from their own perspective—a cultural perspective rather than an audiological one. Thus, some members of that group protest that Gallaudet's "first deaf president," I. King Jordan, is not deaf, since even though Jordan claims to be audiologically deaf and uses sign language, he did not suffer a loss of hearing until he was an adult. Many members of the Deaf society do not view someone who once had hearing as deaf, even if that person is audiologically more deaf than they are.

I, too, have my own definition of deafness. To me, people who can correct their hearing loss to the point that they can carry on a fairly normal conversation on the telephone are not deaf, any more than people with serious vision problems who can correct those problems with eyeglasses are blind. So that's *my* definition of profound deafness—the inability to use the telephone. Audiologists, however, disagree with that definition.

So what's in a label? Two things. First, a label tells society something; it tells society what this person is all about. Second, a label tells the individual something; it tells the individual what he or she *should be* all about. The difficulty lies in finding the label that accurately portrays us as we think we should be portrayed. The impossibility lies in finding a label that means the same thing to everyone. In this game there is no winner.

Chapter EIGHT

I went to college to find a husband, just like all of the eighteen- and nineteen-year-old girls I knew. In the 1950s and 1960s marriage was what life was about for women. And what better place to find a good husband than college?

So in college I began to date. But it quickly became clear that dating and finding a husband were going to be a bit more difficult for me as a deaf person pretending to be hearing, or at best slightly hard-of-hearing. The most obvious difficulty was my inability to use the telephone. I solved that problem by having a sorority sister pretend she was me on the phone when boys called to ask me out (and prayed that she would say yes when I wanted to say yes and no when I wanted to say no). But this solution didn't work very well for chatty calls. I began to get a reputation for being a nontalker.

Alas, I couldn't take a sorority sister with me on dates, which were often disasters. I would be picked up after dark and taken to a dark car in which we would drive to a dark bar or fraternity party from which we would return in a dark car. Conversation via lipreading was pretty much impossible. To be on the safe side I said no whenever my date seemed to be waiting for a response on my part.

Between the phone and the darkness, dating at Syracuse was pretty much a nightmare for me. (There must be quite a few fraternity types from Syracuse who still recall me as a very strange character.) And so I began dating men from the all-male colleges so prevalent in the East at that time—Colgate, Hamilton, Dartmouth, and so on. Life became easier. We wrote letters rather than using the phone. And weekends at another college were spent at least partially in daylight or a lighted room.

In the fall of my sophomore year, I fell for a Syracuse student, one of the houseboys at Chi O, that cheerleader named Gary. He was a senior and a fraternity man. I liked him very much. Because he knew from the cheerleader tryout fiasco, and from working at Chi O, that I had a hearing problem (though, in keeping with my policy of never telling people about my deafness unless it was absolutely necessary, he didn't know the full extent of it), he was aware that I couldn't use the telephone, at least. I knew my hearing loss bothered him somewhat, but it didn't seem like a major issue.

Gary was sexy and smart and full of life. The first time he kissed me, after a movie, I thought I was falling in love. That dropping in the stomach when our mouths met—was that what falling felt like? A few dates later, I was convinced this was real love.

Toward the end of the year, after Gary and I had been dating for a few months, one of my sorority sisters asked me to go on a blind date. She reminded me that I owed her a favor, which was true, but I had no desire to see anyone but Gary. The guy's name was "Bob" Tucker (I've changed his name for purposes of privacy); he was a student at Hamilton College, a small, elite, all-male college about a two-hour drive from Syracuse. Bob was good friends with the boyfriend of this sorority sister and was in town unexpectedly, thus dateless.

"Bonnie," she said, "he's really a doll. Most girls would give their right arm for this opportunity."

"So why don't you find one of them to go out with him?" If there were so many, I didn't see why she had to force me.

"It's short notice. Everyone's got plans," she said. "And besides, you owe me. Come on. Please?"

Since I had no plans, reluctantly I agreed. My objective was to put in the time and get the evening over with as quickly as possible.

Bob was not what I expected in a blind date. The sorority sister who came to tell me he had arrived said, "My God, who is that Greek god?" With brownish-blond hair, big dark eyes, and the body of an athlete, he was very intelligent and also charming. Surprisingly, in spite of all this and a basically pleasant evening, I remained uninterested. I guess I really was in love with Gary. But my disinterest was a new experience for Bob Tucker. He was used to girls falling all over him, could have anyone he wanted. My indifference, my impatience to get home, must've intrigued this "big man on campus." President of everything in high school and equally popular in college, he had probably never come across a girl who had not fallen immediately for him. For once he had to chase. It must have been the challenge that caught Bob's interest, for I was a perfectly ordinary college female, not beautiful by any stretch of the imagination, not particularly athletic, and not very skilled in the arts of dating or charming men. But I was hard to get.

Although I dated Bob a couple of times, for the most part I turned down his invitations, spending my time with Gary whenever Gary wanted to spend time with me (which was never as often as I hoped). As the year came to an end, Gary asked me to stay and watch him graduate and then spend a few days visiting his family in Pittsburgh. I was excited and nervous to meet them. I so wanted to make the right impression.

A few days before graduation I happened to be with Gary when he was talking to his mother on the phone, making arrangements. He was just out-side of the room, and he didn't realize I could see him and read his lips from where I sat.

"She has a hearing problem," I saw him say. And then, defensively, "It's not a *big* problem." His mother was obviously upset. They talked a while longer, Gary's demeanor becoming more defensive, more strained, burdened. Eventually he bowed his head with the weight of the whole thing, and I couldn't lip-read anymore. I was crushed to realize that I was someone people had to be warned about. But I'd been through worse tri-als and was determined to weather this one. I would be so charming his family would have to like me.

Gary hung up and joined me in the other room. The conversation I'd observed was never discussed.

Shortly after that, we went to a fraternity picnic with a large group of people. As it turned dusk, Gary told me that we couldn't see each other anymore. His face was heavy with discomfort, so much so that he looked down, away from me, as he explained the reasons for the breakup. I could've asked him to look up, but I could tell two things: This wasn't easy for him; and he meant whatever he was saying—there was no turning back. At any rate, it was now too dark to lip-read. No sense asking him to re-peat—I wouldn't be able to see what he said. The specifics didn't matter, I thought. The important thing was to keep my composure. But I'd seen that conversation with his mother and couldn't help wondering how much, if at all, my deafness had influenced Gary's decision.

I've often fantasized about the contents of that parting speech. What did he *say* were his reasons? Did his explanations touch on my deafness? Did my deafness, in fact, have anything to do with his decision? I'll never know. (Many years later, when I was practicing law, Gary and I met for a long lunch. During the course of the several hours we spent reminiscing and talking about our current lives and families, I never got the courage to ask him about that.)

I spent the summer after my sophomore year of college with a broken heart.

I was still feeling sorry for myself in the fall, when I ran into Bob at a Syra-cuse college hangout shortly after school began. He'd eventually given up on me, but now he saw that I was more open to getting to know him, more available. We began to spend a lot of time together. Unlike Gary, Bob knew nothing of my deafness, and, for a long while, I wasn't about to tell him.

During my junior year I frequently went to Hamilton for the weekend. I and dates of other Hamilton men would stay in one of the fraternity houses while the occupants moved out for the weekend. Bob played on the baseball team, and sometimes when he had an out-of-town game I would arrive on the last bus on Friday afternoon before he had returned from his game.

One weekend Bob knew that I would have to arrive about four hours before he returned to the Hamilton campus, so he arranged for two of his fraternity brothers to meet my bus and entertain me for a few hours. When those two nice guys picked me up at the bus stop, they were all excited. It seemed that Hamilton College had just finished building and equipping a new music room, complete with one of the very first state-of-the-art stereo systems. They couldn't wait to take me there. Although I had no idea what they were talking about, I agreeably followed them to see this new wonder of the world.

Upon arriving at what looked like a comfortable, large living room, Bob's friends sat me in an easy chair, sat themselves down on a couch next to my chair, pushed a few buttons here and there on the wall, and proceeded to sit there with rapturous looks on their faces for two of the longest hours I have ever experienced. What torture. It brought back early memories of my parents and eldest brother sitting silently in front of the radio for hours. While intellectually I knew that someone was saying something or playing music on that little brown box, I often wondered just how my family could remain glued to that stupid machine.

My friendly hosts had no idea that I could not hear. At first I did not want to tell them, because I had not yet told Bob, and I felt that courtesy dictated that I tell Bob that I was deaf before I told any of his friends. After an hour, however, when they showed no signs of ever cutting this music session short and it appeared that we were in for a very long afternoon, I had second thoughts. At that point, however, it was impossible. I had been imitating their looks of rapture for an hour, pretending that I was enjoying this new toy as much as they were. If I were now to tell them I was deaf, who would be more embarrassed and feel more stupid, I or they?

And so we sat.

I concluded that the time had come for me to tell Bob that I was deaf. We had, after all, been dating steadily for several months. But before I could muster my courage to break what I feared would be the dreadful news, fate intervened.

Spring was finally coming. The endless snow had almost disappeared. Bob came to Syracuse for a weekend with some of his fraternity brothers. He and I, his fraternity brothers and some of my sorority sisters, went to a party. While I danced with one of his friends he danced with one of mine, Janet, from my sorority. Every sister in my house thought Bob was a dream; some, I'm sure, couldn't help wondering why he was with me.

I had my eye on Janet and Bob as they danced. I was growing more fond of him every day and doing my best to make the relationship last. As

I watched them, they looked over at me. Janet said something, and Bob looked surprised, then shocked, then completely stiff. Just then the music stopped. I learned their conversation had gone like this:

"It's amazing what a good dancer Bonnie is," Janet said. Bob nodded. "I mean, to be that good when she can't even hear the music," she continued.

"What are you talking about?" Bob said. This must've been the look of surprise I'd seen on his face.

"That she dances so well when she doesn't hear the music—I think it's amazing."

Bob's look of shock. "What?" he said, dumbfounded.

"Bonnie has a hearing problem. Don't tell me you didn't know." This was when I'd seen him go stiff, as the music stopped.

Bob came over, grabbed me, and pulled me to the hallway by the bathroom. He was livid.

"Tell me it's not true," he said.

And though I knew he could only be referring to one thing, I asked him, "What?" My stomach was feeling the way it had after cheerleader tryouts, the way it had at the fateful picnic with Gary. The snacks I'd eaten earlier swam around inside me, threatening revolt.

Bob just looked at me. "I think you know what I'm talking about," he said. "There's something you haven't told me."

"Yes, but I was planning to," I said.

"Planning to? When, Bonnie? For God's sake, we've been dating each other for over six months!"

I couldn't say anything to this.

"So it's true then," he said.

"Yes."

We didn't leave the party, though we might as well have, because we spent the rest of the evening in silence. When Bob took me home that night, he was still angry.

"It's like lying, Bonnie," he said to me.

"I know," I said. "I'm sorry."

"I think we shouldn't see each other anymore," he said.

I didn't respond, just got out of the car, went into the house, and cried myself to sleep. It seemed there was some balance to be struck, and I couldn't ever find it. If I revealed my deafness to people, doors closed in my face; if I concealed it, people felt betrayed. For a nineteen year old, it was a tremendous weight to carry around. Instead of becoming easier with time, my response to my deafness had grown increasingly complicated.

In just a few weeks, as if nothing had happened, Bob wrote and we began to see one another again. My deafness was not mentioned. It seemed Bob was content to ignore it, to pretend it didn't exist. The subject, apparently, was taboo. I was grateful for and comfortable with the pretense and experienced at going along with the charade. I'd been playing that game my whole life.

At the end of my junior year, Bob gave me his fraternity pin; we were semiengaged. Affection grew, as did our attraction to each other. We spent more and more time together. That summer I stayed in Syracuse to be near Bob. I lived in an apartment with three of my sorority sisters and was able to see him just about every night. Not surprisingly, things got pretty steamy. But we were true products of the 1950s. Nice girls didn't have sex before marriage. If we wanted to make love, we'd have to get married. I pushed for marriage. Bob wavered. Finally, in the middle of the summer we eloped.

Neither set of parents would've condoned this, we thought, nor would school authorities, so we saw no alternative. You had to be twenty-one in the state of New York to marry without parental consent; we were not. So we took the train to Raleigh, North Carolina, and were married before a justice of the peace in the local courthouse on July 15, 1960. The train ride back was our honeymoon.

Our game plan was to keep our marriage a secret until we both graduated from college. Bob lived at his fraternity house at the Hamilton campus in Clinton, New York, while I lived at my sorority house at Syracuse. I took a bus to Clinton every weekend, where we had rented a room from a prudish middle-aged lady who took in boarders. She strongly disapproved of us, although she reluctantly agreed to rent us a room after studying our marriage license very carefully.

That apartment reminded me of the place I'd lived as a child with the spinster landladies. There was that same sense of not belonging, of home not really being home. We spent our weekends in the upstairs bedroom of the house of a critical landlady who would not even allow us to use the kitchen for fear we would contaminate the morals of other members of the household. It was not an auspicious beginning.

Was I happy? I don't know. I think mostly what I felt was a satisfaction: this was what hearing people did. They met someone, fell in love, married, and lived happily ever after. I'd always wondered if I would take those steps into "normalcy," cement that bridge I'd been building between me and the hearing world. Bob was considered an excellent catch; in a way he was the trophy of my success. I was ready for whatever challenges married life would throw my way.

THE FEEL OF SILENCE

"Is deafness all that bad?" asked a friend to whom I was talking about writing this book. "Yes," I replied. But I was not quite truthful. Deafness, in and of itself, is not so bad. Sometimes I kind of like it. A part of me feels sorry for you hearing people who have to live with a constant barrage of noise. How can you hear yourselves think?

No, deafness isn't so bad. What's *bad*, if that term must be used, is the reactions that hearing people have to my deafness. If I lived in a vacuum, deafness could be quite pleasant much of the time. But I don't live in a vacuum.

"**W**hatsa matter, lady, are ya deaf?" I've had that phrase shouted at me by passing drivers as they pulled alongside my car, furious that I hadn't responded to their horns; by passersby righteously indignant that I hadn't moved when they'd said, "Excuse me, please"; by store clerks who had been trying to attract my attention; by seatmates in planes or buses whose attempts at casual conversation had met with silence.

How should I respond? A simple yes, which I tried only once, sent the speaker into such paroxysms of embarrassment that I never had the heart to do that again. A sweet smile seems to be the most diplomatic response.

Demeaning. That's what deafness is. It strips one of dignity. It makes one inferior. Hearing people are always in a superior position simply by virtue of being able to hear. Deaf people have no choice but to rely on the hearing to act as intermediaries.

Deafness means a loss of power.

Deafness makes even the most independent person dependent. Deafness acts as a magnifying glass. It makes everything seem larger than life. All of the trivial irritations of everyday life are blown out of proportion and magnified a thousandfold.

Deafness holds one in check. It controls the whole of one's personality. It stifles even the most gregarious. If not hamstrung by deafness, I would speak to strangers everywhere. But deafness prohibits such spontaneous friendliness.

Deafness means isolation.

Deafness is a state from which there is no escape.

"**I**sn't she remarkable?" they ask. "She's deaf, and look at what she's done."

Oh God. They are putting me on a pedestal again. How soon will it be before I fall? How long will I last this time?

Because I always fall. And the higher the pedestal, the further I topple.

The second life

WIFE AND MOTHER

Chapter NINE

Somehow, a secret weekend marriage didn't feel like a marriage at all. It felt more like having a license to engage in sex. Every week we led our separate lives in separate cities, but on the weekends in our secret apartment we were husband and wife. Keeping the secret was the most difficult part. We couldn't let people know that I was going to Clinton every weekend. Hamilton men didn't leave their fraternity houses on a weekly basis to accommodate their dates, and women simply didn't visit Hamilton except when the men vacated their fraternity houses. Also, it was commonplace for Hamilton men to leave Clinton fairly frequently on the weekends and head for the big cities where the college women were. We were forever having to think up stories to tell people where we were on the weekends, particularly when Bob's friends came to Syracuse and he declined to join them.

Our regular weekend disappearance was, as far as his fraternity brothers knew, Bob disappearing by himself. Increasingly baffled by his unavailability for the usual party scene, and by his continued refusal to go to Syracuse, where they assumed he'd want to visit me, his friends became suspicious.

After we'd been meeting at our weekend apartment for several weeks, we finally did attend a party at Bob's fraternity house, in celebration of a football victory. Bob and I were faithful to our vows of secrecy. No one knew, not even our roommates.

Well into the evening, one of Bob's fraternity brothers approached me. Dan had always been especially kind to me. He looked confused and upset, guilty almost, but there was a determination in his face, as if he were about to set some matter straight. I smiled at him. He was fairly drunk.

"Bonnie," he slurred, "I care about you, you know that, right?"

"Yes," I said. Usually, the more someone drinks, the more rubbery their speech gets, but the intensity of Dan's expression was very articulate—I was reading him loud and clear.

"Well, I hate to be the one to tell you this, but I think you should know."

"Go ahead," I said. "What is it?"

He looked down, dug the toe of his shoe into the carpet, then took the last swig of his beer. As though fortified by that swallow, he unleashed the news. "We think Bob's got a mistress," he said, looking away. I tried not to smile. "He disappears every weekend, and no one knows where he goes." Dan was so earnest, so sorry to be the bearer of bad news, you would've thought he was the errant boyfriend. His face was apologetic, contrite.

"Really?" I said. I feigned distress. "Thanks so much. I'll talk to him."

Our families were as unsuspecting as our friends. After we'd been married for four months, we spent Thanksgiving with Bob's parents, who owned a motel in Skaneateles, New York, a lake community about an hour from Syracuse, and lived during the winters in Baldwinsville, a Syracuse suburb. Bob, of course, had told his parents I was deaf. Like Gary's mother, Bob's mother had other ideas when it came to the right wife for her son. Though she was very polite to my face, she presented a different side when she thought I couldn't see her. The first night after dinner, as I sat on the living room couch, I inadvertently "eyesdropped" as Mrs. Tucker spoke to her husband. "Oh, he'll never marry her," she said. "He's too smart to marry someone who's deaf." I was glad at that moment for our secret, glad to postpone indefinitely the moment of their inevitable dismay. Any hopes of ever having a close relationship with my in-laws vanished.

In early February, I got a flu that hung on. I was tired, had no appetite, and when I did force myself to eat I couldn't keep anything down. Bob said it was probably sheer exhaustion from the stress of senior year. I assumed it was an intestinal virus and went on with my studies, sure it would go away. It got worse. I thought that if I threw up one more time I would die.

In desperation I finally went to the doctor. He ran some tests and gave me something to take for the nausea. The next day I went back for the results, feeling no better. The nurse took me into an examining room and shut the door. Did I have a dreadful disease?

The nurse looked at me with that same sympathetic look that had been on Dan's face. "I hope this isn't bad news," she said, "but . . . you're pregnant." The poor nurse thought she was telling me I was an unwed mother. And I was shocked, but not for the reasons she'd assumed. I had visited Planned Parenthood before Bob and I took the train to North Carolina, had been using a diaphragm faithfully, and had never considered for a moment that I might be pregnant.

Bob was as surprised as I was, at first, but quite quickly we got used to the idea. We both wanted children. So we'd be parents a little earlier than we'd planned—we'd manage.

In May I would graduate, but Bob had another year of college to go. It wasn't until his graduation that we had planned to figure out what to do next, how to go about informing people of the nuptials that had already taken place. Now we had to tell everyone. My parents took the news with good grace and held a party for us at their home to announce the marriage. Bob's parents were noncommittal. The powers that be at Syracuse, however, were incensed, and for a couple of weeks my expulsion seemed inevitable. Fortunately, the dean of the journalism school intervened. I was just beginning the last semester of my senior year, he argued, and it was preposterous not to let me finish. But my old friend, the dean of women, was adamant. No pregnant woman was going to impugn the morals of *her* university. So a compromise was reached. Syracuse University had a branch program in Utica, New York, about twenty miles from Clinton and Hamilton College. Bob and I would live in Utica, and I would take my last semester of classes on the Utica campus, still receiving my degree from Syracuse. Bob, of course, would continue to attend Hamilton. He wasn't pregnant, and expectant fathers did not need to be hidden or ostracized.

And so we moved to Utica and found a tiny apartment in a seedy part of town, up a steep narrow staircase over a bar. We had no money to live on except what we earned from our part-time jobs. As far as we could tell, the rest of the people on the block were on welfare. It was not the ideal place for a young pregnant woman to spend her solitary evenings while her husband was at school and at work, especially a young, pregnant, deaf woman who would not hear an intruder approach. Bob decided what we needed was a dog to protect me.

I didn't want a dog. I particularly didn't want a big dog. I have an irrational fear of big dogs (probably stemming from the time that a classmate in grade school had her ear bitten off by a strange large dog). Bob, however, loved big dogs, and the shaky neighborhood we lived in gave him a plausible excuse for bringing one to our tiny apartment. I lost the argument (which should have told me something—I was to lose most of our arguments during seventeen years of marriage) and went with Bob in his old car to a farm on the outskirts of town to pick up one of the largest puppies I have ever seen. He weighed 90 pounds to my 105.

It took some doing to get that dog in our car. He didn't want to go. But getting the dog in the car was nothing compared to getting him into our apartment. Because Duke, as Bob immediately named this half-German shepherd, half-Labrador monster, had been trained by his previous owners never to step foot inside a door. Bob dragged the dog, pushed the dog, pleaded with the dog. Duke would not budge from the doorstep. And when Bob tried to carry him, Duke struggled so hard that his ninety pounds felt more like twice that weight.

Bob gave up temporarily and leaned against the wall to think, to catch his breath. I couldn't help feeling hopeful.

"I guess we'll have to take him back," I said. I tried to be respectful of what I knew would be Bob's disappointment.

"No," Bob said. "He'll cooperate. Won't you, Duke?"

I appealed to Bob's sense of reason. "He's going to have to go to the bathroom, Bob. Even if we get him up there, we'll have to do this several times a day," I said. But Bob was stubborn.

"Come on, Duke," he said. And then, "Bonnie, pick up his hind legs."

"You've got to be kidding," I said.

He wasn't.

We carried that oversized puppy up the long steep flight of stairs, me responsible for the tail end. As soon as we got the dog inside our front door, he did what any sensible terrified being would do: ran to the bedroom, hid under our bed, and refused to come out. By this time Bob and I were exhausted and ready to go to bed. There were limits to what I'd tolerate. A big black monster dog underneath my bed all night went beyond them. I put my foot down.

"Either the dog goes or I sleep elsewhere," I said.

I slept on the lumpy living room couch while Bob and Duke shared the bedroom.

The next morning when Bob left for school and work Duke was still under the bed. Bob knew I had no classes that day, so he breezily threw the dog's leash on the table, reminding me to take the dog for a walk. Since Duke wasn't coming out from under the bed for anything, I wasn't worried. He could stay there all day for all I cared.

Bob's car had barely pulled away when Duke appeared beside the front door of our apartment, crying and howling. And though I couldn't hear this, it was impossible not to see it; that apartment was *small.* Duke got more and more panicked, and after an hour and a half I couldn't stand it anymore. I lashed one end of the leash to Duke's collar, slipped the other end over my wrist, and opened the door. Mistake. Duke took off like the desperate animal he was, and I tumbled down the steps after him.

Once outdoors Duke calmed down a bit, and I was able to get my bearings. Moving along at a slower clip, we proceeded to the park a block away, where we spent a pleasant half hour with the derelicts and winos.

When it was time to go back home, Duke remained unpersuaded that it was permissible to enter the premises. After twenty minutes had passed, and the two of us were still parked in front of the staircase to our building, I gave up. I walked into the bar with Duke still lashed to my wrist and asked the first patron I came to if he'd like to earn two dollars by helping me carry Duke up to our apartment. Two dollars looked pretty good to an unemployed laborer on his third or fourth beer at 10:30 in the morning; he accepted with alacrity. By the time we got Duke into the apartment (where once again he promptly dived under the bed), I was long past the point of being concerned about bringing a strange male into my apartment. This was the dog that was supposed to be for my protection?

Actually, as it turned out I didn't need much protection from the patrons of the bar below us, for shortly after Duke came to live with us the bar was sold to a new owner and became a gay bar. On quite a few occasions Bob was approached; once someone left him a note on his car. But no one bothered me, except, of course, Duke.

Kevin was born several weeks late. He obviously didn't want to leave the comfort of the womb; his birth ultimately had to be medically induced, as he was so large and so overdue the doctors were concerned. This was long before natural childbirth and Lamaze classes became popular and before fathers were allowed in the delivery room (Bob did not witness any of the children's births). Fathers were, however, permitted in the labor room during the initial stages of labor, and thus Bob witnessed my growing discomfort.

I doubt that he enjoyed that experience. I was not a good patient. I'm actually a terrible coward when it comes to physical pain. And being deaf didn't help—it's hard to lip-read what people are saying when you are in the throes of a labor pain. Lipreading takes *concentration*. But while it was difficult for me to lip-read either Bob or the medical personnel giving me instructions, it was virtually impossible to lip-read the doctors who spoke while sitting at the foot of the bed looking at the lower part of my anatomy rather than at my face.

At least I only had to struggle with lipreading through the red heat of pain until they wheeled me into the delivery room and put me to sleep as they did in those days. Deaf women today have to do this throughout the entire "natural" delivery. I don't know how they lip-read (or watch someone signing) instructions to breathe in, breathe out, relax, and so on, when they are in agonizing pain. Or does the need to focus on watching what is said distract from the pain? Somehow I doubt it.

The last thing I lip-read as they wheeled me into the delivery room was a nurse saying, "No, don't take her glasses off until she's completely under—there's a hearing aid built into them and she needs them to hear." (That nurse, and the doctors too, I think, never quite understood the concept of lipreading. I think the medicos shouted louder when they thought I didn't understand them.) And then I awoke and was handed a beautiful nine-pound boy. (This is not just a proud mother talking. He was so big and pink and healthy looking the hospital used him for a demonstration baby when teaching new mothers how to diaper, bathe, hold, and care for their newborns.) I'd have done it all over again like a shot.

Once Kevin was born, there wasn't room for all of us in that tiny apartment. We rented the ground floor of an old house on a corner of the main thoroughfare in Utica, in a slightly better neighborhood. It had two advantages: no stairs and a very small grassy area for Duke. The grassy area proved to be his downfall, for Duke had two problems, one physical and one emotional. Physically, he suffered from the aftereffects of chorea—a fact we learned several weeks after we acquired him. That illness had left Duke with a jaw that snapped up and down of its own free will, at the same time emitting a great deal of saliva. This made Duke look like a mad dog (and I still harbored the secret fear that his madness would one day manifest itself in some inappropriate manner). Emotionally, Duke was a friendly creature. He loved people, especially children. And he showed that love by jumping all over everyone. The children in the immediate neighborhood loved Duke in return, and they would occasionally come to the house just to play with him. Children who didn't know Duke, however, were terrified of him. Duke's physical and emotional characteristics simply didn't complement one another.

One day a police officer arrived at our front door with a formal order. Because our apartment faced the main thoroughfare of town, children from all over Utica had to walk past our apartment to get to school. Numerous parents had complained to the police that their children were forced to cross the dangerous main street of town to avoid walking past a "mad, vicious dog." The order from the chief of police was quite clear. Duke had to go, or we had to go. Since even Bob had to admit that we had nowhere else to go, Duke was returned to the farm. And my attention was diverted to worrying about my son instead of my husband's dog.

I was surprised how little I knew about how to care for babies. I didn't even know how to change a diaper. When Kevin was born, my mother came to help out for two weeks.

"Be very careful," she said, during the first lesson on diapering, "not to prick him with the pin." She showed me how you keep your fingers between his skin and the pin, so that if it pushes through suddenly, it's you who will bleed, not the baby. This was easy enough and made perfect sense. I wanted her to tell me more. Everything she knew.

"When the point of the pin seems dull," she said, "run it through a bar of soap like this." I remembered seeing her do this when changing baby Richard. "The soap," she explained, "sharpens the tip." I tried this, running the point of the safety pin through a bar of soap in my hand, careful not to scratch myself. It worked; the pin slid into the thick cotton without resistance. There were tricks to this trade! I was relieved.

I learned how to hold up Kevin's head, never to leave it without support. How to bathe him in shallow tepid water, with gentle soap. I learned that sometimes when the baby screamed, mouth wide open in what I imagined to be the worst sort of empty wail, the baby wasn't dying, the baby needed to burp. Mother showed me how to put a clean folded diaper over my shoulder, then the baby, then gently pat his back.

At night during those first two weeks it was my mother, not Bob, who was alert to the baby's first whimper and would bring his small self to me, a bundle of warmth, hungry. As I fed him the bottle of formula she'd prepared, she sat up with me, and in the silence I imagined we were both wondering the same thing—however would I manage all this once she left? What she couldn't show me was how to raise a baby that I couldn't hear. Lurking, I imagined, in the back of both our minds was the reminder that she hadn't thought it safe for me to care for others' children; how was I to care for my own? These fears remained unspoken, as had every lifelong fear about my deafness. Don't mention it, and maybe it will go away.

When Bob and I and Kevin took Mother to the train station, she and I both cried. Bob looked at us uncomfortably, pretended not to notice. Kevin was oblivious to the fact that his mother was any different from any other mother. I was meeting all his needs, wasn't I? To love and to nurture and to feed and to protect—are those roles dependent upon hearing? My mother hugged me, and I tried not to break into a sob. Once I'd been her little girl; now I held a child of my own.

"Bye," I said. "Have a safe trip." Mother nodded, too choked up to speak. She kissed Kevin's forehead. She and Bob exchanged an awkward embrace. As she walked away, I felt the instant largeness of her absence. I was to accomplish this alone, without hearing, without help—for in those days fathers were not expected to share in child-rearing.

"Thanks," I called out after her. "Thanks for everything."

As we walked back to our old car, I promised myself I would manage. I would compensate for my deafness, the way I had in other areas of my life. It was my inadequacy, and I would see that it intruded as little as possible on my family. I would not burden my husband with it, or my child.

I needn't have worried so much. We muddled along alright. I put Kevin in a bassinet on wheels and wheeled him from room to room with me. He was always in my line of vision. When he got a little older, and it was necessary to put him in his own room to take a nap or go to bed for the night, I checked on him every ten minutes, like clockwork, unless Bob was home or someone was visiting who would hear him cry. I have no way of knowing, of course, how many times Kevin awoke immediately after I left his room and cried for the full ten minutes before I returned. I can only hope it wasn't too often.

I was misinformed by my very elderly doctor that after childbirth my old diaphragm would work fine, and fourteen months after Kevin arrived, our daughter Ronale was born (her name is pronounced ronna-lee). I felt more comfortable with her, partly because I had my systems down by that point, and also because Kevin was a reliable sentry. As young as he was, Kevin understood the importance of letting me know whenever he heard the baby cry. The responsibility made him feel important. When Scott was born years later, when Kevin was six and Ronale five, I had both Kevin and Ronale to depend on. On more than one occasion I explained to them what serious business this was; they both clearly understood, and they vied with one another to be the one to tell me Scott was awake or crying.

I never had to tell any of my children to look at me when they spoke, however. It didn't take them long to figure out that if they wanted me to respond to what they said they had to face me when they talked and make sure I was looking at them. A child who is demanding Mother's attention will do whatever it takes to get that attention. If the children didn't think I was paying sufficient attention they'd place their tiny hands on my cheeks and turn my face in their direction.

All three of my children spoke fluently at an early age. And while the speech of little children is usually impossible to lip-read (aside from the lack of clarity, children often fidget when they speak), I was always able to understand everything my children said. I suspect this was in large part because my children made sure they spoke clearly; because they wanted to ensure my full attention to their needs and desires. Children are remarkably adept at figuring out how to get what they want.

I vividly recall the first time Kevin answered the telephone. He was sixteen months old. He picked up the receiver, said hello, and, after a pause, looked up at me and said, "Gramma says when will daddy be home?"

As precocious as he was, Kevin couldn't be expected to handle telephone tasks. One morning after Bob had left for class, Ronale woke up with a fever. I could tell just by holding her that she was burning up, and the thermometer convinced me that she should see a doctor. Since I couldn't call the doctor's office to make an appointment, we would have to just appear.

It was miserable winter weather outside, my only transportation was the bus, and there was no one to leave Kevin with while I took Ronale to see the doctor. Her fever seemed to rise by the minute. I did the only thing I could do—bundled both kids into their snowsuits, put on my own coat, hat, and gloves, and headed out, Ronale in one arm, the other extended to hold Kevin's hand as we crossed busy streets on the way to the bus stop.

When we finally walked in the doctor's office, the waiting room was spilling over with sick children. Every child in Syracuse had come down with something overnight and it seemed they all went to the same pediatrician we did. I waited in line at the window for my turn to speak to the receptionist. The chorus of coughing—a crazy facial dance I could see rather than hear—made me nervous, and I kept Kevin as close to me as I could. I noted that there were at least ten names on the list of patients waiting to see the doctor.

"Did you have an appointment?" the receptionist asked.

"No," I explained. "She just woke up with this fever. She was fine last night. I can't hear on the telephone, so couldn't call to make an appointment."

"The doctor will see you eventually, but as you can see, we're booked with patients who have appointments. He won't be able to see you till the end of the day."

When I turned around and imagined myself and my children wedging ourselves in amongst the various illnesses, I started to feel sick myself. And claustrophobic. Kevin was eyeing a truck on the floor that a baby was drooling all over. How could I expect him to sit here for hours and not play with the toys? But the germs in this room were thick.

I tightened my grip on his hand and turned back to the woman at the little sliding window. Her side of the office looked amazingly sterile by comparison.

"Is there no way the doctor could see us within the next couple of hours?"

She gauged the list with a sweeping glance; it was growing.

"Maybe after lunch?" she said tentatively, as if even that was a generous estimate.

Could we wait three or four hours in this place? And what would I do for the kids' lunch? As much as I hated to go home on the bus, only to turn around three hours later for the same bus ride back, I saw no other option. I looked at the woman again. "Can we make an appointment for four o'clock?" She dutifully penciled my name in the appointment book.

And we marched out into the cold where the air, though biting, circulated, and I was able to breathe deeply again. I was totally frustrated.

The children, too, must have been frustrated sometimes. Once they were walking, I couldn't keep them in the same room with me all the time. And if they were in another room and needed me, they couldn't call me. If they cried, I wouldn't hear them. While I checked on them regularly and tried to keep them next to me as much as I could, it simply wasn't always possible. I understood the hazards of this when Scott, just thirteen months old but a whirling bundle of energy, pulled the door handle to a sewing cabinet built into the wall of our family room.

As the cutting table swung down out of the wall, one was supposed to open the leg folded underneath it so the table would stand on the floor. Scott didn't do that. As he tugged on the handle with his right hand, the table popped out of the wall, bypassed the floor, and swung flat against the wall, chopping off part of Scott's left thumb, which was resting underneath the hinge where the table pulled out from its cabinet. I, of course, didn't hear Scott's screams of pain and terror and didn't know he was hurt until he came running into the kitchen cradling his bloody left hand to his chest. How outraged Scott must have been that I didn't rush to his rescue but left him to wander the house to find me. To make matters worse, Bob had taken our only car to work and I couldn't call for help; I had to carry Scott to a neighbor and have her get assistance. Ultimately the neighbor drove us to the hospital and then came back and found the tip of Scott's thumb on the drawer knob of the sewing center.

Despite the difficulties inherent in deaf parenting, I loved being a mother, and I spent the same sort of focused time with my children that my mother had spent with me. I read to them for hours, as they sat entranced. Children's books often revolve around sights and sounds, an introduction to the world around them. Some of these books were nonsensical to me, but I read them anyway.

"Bow wow," says the dog.

"Meow, meow," says the cat.

"Moo, moo," says the cow.

"Neigh, neigh," says the horse.

"Toot, toot," honks the car.

"Clang, clang," goes the fire engine.

"Screech, screech," wails the . . . (I forget. What goes "Screech, screech," anyway?)

"Bang, bang," goes the gun.

I hoped that what I was reading made sense to them. And I hoped my rendition of the sounds wasn't too far off.

Nighttime was more challenging. Bob was in law school during the day and worked two to four nights per week as a private investigator. At that time the only ground for divorce in New York was adultery. Bob's job was to follow an allegedly errant husband or wife to a motel, sit in his car outside the motel until the unsuspecting spouse and companion left, and in a notebook record the times, places, and details that would eventually serve as the requisite proof of adultery. Bob would sometimes spend most of the night in a cold car, studying, while waiting for his suspects to exit the motel.

On the nights he worked, there was no one to tell me if Kevin or Ronale was crying. We desperately needed the money from his job; we were living on student loans and the generosity of my parents, who kept the kids clothed. So I had to develop a system. I slept in half-hour shifts and checked on my babies in between. Most of the time, this appeared to work, though again I have no way of knowing if the babies thought it worked. Did they cry out with nightmares that I never heard? Every now and then I wonder if they may have been left to suffer through some traumatic episode alone. Did I scar them for life?

I never became overly confident as a deaf mother, but I did start to worry less, to relax. We were managing fine and our poverty was temporary; we knew this.

I'd learned in college to awaken by an inner alarm clock. When I slept in those twenty- to thirty-minute spurts, I programmed myself to wake that often. It became habit, and my dreams adjusted accordingly. Like magic, my eyes would startle open at these regular intervals, and I'd half sleep-walk into the children's room to witness the steady rise and fall of their breathing.

One night when Bob was working I was especially tired. Ronale was one year old at the time, and Kevin about two. I'd had trouble sleeping the night before and hadn't had a chance to nap during the day. When I lay down for my first twenty minutes of slumber, my inner alarm went on a holiday. My mind and body were so exhausted that neither was capable of telling the other what to do. I dreamed about the math rhyme, and the way I used to perform it on command, how easy it became after all that repetition, and how predictable the applause of the adults. "Multiplication is vexation. / Division is as bad. / The rule of three perplexes me. / And practice drives me mad." It'd been years since I'd thought of that rhyme, yet in the dream it all came back to me, and I was still the little girl with brown curls who could please, simply by being dressed up, put on display, like a little windup doll. I said what I'd been taught—they clapped. It was easy to be a star. Life had not ever been as easy since. I wallowed in that time of no responsibility. The rhyme played over and over in my dream.

It was midnight when I woke with a start and looked at the clock. I'd gone to bed at ten. Two hours since I'd checked on my sleeping toddlers. I grabbed my glasses, put them on, and went to see that everything was alright.

Ronale's crib was empty. Every fear any mother has ever imagined popped into my head. She'd been kidnapped. She'd fallen out of bed and was now plummeting down a fatal flight of stairs. She'd discovered the cleaning supplies and was having a taste of something poisonous. I ran to find her.

What I found was Ronale in her pajamas in the kitchen, in the middle of the floor, playing with a set of steak knives like they were so many pickup sticks. The blades looked sinister under the harsh light I'd left on in the kitchen. I gasped; she looked up, startled. Then she held out a knife to me, like a toy she was willing to share.

"No, no!" I screamed, grabbing the knife from her hand and whisking her away to check for gashes, for punctures. She'd managed to pull the silverware drawer out far enough that it fell onto the floor, and she'd been sitting in the middle of forks and spoons and knives. The drawer could've killed her, had it fallen on her head. I checked her head for bumps. I checked her mouth, forcing her to open wide and let me look; she started crying. Ronale was at the age where every foreign object goes first into the mouth. I was sure she'd slices her tongue to slivers, sure I was the most negligent, irresponsible mother in the world.

I found no blood; both eyes were intact; nowhere on her body were there wounds. But still I couldn't forgive myself. My reaction had made her cry, and as I tried to comfort her I began to cry myself. You don't have to be hearing to know that a wooden drawer full of silverware makes a noise when it drops to the tile floor, probably a pretty loud noise. A hearing mother would've caught this accident in a much earlier stage. I said a prayer of thanks that my baby was all in one piece and vowed I wouldn't close my eyes again unless Bob was there, as our collective ears.

When I'd calmed Ronale down, I put her back into her crib with firm instructions. "*Never* climb out again," I said. "You could get hurt."

Until Bob showed up in the early morning, I didn't let myself lie down. When I told him what happened, he acted indifferent. After all, he was exhausted too, and Ronale hadn't actually been hurt. But what his reaction said to me was that this was my problem, not his. It was up to me to find a way to solve it. Fair enough.

Every time the children napped, I rested (though I couldn't sleep lest I forget to check on the babies at ten-minute intervals). I was saving up my energy for the long nights when I would hold vigil outside Ronale's door. This went on for three nights, during which Ronale climbed out of her crib at least twice per evening. There was no holding her down, no dissuading her one-year-old mind. She'd learned how to get out, and there was a whole world out there to explore, so many new things to put in your mouth! I was soon suffering severe sleep deprivation. Finally, I purchased a small halter, an offensive item that looked like something you'd use to walk your dog. The first time I put it on her, she screamed for ten minutes, while I watched in dismay. But it kept her inside the crib.

I used the halter only when Bob was working, and only on nights when I could no longer trust myself to stay awake. I'd try to slip it onto her upper body without waking her, but she always woke up, and she always screamed. That harness was her nemesis and mine, but a necessary evil. Each time I left her room after harnessing her in, I was crying.

As the children got older, other, less tangible problems surfaced. Sometimes my deafness embarrassed my children, which in turn embarrassed me. They were always telling me to speak louder or softer. When I spoke too loudly in a quiet place, which inadvertently I frequently do, they would be mortified. And when other people were forced to ask me to repeat what I was saying several times since I was speaking too softly in a noisy environment, the children found that embarrassing in a different way.

Sometimes I resented my children's constant instructions, which led to friction between us. Even when they were very small, for example, every time I drove them someplace the kids would tell me at least once, and more often two, three, or even more times, "Mom, your signal light is blinking—turn off the signal light." And they were always right; the signal light always *was* blinking. But I was not grateful for their friendly assistance.

"What do those kids do," I silently muttered, "sit and watch the signal light during the whole trip so they can catch me up when I forget to turn it off? Are they deliberately trying to torment me?"

Finally one day I had had it. "For heaven's sake," I shouted, turning around to face them. "Stop it, will you? Just stop looking at the damn signal light and you won't know it's blinking." "But Mom," said my daughter, "it just keeps clicking and it drives us crazy."

I had never imagined that the turn signal on a car made a noise.

Other times I was more puzzled than offended by the children's instructions. When touring a castle on a famous estate I exclaimed to the children about the various sights. Scott pulled me down so that my face was at his level.

"Mom," he said, "you have to speak very quietly in this castle. Everything echoes."

Obligingly I began to whisper, as well as I could. I'd seen echoes described in books, of course. But I didn't really understand what an echo was. What does an echo sound like? And how does one know where or when an echo will occur? The kids tried to explain, but their explanations left much to be desired, I thought.

The children apparently became inured to some of the ramifications of my deafness, however. My mother stopped by one day when the children were in school and ran around the house to (1) turn off the fan over the stove (which was on high and very noisy); (2) redistribute the clothes in the washer, which were out of kilter and causing the washer to emit an unpleasant clanging noise; and (3) turn off the oven timer, which I had apparently accidentally set while cleaning the oven.

"If you weren't deaf before, you would be now," Mother caustically remarked.

The children had never mentioned any of those noises to me. I guess they'd become accustomed to them.

They tell me that the new appliances talk to you. The washing machine tells you when to put the soap in or when the spin cycle is out of whack. The dishwasher tells you that the dishes are dirty or clean or whatever. God. Now that my children are grown and on their own, will I have to hire a maid to talk to my appliances?

Later would come the unique joys of being a deaf mother of teenagers. The kids would play the stereo at its highest volume, without fear that I would tell them to turn it down. They would talk on the telephone at all hours of the night or day, knowing that I would not hear them. One of them even discovered that he could climb out his bedroom window and creep in late at night and I wouldn't hear any of it. The kids knew when they had it good.

I didn't always have it so good. I recall a beautiful spring Monday. I was driving down the city streets with all the car windows open on my way to work in the early morning. I stopped for a traffic light and noticed the drivers in the cars on both sides of mine staring hard at me. Was I drooling? Had I forgotten to comb my hair? What could be wrong with me that I was attracting so much attention?

At the third traffic light a bleary-looking man in the car in the next lane stuck his head out of the window and asked, "Jesus, lady, couldn't you turn that stereo down a little this early in the morning?"

I reached for the dial. Sure enough, my teenagers, who had used the car over the weekend, had left the radio on full volume.

I think the biggest yet most subtle problem that arose from my deafness was the slight shift in the normal balance of power (if *power* is the accurate word) that resulted. The children found it necessary to tell me what to do at times. "Speak louder." "Speak softer." "Turn off the signal blinker." "Don't turn away, because the lady is talking to you." "Someone's calling you—turn around." "Someone's talking—you're interrupting." "Pull over to the side of the road—there's an ambulance coming." This occasional authoritative role sometimes carried over to inappropriate occasions. My children were always more likely to argue with me than with their father or other adults. And they were quick to criticize my behavior or thoughts. Their ability to hear placed them in a superior position at times, and that slight feeling of superiority carried over to other situations. I never found a way to deal with that recurring irritation.

But I'm getting ahead of myself.

For several years when the children were young, money was a major problem. Before becoming a law student, Bob ran a small business leasing artificial plants and flowers to offices and restaurants. After a year of this, he'd saved enough to start law school at Syracuse University, with the help of several student loans. We moved into married students' housing. While he worked nights, chronicling the precise logistics of the failing marriages of strangers, our own marriage was less than ideal. Not that I complained. In fact, at the time I'm not sure I even noticed or thought about it. I don't remember ever feeling like I was in love with my husband. I appreciated him, and the stamina it took for him to get through law school while working nights and supporting a growing family. But I can't say I was madly in love.

I tried hard to get a job working the night shift on the assembly line of a local factory, without success. Although I was smart enough not to tell the interviewers I was deaf, the comprehensive physical exam included a hearing test. I thought I was being very clever when I tried to bluff my way through it. Watching the test giver closely through the glass window, I raised my hand to indicate that I'd heard a sound every time I saw his arm move on the machine. I was not as clever as I thought; the test giver was no dummy. He quickly figured out that I couldn't hear, and I was turned down for the job. In the words of the personnel manager, it was "too dangerous" for a deaf person to work in a factory, any factory, since "things often fall from above" and "hazardous settings are frequently created" that a deaf person wouldn't be aware of.

Baloney. Pure paternalism. But they called the shots. So, to do my part to keep our family afloat, during the days I took care of other children in our apartment, now feeling so comfortable taking care of my own children that I had no qualms about taking care of more. During the evenings I worked several nights a week at my old workplace, the Syracuse education library.

Money was not our only problem, but it was the most visible one. Living on approximately $3,000 a year, we spent virtually no money for anything but the barest necessities—the cheapest food and housing available. We ate a lot of macaroni and cheese, my mother's old stand by.

It was easy to blame any lack in the marriage on our lack of money. There was no money for entertainment, and we couldn't afford a sitter so we didn't go out at all. Between our jobs and Bob's school schedule, sometimes weeks would go by where Bob and I didn't have any meaningful exchanges. I focused on the children; he concentrated on law school. Nobody ever said married life would be romantic, right? And once he got out of school and began to make some money, everything would change, I was sure.

And so we alternated nights with the children—if Bob was off, I worked, and vice versa. The law school years plodded along this way, an exercise in endurance.

In early March of Bob's last year in law school, we woke up one morning to a blizzard that had raged all night, leaving the roads unpassable (New Yorkers still refer to this as the "blizzard of sixty-six"). There were traveler's advisories, the university was closed, everything was on hold.

At first it was pleasant. Bob got an unexpected day off and caught up on his sleep. The house seemed cozy compared to what was happening out the windows, and the children were entranced with the world turned white. I made hot cocoa and got out more blankets; the kids and I sang every song we knew. I sang off-key of course, but the kids never let on that they noticed.

The next day the weather worsened. The city remained shut down, and driving was not advised. The kids, used to spending some time each day outdoors, grew stir-crazy. The drifts were so deep that I wouldn't let them out to play in the snow at all, for fear they would disappear. Bob wasn't used to being home two days in a row, wasn't used to the children on a twenty-four hour basis, and began to be antsy himself. The apartment was tiny, not a place for four people to be caged, two of them under five years old. The novelty was wearing off.

The third day of the blizzard we ran out of milk. The fourth day we were down to peanut butter sandwiches on stale bread—breakfast, lunch, and dinner. The kids were cranky and had runny noses. I felt a growing claustrophobia. The snow kept coming down.

On the fifth day of the blizzard, after I had an inane argument with Bob about how thick to spread the peanut butter, or something equally ludicrous, he went to the bookshelves, pulled out the road atlas, and opened to the double-page spread of the map of the whole United States.

"What are you doing?" I said. The children gathered around, always curious when a book was opened.

Bob looked serious, as if he'd had a revelation.

"Bob," I repeated, "are you leaving us?" I was kidding, but I was curious about why he was studying this map so intently.

"Pick a spot," he said to me, "any spot, where the sun shines three hundred days a year."

I looked at him to see if he was serious.

"We are *out* of here," he said.

And so we were. During the spring break from school Bob flew to Phoenix to interview for jobs with law firms. He returned with job in hand, ecstatic to be on the way to warm country. Two days after Bob's long awaited final law school examination, we were on a plane for Phoenix. We didn't even stay for the law school graduation ceremony. Bob was too impatient to begin our new life.

We took off for Arizona with very few possessions—our clothes, books, the children's toys, and a few boxes of dishes, kitchenware, and treasured junk. We didn't have any furniture worth moving, and our old car wouldn't have made it across the country. Bob figured his law school diploma could follow us easily enough. Our real life was about to begin.

THE FEEL OF SILENCE

I am not temperamentally suited to be a deaf person. Deaf people need a tremendous amount of patience; I am one of the least patient people I know. God dealt me a double whammy. If he was going to make me deaf, the least he could have done was give me the patience to go with it. I don't have the patience to be deaf, to put up with the day-to-day annoyances and frustrations. I am too independent to have to rely on other people to tell me what is happening, or to make phone calls for me.

The ideal deaf person would sit quietly with hands folded and wait patiently for someone to announce what is going on. I don't recall ever having done that and doubt that I ever *will* do that. I am simply incapable of it. Yet I hate to grab someone by the arm and ask, "What is he saying?" because it is obvious to me that the person whose arm I grab does not want to repeat to me what the other person is saying. And I resent having to ask. So usually I don't. I just fume.

Chapter
TEN

We moved to Arizona on Memorial Day. The kids were wearing snow-suits as we boarded the plane at Syracuse; we got off to face 100-degree temperatures in Phoenix. I had no idea what I had let myself in for.

For a city girl Arizona was quite a change. While the state wasn't ex-actly wild in 1966, it was considerably wilder than it is now. There were lots of open spaces. And Bob was determined to have our share of them. We rented a house in a working-class neighborhood for a year, until we found a small house in the center of Phoenix that we could buy with less than the $1,000 down payment loaned to us by my grandfather. I thought I could redecorate the house for no money but lots of work (pleasure to me) and resell it for a big profit. We were lucky. I was right. After a little over a year we were able to sell it for enough to allow Bob to leave the large law firm he had been working with in Phoenix and start his own firm with an-other lawyer. We were also able to embark on Bob's goal of owning part of the Wild West.

We started with an acre. On that acre, in addition to our house, we had four horses, three dogs, three cats, birds (I can't remember how many), un-countable gerbils, and a varying number of Arizona reptiles—assorted lizards, Gila monsters, and the like. Five years later we progressed to two and a half acres, where we also had scorpions and an occasional tarantula, and where Bob even killed a rattlesnake in our garage. The howling of the nearby coyotes kept everyone in our household awake at night except me.

Bob was still partial to German shepherd-sized dogs, so we always had at least one, usually named Duke. One Duke lived with us for at least seven memorable years.

Since I couldn't hear a doorbell or a knock at the door, when I was home alone I always left the doors unlocked, so visiting friends could walk in and find me. Duke, however, was once again supposed to protect me. At least that was the line Bob fed me every time I recited the complaints of those the dog scared half to death—such as the pool worker whom the dog chased and cornered in the yard, causing the poor man to make an unfor-gettable flying leap over our six-foot fence. Unfortunately, Duke never got smart enough to distinguish friend from foe. My friend Mary would pull her car into the driveway, hoping to dash into the house before being cornered. Often, Duke would get to the car first. Front paws on the car window, fangs bared, he would bark at the top of his lungs, daring Mary to open her car door. Only a few of my friends were ever brave enough to call Duke's bluff. And one who did discovered that Duke was *not* bluffing. He bit. My friend must have borne some resemblance to either the mail carrier or the paper carrier, both of whom Duke reviled.

As if Duke wasn't bad enough, we had horses to cope with. One of the horses was mine, always a nag, since I wanted no part of the fancier horses Ronale rode competitively for 4-H or the thoroughbreds Bob trained and rode in such perfect form. My nag and I went riding three or four times a week. Note the way I phrase that. I don't say "I rode the horse" because, much as I learned to enjoy riding, I never got over my fear of horses. So if I wanted to go left, but the horse wanted to go right, we went right—always. And the horse knew who was in control.

While Arizona was full of open spaces in the 1960s, I still had to ride my horse about a mile through the alleys behind the houses to get to those open spaces. Often I rode a few blocks to pick up a friend on her horse. Before I learned to be ever vigilant and keep a tight rein on the horse while still in "civilization," I suffered through a few instances when my mount bolted at a loud noise, such as the slam of a garbage pail cover, that I, of course, had not heard in time to restrain the animal. But the first time my friend shot at a rattlesnake was the worst. I didn't expect noises fifteen miles from the nearest house.

City living seemed a lot easier.

During the years I spent as housewife and mother, my deafness was never discussed in my family; not between Bob and me, and not between my children and me. I found that quite acceptable, because my deafness had never been discussed between my parents and me or between my brothers and me, either. My children knew that I was deaf, but they accepted it as a matter of course, and a certain amount of compensating went on, even with the them. At times the chidden were especially protective of me.

Once we were at the grocery store, going through the check-out line. Kevin would've been about ten years old. I'd misplaced my check-cashing card and was rooting through the mess of my purse to find it. I must've had my head down for a full minute before I noticed that Kevin was talking to the clerk, with a somewhat defensive look on his face. What I caught of what he was saying was, "My mother isn't being rude. She's deaf."

Apparently the clerk had been assuring me that I didn't need to show my card, that she recognized me as a regular shopper. She'd said this over and over, while I kept searching through my purse, and eventually she'd gotten irritated. Kevin told me later that, after several attempts to get my attention, the woman had finally said, "Ma'am, the least you can do is acknowledge I'm speaking."

I remember another day when Kevin came home from third grade visibly upset. At first he wouldn't talk, but when I persisted he told me what was bothering him.

"Mrs. Ruffner said blind is worse than deaf," he blurted out. It was clear he disagreed.

"Well," I said. "How did this come up?"

"We were talking about all the things that can be wrong with people," he said. "And then she said, between being deaf or blind, the worst handicap was being blind."

"What do you think?" I said. I knew very well what I thought, but I wanted to hear how Kevin viewed this.

"I think deaf is worse," he confessed.

"Why is that?" I asked, trying to sound indifferent.

"Because," he answered, "you don't have to see to be able to talk to people, but if you can't hear, you can't be a part of everything. You miss stuff. You're left out."

"That's true," I said.

I was shocked at the sophistication of his analysis. I'd thought of this many times myself and agreed wholly with my son. But I doubted that most kids his age had ever given it much thought or had any context in which to ponder the question. As Helen Keller recognized, though blindness makes you less mobile, deafness inhibits your ability to interface with the rest of the world. While blindness cuts you off from things, deafness cuts you off from people, from communion.

I wanted to take away the heaviness of that moment for my son. He was too young to be worrying which disability he would choose. His favorite after-school snack was popcorn, and I quickly made a batch, with lots of butter the way all three kids liked it. And even though I let them watch television while they ate the popcorn, which was a special treat, Kevin's expression never lost that seriousness. It seemed an unreasonable weight for a third grader. Later, as I was having a terrible-twos battle with our most recent offspring, Scott, it occurred to me how blessed I was to have three hearing children. Not only hearing, but seeing, speaking, feeling, breathing, feisty individuals. I was proud of them, so attached to them, and I vowed anew never to let my deafness stand in the way of their progress.

I went overboard in some cases, with pressure from Bob. When I'm present at a conversation, I can't always figure out who is talking in time to look at the speaker, and it's impossible for me to see the lips of all the speakers at the same time. Because Bob, with my acquiescence, insisted that *no* concessions be made for my deafness, the children were taught to proceed with all conversations without thinking about whether I was able to follow.

The fault is mine. If there is one thing I would change about the way I raised my children, it is that. If I had it to do over again, I would insist that my children see to it that I am part of all conversations at which I am present. I should have altered that policy at the onset, rather than feeling that I must adhere to it in the overzealous belief that I should ask *absolutely* nothing from hearing people—particularly my children—because of my deafness. Not for my children a childhood spent interpreting for a deaf parent. I'd have no part of that. But, in my zeal, I think I overlooked the happy medium.

Through all the years my children were young, I don't think I took a single uninterrupted bath. This too was a product of my response to deaf motherhood. Afraid that some emergency might occur while I was in the tub, I *always* left the bathroom door unlocked. If I locked it, how would the children reach me if one of them fell, was cut and needed stitches? I tried for years to explain to my children that the door was unlocked only for emergency reasons. Inevitably, however, every time I took a bath they would open the bathroom door several times to tell me, "He hit me." Or "she's teasing me again." Or "the paper boy is at the door." Yet I could never bring myself to discipline them for interrupting me in the bathroom. Had I been able to hear, they would have been able to yell at me through the door. In retrospect, I think I was wrong. I should have put them on bread and water diets and banished them to their rooms for a week every time they interrupted me without *good* cause.

The same fear of calling attention to my deafness ruined much of the pleasure I might have derived from our family's frequent dinners out. For years I put up with sitting in dark restaurants, unable to lip-read a word anyone said as my family talked around me. I won't do that anymore. Now I ask the waitperson for extra candles or lamps. If I can't get the table light enough so that I can hear what is being said, I leave. Sometimes this is awkward. In a very fancy restaurant with my parents and my brother one night, for example, my mother asked for extra candles. The maitre d' said they had none. My folks particularly wanted to eat there, however, we had reservations, and so on. So I said the light was fine (it was really not as impossible as most places). As it turned out, however, the server did bring us a lamp. Even five years ago I could not have asked for more light. Some mistaken notion of pride (or maybe shame?) would have prevented me from asking for help.

THE FEEL OF SILENCE

"Let us pray," the chaplain says. And every head in the audience bows; every eye in the audience closes. Except mine. I bow my head at half-mast and keep my eyes wide open. Else how will I know when the prayer is over and it's time to look up again?

I love the water. If I had my druthers, I'd live in a small house right on the ocean in Southern California. Unfortunately, I don't have my druthers.

Despite my love of water, or maybe because of it, some of the most difficult riddles arising from my deafness have involved water.

At a meeting once someone tried to describe for me the speech of a woman whom I was unable to understand. "She sounds like she is talking with her face underwater," I was told.

I've tried to picture it. I've even tried to talk with my face underwater to see how it feels. It's very vexing. Although I now know how it feels to talk with one's face under the water, I still have no comprehension of how it sounds.

Many people have remarked to me about the hypnotic quality of the sound of water. What causes that? Is it the repetition of the same sound that brings the hypnotic effect? If that is so, why doesn't every repetitive sound have a hypnotic effect? It must be something about the particular sound of water that, repeated, has a hypnotic effect. What can that something be?

I once went to an encounter group meeting with a friend. "Close your eyes and picture yourself in another place at another time," the leader spoke in a soothing voice. I lowered my eyelashes and watched the leader out of the corners of my eyes.

I didn't get away with it.

"Your eyes are *not* closed," he snapped.

I explained.

"You can't get the full benefit of this with your eyes open," he said with an exasperated look.

I don't think I could be hypnotized.

Chapter ELEVEN

As much as I tried to keep my deafness out of the forefront of my life and mind, there were times when it snuck up on me. One startling development involved the discovery that my youngest brother was severely hearing impaired. When Richard was twelve and I was twenty-two and the mother of two, my parents discovered that Richard had an eighty-decibel hearing loss in both ears. We were all shocked. Did deafness run in the family, we wondered? Was this a genetic problem?

I put the question before our family doctor. "No," he assured me. "I do not see a genetic pattern here. The development of your deafness and your brother's deafness was too dissimilar." Wanting to be reassured, I acquiesced in the doctor's decision and pushed the too horrible thought into the furthest recess of my mind. Even a remote possibility that my children might become deaf was not to be contemplated. My parents must have felt the same, because none of us sought further advice about the possibility this might be a genetic problem.

How naive we all were. There's nothing like willful blindness. It wasn't until many years later, when my father began losing his hearing at about fifty, too young to attribute the cause to old age, that we finally acknowledged the obvious. By then, however, all three of us, myself and my brothers Jim and Richard, had all the children we intended to have, and luckily all of our children were—and are—hearing.

So once again I went about my normal life, pretending as well as I could that I wasn't deaf. I remember Scott's fourth birthday party. His nursery school classmates were invited. After the party, the parents came to pick their children up. One little boy was in the midst of what he thought to be an important project in our large sandbox. He begged his father to let him stay and finish. The father and I chatted for about fifteen minutes, after which he finally managed to drag his reluctant son out of the sandbox. As they were leaving, the father turned to me. "You really are a nice woman," he said. "I enjoyed talking with you."

His expression was so surprised that I had to say, "Thanks, but why do you look so amazed?"

He mumbled sheepishly, "Well, you know . . . every time I've tried to talk to you before, you've ignored me."

The best part of housewifery for me was the time it allowed me to spend with my children and the time I spent alone at home while they were in school. I'd always been a homebody and loved to create projects for myself. Over the years in our different homes I designed, made, and painted furniture, painted walls, made shutters, built gardens bordered by old railroad ties. My garden was my haven—I grew petunias, marigolds, zinnias, vincas, and geraniums and at various times had literally hundreds of houseplants. Any plant that could tolerate a desert climate got a chance in my house.

It was with my children or plants that I was always happiest. When it comes to gardening, deafness is certainly preferable to blindness—flowers don't speak or sing or lecture or argue, but what a loss it would be to never witness their freshness, their fullness, the perfection of a bud recently opened, the lively accompaniment of the dance of bumblebees. And the smells! I've never taken the sense of smell for granted. In the garden I experienced my world as fully as any hearing person could, perhaps even with heightened senses. It was a pleasure dependent on no one, and no one could take it away from me.

In the kitchen, I painted the cabinets in southwestern designs—animals and figures. I became a competent cook and loved entertaining. When you're in charge of getting a nice meal on the table for your guests, you can get away with less socializing. I preferred entertaining this way.

In terms of arts and crafts there was probably nothing I didn't try. Decoupage, painting, wood carving—I even placed a carving in a nice gift shop, though I never took art seriously enough to pursue it, probably because, while I have a vivid imagination, I'm not much of an artist. I have almost no real talent and even less patience. Arts and crafts were simply hobbies.

When we finally built our own house, I worked with the architect to come up with a design that would suit our special needs as well as our budget. The design I drew had the pool in the front courtyard, with the house U-shaped around it. Every wall had large glass panels, so I could see the children in the pool from every room in the house. That would make up for not being able to hear them. Even the hallway had glass panels looking out to the pool. By myself I designed the patio and courtyard and laid thirty-five hundred bricks. I found working with my hands enormously satisfying and was perfectly content not to have a career. This *was* my career. What could be more fulfilling? I had three wonderful children, a successful and responsible husband, and time to dabble in all my favorite pastimes.

The worst part of housewifery was undoubtedly the little errands that have to be run. For one who doesn't hear, the simplest tasks become nightmarish. And certain times of year are particularly bad.

One year a couple of weeks before Christmas, the kids were all in school, and I was determined to get the rest of the shopping done and the out-of-town packages mailed. I headed for the mall, where recent technology had not taken deaf shoppers into consideration. With trepidation I approached the check-out counter with my pile of gifts. Would the cash register face me, allowing me to see the total I owed? Or would it be one of the new "improved" registers, positioned so that only the clerk can see the amount? I stood with my pen poised over my checkbook, ready to catch the amount on her lips.

"Sixty-seven fifteen," she said quickly. "Will that be cash or charge today, ma'am?"

"Check," I answered. "What was the total again?"

"Sixty-seven fifty," she said. The amount was changing. ("Teen" and "ty" are indistinguishable on the lips; try it and see.)

"I'm sorry," I said. "Is that fifteen or fifty cents?"

"Fifteen," she said. There was a long line behind me and the clerk didn't hide her irritation.

"Did you say one five or five oh?"

"Fifty!"

"Yes, but is that one five or five oh?"

So we went, around in circles.

And then I took off in the car, headed for the dry cleaners to pick up Bob's suit. Pulling up to the drive-in window I took my place as the fifth car in line. A glance inside revealed an even longer line there, so I settled in for the wait.

I had a stack of packages in the car to take to the post office, some of which I had not yet addressed. I took out my pen and propped package after package on the steering wheel in front of me as I wrote. It took me awhile to notice that the people in the cars ahead of me were staring in my direction. I turned to look behind me, at whatever they might be looking at. There was nothing unusual, just a growing line behind me. The looks became more angry and insistent. Kids in the backseat of the car in front of me stuck out their tongues. Why the hostility? Wasn't this Christmastime, for heaven's sake?

I saw the clerk in the cleaner's abandon her post, walk past the long line of customers and out toward my car. The people inside were mad, the people outside were mad, but no one was as furious as this lady who approached me, yelling as she marched.

As she came closer to me, I saw her say, "What's the matter with you?

For God's sake, if you can't wait your turn then just leave. Who do you think you are?"

I was close to tears. I *was* waiting my turn.

"Stop blaring that horn," she yelled.

Oh Lord. The whole time I'd been sitting there, either my boxes or my elbow were leaning against the horn, and it had been constantly blaring.

"I'm so sorry," I said, feeling like a fool. "I'm deaf; I had no idea my horn was blowing."

She looked at me with disgust. "Don't give me that bullshit," she said. "You've been coming here for years; don't you think I'd know if you were deaf?"

What could I say? I was quiet, defenseless. I shut up and drove off to mail my packages, Bob's suit forgotten.

At the main post office, ten workers stood behind ten windows. The place was packed, as I'd expected. Bodies were crammed along every wall, outside the doors, in every conceivable space in the room. Boxes and packages were stacked next to the people waiting. In every customer's hand was a pink slip with a number. I grabbed my own from the little machine. Ninety-nine. The sign on the wall told me that the lucky person holding number twenty-six was being serviced. He'd probably been here since noon.

I found six inches of unoccupied space within view of the sign and began to play the waiting game. Fifty-five minutes later the number eighty-nine flashed on the sign. Now I stared in earnest. My eyes darted from window to window, trying to read the lips of each postal clerk as he or she yelled, "Niiinetyyyy!" "Niiinetyyyy-fiiive!" "Niiinetyyyy-siiix!" I missed a few. My eyes couldn't follow the lips of all ten clerks or predict which one would yell next. I saw "Niiinetyyyy-seeevenn!" and pushed closer to the windows. I looked at the sign. It read one hundred. Shit! I rushed up to a window as a woman turned to leave, clutching her purse. The sign now boasted the number two; the whole sequence had started over.

I shoved my piece of paper containing the number ninety-nine at the clerk. It was crumpled and wet from the sweat on my palms. "I've been here the whole time," I said. "I don't know how I missed it."

The clerk ignored my crumpled number, took instead the paper containing the number three from the man at my side. The man elbowed his way in front of me.

The clerk said, "You'll have to pull a new number, lady."

Every injustice came back to haunt me; I felt the heat rising in my face. I didn't care at that moment if it was Christmas, or Easter, or Thanksgiving, didn't care if the clerk behind the counter was the second coming of Christ himself.

"Like hell I will," I shouted.

He waited on me, not at all polite or happy about it. The man with the number three shook his head. As I walked out, I knew that to every person in that post office I was rude, the world's worst bitch, and there wasn't a thing I could do to change their minds.

Still, the most pervasive difficulty with being deaf in a hearing world is the inability to use the telephone. This difficulty is the common denominator of my past, present, and (as far as I can predict) future existence. As a teenager, I felt ostracized when everyone but me spent hours a day talking on the phone. Later, my inability to use the phone served as an almost insurmountable barrier to dating. But, to the extent that these types of frustrations are ever subject to measurement, the worst barriers presented by the telephone arose when I was an adult.

Illness among my children necessitated use of the phone. If they were sick at home, often the doctor needed to be called; if they became sick at school, I had to be called to go pick them up. Simple scenarios for a hearing person—the phone is something they take for granted. It was another challenge of deaf motherhood to overcome, and Bob didn't make things any easier.

I remember a time Scott's school tried to call me about an emergency—Scott had hurt himself on the playground. When I didn't answer the phone, the school contacted Bob, who was unable to leave his office and thus gave his authorization over the phone for whatever medical treatment was deemed necessary. Bob didn't attempt to notify me, by messenger or otherwise. So Scott had to endure medical probing and treatment without any parental support, with only the school nurse at his side. I didn't learn about any of this until Scott hobbled in the front door at the end of the school day. I was furious that I hadn't been contacted. I was his *mother*. At first I was outraged at the school's irresponsibility. Then, as the details of the story began to unfold, I was mad at Bob. But finally, the only place I could direct my fury was at myself, for being the kind of mother who could not hear.

Whenever we moved to a new house, I prayed that I would have a friendly, outgoing next-door neighbor, one who would not mind making occasional phone calls, one I wouldn't mind asking. In one memorable instance my next-door neighbor was not friendly. It would have been impossible to ask her to make a phone call. The man across the street seemed friendlier. After he initiated a couple of friendly talks, I steered the conversation around to the fact that I was deaf and mentioned that I was unable to use the phone and needed to find someone who might make a call for me in a pinch. That was the last friendly conversation he initiated with me.

Another time someone plowed into my car while it was parked in the parking lot of the supermarket, badly damaging it. This involved the need to communicate with an endless number of people at rental car places, insurance companies, the Datsun repair shop, and body shops, over a period of three weeks. Since I couldn't just pick up the phone the way a hearing person could, I drove my rental car to the office of the person I wanted to speak to, which might take an hour, often to find that the person was out, that someone else, someplace else, needed to be contacted.

In rare instances when I was expecting an important phone call from a doctor I would gather the nerve to impose on a neighbor and ask if the doctor could call at his or her house. Sometimes I'd set this all up only to have my neighbor go out for the afternoon. So when the doctor called, no one answered, but I was at home, desperately waiting for the call.

I don't recall, in all the years of our marriage, that Bob ever made a phone call for me or repeated a speaker's words for my benefit. Not wanting to burden anyone with my deafness, I didn't ask for his help. Not wanting to acknowledge that I was deaf, he never offered help. We were both at fault. Perhaps if I had asked he'd have willingly helped. I'll never know.

THE FEEL OF SILENCE

The next time you ask someone for directions, pay attention to the speaker's body language. If the speaker is telling you to go that-a-way, he'll face that-a-way as he points in that direction and tells you where and when to turn. That-a-way, of course, is never facing you.

Try my method. As the speaker faces that-a-way, run around to the side he is facing—fast—so that with luck you get there in time to see his lips before he finishes telling you *when* to go that-a-way. Then, as he turns in the opposite direction to tell you to turn the *other* way after reaching an unknown destination, run around again—fast—so that with luck you get there in time to see his lips before he tells you what that unknown destination is. Repeat as often as necessary.

Warning: This is not an infallible recipe; it only works if you are in good shape and the person giving directions has to think a bit before speaking. Whatever you do, don't follow me. I go around in circles even after getting directions, more often than not.

When hearing people get mad and don't want to listen to their opponents, what can they do? They can storm out of the room or the house, if that's possible, but short of that they seem to be stuck. Not me. If I get mad and don't want to listen to my opponent I can simply turn my back or, better yet, close my eyes. Nothing infuriates an opponent more. I know, I know, it's really not fair. And I try not to take advantage of that tactic. But when I want the perfect squelch, have I got it!

Chapter TWELVE

For a while, the Tucker family prospered. Bob quickly became a shrewd and well-respected trial attorney, and with the success of his practice came what we thought of as a lot of money. The children were enrolled in private schools, we built a bigger and nicer home, and we began to take vacations. One winter, we all learned to ski.

From my first experience on skis, when I was just over thirty, I loved skiing. It is the one thing that I do with utter concentration, without allowing worries or distractions to interfere. On the ski slopes I glide along to my own rhythm in perfect harmony with myself. Between ski runs it's another story.

Often when my children were younger, I ended up skiing alone for part of the day while the kids went off to ski with friends. And today I still often ski alone when the people in the group I am with ski at other levels of ability than mine. (I like the black diamond runs but not the double blacks.) Thus I've spent years riding on chair lifts with strangers. Only my great passion for skiing enables me to put up with those chair rides. Sometimes the ski areas are crowded, and "doubles only" are allowed on lifts. Anyone who is alone goes to the end of the lift line, shouts "Single!" at the top of his or her lungs, and waits for someone to shout "Over here!" Naturally when I yell "Single!" I cannot hear a reply. Usually by the time I finally find a partner, people all around me are staring and I feel thoroughly humiliated.

Once my partner and I get on the chair, I turn sideways (as much as that is possible on a ski lift) and try to read my companion's lips as he chats through a frozen mustache or she speaks through a scarf or sweater pulled up over her chin. When it is really cold, people cover their entire mouths and noses with scarves, so I have no idea when they begin to talk, much less what they are saying. Although to this day it remains difficult for me to tell strangers I am deaf, occasionally I have managed, in a burst of rare courage, to blurt out softly that I am a lip-reader, so I have to see my seatmates' lips to understand them. On all occasions when I have made that statement, all attempts by my seatmate to make conversation have ceased immediately. It's often a long chair ride on the advanced runs I ski; thus I prefer to keep silent about the need to lip-read and do the best I can.

I remember riding on a ski chair with Bob the third winter we went on a ski vacation. We'd left the kids at the ski school to ski with a group of other kids, and I turned to ask him what time the group skiing would end. A reasonable question, I thought, but he exploded. "Dammit," he said, "it's freezing on this chair. I want to turn my head this way [opposite me] and let the sun hit my face. Don't talk to me, will you; I can't worry about your lip-reading now." I was stunned, but I shut up. Since that day I have tried to position myself at all times on the side of the chair so that the sun is facing in the direction of my seatmate (which means that my face is usually frozen since I am always turned away from the sun). I'd never thought of that.

On another memorable day the ski area was particularly crowded, the snow was fresh and powdery, and the lift lines were long. Bob and I and the children had skied together most of the time, and we stopped at the lodge for lunch. I'd had a great morning and was feeling exhilarated.

As we entered the lodge, Bob looked upset. After awhile, when his mood hadn't lifted, I asked, "What is it?" The children had gone off to the rest rooms.

"You're just not safe," he said.

"How do you mean?"

"You don't pay attention, Bonnie, and it really presents a hazard out there." He'd waited so long to say this that his voice rose; I knew him well enough to tell by his facial movement.

"What are you talking about?" I asked. "Pay attention to what?"

"The other skiers!" he almost screamed. "They come whizzing up behind you, they say 'On your left!' or 'On your right!' and you just ski on, right where you are, like nothing's happening. Somebody's going to get hurt!"

"I mostly stay to the side anyway," I said. "I've never had a collision yet."

"It's just a matter of time, Bonnie, that's all I'm saying. When someone comes up behind and says that, you're supposed to give them the right-of-way." He was lecturing me. "You have to play by the rules."

As usual, I gave in, not wanting to argue, but I hardly skied that afternoon. Was I really a hazard on the slopes? I didn't (and still don't) think so. I ski well enough that people don't need to pass me that often, and when they do, it seems to go smoothly. But he'd pointed a judging finger at my deafness, and my confidence had shrunk. I spent much of that afternoon trying to figure out how to ski while watching the lips of the people behind me.

Though we still looked like the better-than-average American family, and I still very much enjoyed motherhood, the marriage was disintegrating. I was practiced at burying my head in the sand and did so successfully for the most part. Every marriage has its problems, right?

Bob's irritation with my deafness became more constant. The smallest thing could make him furious. If he'd look up from his morning newspaper to talk to me and I didn't happen to be looking in his direction, he'd be so angry he'd refuse to repeat whatever it was he had said.

When we entertained, it wasn't enough that I give a pretty good dinner party. I was also supposed to keep up, socially. As I maneuvered through the sometimes meaningless conversations, nodding and smiling at what I hoped were the right times, I occasionally blundered. Maybe I blundered more frequently than I realized, or than I care to admit. In one conversation, a male friend of ours was talking for quite a while about his mother's new boyfriend and how he didn't approve of the relationship. I was in and out of the conversation, trying to be both a good hostess and a good conversationalist, and I thought he'd been talking about his *brother's* new boyfriend. (Again, see if *you* can tell the difference without sound.) At an appropriate time, I offered up a theory. "You know," I said, "the current view of experts is that sexual preference isn't something that can be changed at will." The looks I got were first blank, then confused, then incredulous. A friend caught on to my error, leaned toward me and said, "No, he's talking about his *mother's* boyfriend." People let out a few uncomfortable laughs. I tried to laugh along with them.

"Sorry," I said. "I guess I misunderstood."

No one was as unforgiving as Bob in these instances. He walked away in disgust.

When we occasionally went to movies with other couples, Bob would be furious at the end of the night that I hadn't been able to follow the dialogue, had no idea what the movie was all about, and therefore was unable to participate in an intelligent discussion of the movie over dessert. I only went to the movies to please him, to fit in. For me it was an exercise in frustration and always has been, something to sit through.

Bob hated that I couldn't listen to music, that he couldn't call me on the phone, and that we couldn't converse in the dark (he found night-lights unacceptable). One miserable time he stopped speaking to me for several weeks because he was "fed up with having to come find you rather than being able to call your name."

Bob's steadily worsening antagonism toward my deafness should have warned me that the facade of our all-American family was crumbling, but it didn't. On the surface, I continued to compensate, ignoring that which I could not change. I focused on the good things. Bob was very bright. When in the right mood he was good company—intelligent, lively, and witty. He was a go-getter. A hard worker. I admired that, and I respected him. We had a busy, active life. The children were happy. So it wasn't perfect. Was any marriage?

But still . . . Looking for solace I began to think about finding a piano. Not just any piano, but one like the one I'd had as a teenager. My piano had provided so much comfort in high school, perhaps it could do the same for me as an adult, though at the time I didn't think about the piano representing comfort. As I said, I'd become adept at burying my head in the sand.

Unfortunately, locating an old upright piano meant dealing with the classified ads, and that led to my nemesis, the telephone. Coping with the telephone, or rather, coping with the lack of hearing in a world that relies heavily on telephones, has been the most constant demon of my deafness. Alexander Graham Bell, how could you invent such a monster?

How do I love thee, Mr. Bell? Let me count the ways. I loved you when I went to visit a friend and drove in circles for two hours. The man at the gas station couldn't find the street on the local map, so I begged him to call my friend and ask for directions. He looked at me in horror. "Lady," he said, as if I were from Mars, "we aren't allowed to do things like that."

I loved you when, exhausted, I checked into a hotel while driving across the country. I was dying to take a bath, call room service for a sandwich, and flop into bed to eat it in comfort. I took the bath and put on my nightgown before realizing I'd have to get dressed again, go to the lobby, and ask someone to call room service for me.

I loved you when I went to pick up my son at the airport. His plane arrived, but he wasn't on it. I was worried. I knocked on a door that read Security Police and asked the people inside to make an emergency call. They said they were "too busy." The airline personnel I asked to make the call were also too busy. Rather frantic, I returned to the security office and forced my way in the door. The police were "busy" playing cards. "If someone doesn't make a call for me, I'll see to it that you're all fired," I calmly stated. They made the call.

I loved you when my teenaged son would call me at my law office and we would talk via my secretary. He'd ask if he could do this or that, always some unreasonable adolescent request. I'd say no. He'd argue. I'd say no, again. He'd continue to plead his case, talking back to me in his most obnoxious tone. It wasn't bad enough that I had to hear this, deal with it, but I had to watch my interpreter witnessing this embarrassing conversation.

Later still, I loved you when I wanted to call a man I cared about. He wanted to call me. But since we knew we could not talk privately via the interpreter, we did not call one another. One day he finally did call. I was so glad—there was something I desperately needed to tell him—but I hesitated. Could I tell him through the interpreter, invading my privacy and his? I couldn't; this thing remained unsaid.

Oh, yes, Mr. Bell, my love for you is endless. And this love was especially overpowering while I was searching for my piano.

I spent literally months perusing the ads, but they all listed phone numbers rather than addresses. I had a very gracious neighbor and close friend at the time, Sandy, who was never too busy to make calls for me, but I couldn't keep pestering her to call ad after ad about used pianos for sale. I was grateful for Sandy and her generous spirit, and I wanted to save my phone-calling requests for more important things. So I muddled along the best I could.

Bob couldn't understand why I wanted an old piano when we could afford to buy a brand new one. He couldn't fathom why I was dead set on buying a piece of junk. I'd explained it to him and the children, and the kids understood and occasionally made a call or two for me without my even asking. I'd find the newspaper where I'd circled numerous ads, and a price would be written there and an address. It was through this sporadic cooperation that I eventually found my gem. Older than my original piano, if that was possible, it passed the play test. When I took my fingers automatically through "Silent Night," I could *feel* the sounds, the tones, the notes.

"I'll take it," I told the woman. I happily passed over the two hundred dollars she was asking, not even stopping to consider if the price was fair. After my long and difficult search, I would've paid almost anything. Music, of sorts, was a part of my daily life again, and I felt fortified. Though it wasn't the kind of music Bob had in mind, for me it was like going home to something safe.

We continued to take frequent vacations, ski trips and others. One August when Kevin and Ronale were about eleven and ten, and Scott about five, we rented a house with another family in Coronado, California. The kids and I loved the ocean, though Bob mostly played tennis, a sport he excelled at. I went along with whatever entertainment the children were interested in each day.

One day Ronale and I rented bicycles and took a long ride through the charming town. We were talking, telling each other stories as we often did, and laughing. We'd been to Coronado before, and we loved it. As we rode side by side, talking, Ronale turned toward me every time she spoke, so I could read her lips. It was habit; we were both used to this method of communication.

I think she was trying to tell me to look at something up ahead, but

I didn't get the time to understand what she was saying. In the middle of a sentence, Ronale had ridden her bike through a plate glass store window.

I screamed as I saw the glass give, breaking and shattering into millions of tiny weapons. I was off my bike in an instant, in time to catch the biggest piece of glass before it hurt her. I pulled other pieces of glass away from her where she'd landed on top of some display lamps that had been in the window. I saw blood immediately and the broken lamp underneath her. We had no idea what the extent of her injuries were. While the store-keeper called an ambulance, I cradled Ronale's head in my lap and picked shards of glass from her hair. I was reminded of the night when she was only a baby, when I'd found her playing with knives on the kitchen floor. I waited for the ambulance and choked on silent tears.

"It's going to be okay," I kept saying to her, as I stroked her face, which, remarkably, was uncut. The blood pooled around us as the flashing lights of the ambulance signaled rescue.

I hardly remember the ride to the hospital, but when we got there I had a nurse call the house we were renting and one of our friends went off to fetch Bob. He was at the tennis court in the middle of a match. He arrived at the hospital in his tennis whites, to find me and Ronale a mess, bloodstained. Ronale was being stitched up; the cuts had turned out to be relatively minor, not nearly as bad as the amount of blood had suggested.

He took me out of the room to lecture me, to complain once again about my being deaf. If I hadn't been deaf, Ronale wouldn't have had to look away from where she was riding to face me when she talked. (Did he imagine I hadn't thought these same things?)

When he was finished, he peeked in at Ronale, then, upset and irritated, stormed out the door to resume his tennis match. When we were ready to go home I had the nurse call my friend, and she came to pick us up. Looking at Ronale's bandages, at the stitches like small zippers on her skin, I felt the greatest guilt of my entire life.

THE FEEL OF SILENCE

Being deaf is sometimes like picking your way through a mine field. No matter how carefully you walk you usually won't be able to avoid some kind of trouble. I've carefully vacuumed an entire room before realizing that the plug was not plugged in and thus the room was just as dirty as before I began. I've left the water running in the sink or bathtub and flooded the entire kitchen or bathroom floor more times than I care to remember. I've "started" my car in front of a group of observers when the car was already running (thereby looking like an idiot in the process) too many times to count. I've ground up the silverware in the garbage disposal (and destroyed the disposal) at least once a year for the past fifteen years. I've dropped my keys a dozen times on the sidewalk and walked on without picking them up. Such is the mine field of deafness.

Chapter
THIRTEEN

R onale healed with hardly a scar. Between Bob and me the scars were deep, but we continued to neglect them. Years went by without a real confrontation, but Bob's bitterness festered. I wasn't without some bitterness of my own, but I was used to this marriage in much the same manner that one gets used to an uncomfortable pair of shoes she's unwisely purchased but can't afford to replace. So I was genuinely shocked when Bob remarked one morning, while brushing his teeth, that he wanted a divorce.

"What?" I said. "Are you serious? Why?"

He said because I was deaf.

I didn't believe him, for reasons of self-preservation. How could he want to divorce me for something that I was powerless over? Hadn't I tried to make my deafness as unobtrusive as possible? Hadn't I been as good as everyone else at ignoring it? In what ways, I wanted to know, had I failed him? The answer he gave me was always the same. He wanted a divorce because he was tired of having a deaf wife.

I still refused to believe it. I suspected everything it was possible to suspect—midlife crisis, another woman, or something else he wasn't telling me about. Having never openly acknowledged my deafness as a major problem, I refused to believe that someone else would do so.

"Will you go with me to a psychologist?" I said.

"I don't see why, Bonnie, I've made up my mind."

"A psychologist might be able to help us," I said.

"I'm not crazy," he said. "I just want a divorce."

"But all this time, the children, won't you go for them?"

After days of my badgering, he agreed to go. The doctor saw us separately and together and then called me in again.

"It's a difficult thing to hear," he said, "but your husband is quite clear about this. He wants a divorce."

"But it must be something besides the fact that I don't hear. Another woman or something."

"No, I'm afraid he's very clear about that, too," the psychologist said. "And though it may sound terribly uncompassionate, it's what he wants.

He's simply tired of your deafness." All I could think then was that one doctor can be wrong. I persuaded Bob to go with me in search of a second opinion. This time we went to a reputable psychiatrist. He also saw us together, then separately.

When he echoed what the other doctor had said, I let it sink in for the first time. The man I was married to, the man who I assumed loved me, was leaving me for a reason beyond my control. In the harsh and immediate reality of this, there was no more room for denial, but without denial, my lifelong strategy, how was I to proceed?

My sorrow went way past losing Bob. It was everything he represented—marriage, family, normality. All the people I knew—hearing people—were married. It was through marriage that I became *more similar, less different.* I had to face not only a divorce but the idea that my deafness was at the root of the divorce.

I tried to live with it. I really did. But it was overwhelming. Divorce, to me—and I suspect to many other women who are products of the fifties—gave truth to the old cliché. It was a fate worse than death. It meant FAILURE, in capital letters. It would make me twice a misfit, twice an outcast. Now my deafness would be much harder to hide. I would be really visible.

Divorced and deaf. Deaf and divorced. It was hard to tell which was worse, but the combination was unthinkable. Yet I couldn't stop thinking about it. It. It. "It" encompassed so many variables. The most graphic, the most frightening of those variables was obvious. Since my deafness was so unbearable to live with, I would have to live alone. Could I do that? Did I even want to do that? For how long?

When I finally gave up, I really gave up. We agreed that Bob would move out after Christmas, to avoid ruining the children's holiday. On New Year's Day he left. I could hardly make myself eat; it was as though I'd been turned inside out, and every raw nerve was now exposed to the elements. I went through my days in a fog.

At the doctor's office, I complained of insomnia. When he heard I was going through a divorce, he didn't hesitate to prescribe sleeping pills. I never took them.

At the second doctor's office, and the third, I said the same thing—not sleeping well, distraught, anxious, depressed. They all wrote out prescriptions for temporary oblivion. And though sleep was hard to come by and the only respite from agony, I resisted the urge to take those pills. I hid them in a safe place and waited.

A few weeks after Bob moved out, he started taking the children on occasional weekends. Around the kids I tried to act normal, getting their meals on the table, remembering to give them lunch money, and so on, but the minute they were out of my sight I gave in to collapse. After I saw them off one Saturday when they were visiting Bob, I was in a vegetative state. I didn't know or realize exactly what I had planned, but I went through certain motions as though I'd thought it out carefully. After straightening up the house and watering my plants, I took a bath, dressed, put the sleeping pills in my purse, and drove to a hotel. I chose one on the other side of town, where I'd be sure not to see anyone I knew.

The rest feels now like a slow-motion film. I got my room, put the key in the doorknob, and locked the door behind me. I went to the sink and opened one of those sterile glasses, filling it with tap water. Then I started swallowing pills on my empty stomach—blue ones, light green ones, small yellow ones. The colors made an interesting pattern in my cupped palm. I took them singly at first, then started taking three at a time, imagining they were some magic potion that would make me immune to further pain.

When I'd swallowed what I thought was sufficient, I lay down on the bed. I looked at my watch. It was almost seven. Darkness was falling outside.

What came to me as I waited was utter and complete panic. It started with some mundane thought—I should've reminded Ronale to return her library books. I was leaving my children, whom I loved dearly, with one parent, *that* parent. How could I leave them with only Bob to see to their needs? Sure, he would provide for them financially. But I did much more than that. How could I leave them in the care of this man I was growing to detest? He couldn't provide for them emotionally.

The panic at first was visceral, a churning in my gut. Then it took on a visual form—bright and blinding light behind my eyes. I looked at my watch again—7:15. Drowsy already, I went to the front desk and asked them to call me a cab.

When I sat down to wait, I could hardly fight off the chemical exhaustion that wanted to take over my body, my life.

"Are you okay?" the clerk said.

"Yes, just sleepy." I managed to get a few words out.

The clerk had to jostle me when the taxi came, but I walked out of the hotel on my own two legs, looking perhaps a little drunk.

"Are you coming back?" the clerk asked.

"What?"

"The room. Are you checking out or what?"

I must've nodded, because he took the key from my hand, then closed my backseat door.

When the driver turned and looked at me, his face swam in front of mine.

"Where to, ma'am?" he said.

"The nearest hospital."

I was so tired, but they wouldn't let me sleep. I vaguely remember being forced to throw up, and I vividly recall spending hours with the nurses taking turns walking me up and down the halls. About noon the next day, they finally left me alone. I put my street clothes back on and prepared to leave, as easily as I'd left the hotel the night before.

"I'm sorry, miss," one nurse said. "You'll have to see the doctor. Usually with a suicide attempt we keep you here for forty-eight hours' observation."

"Nonsense," I said. "I've got three children I need to pick up later today, and I don't have forty-eight hours to spare. I'm absolutely fine."

She made me sit down, kept insisting I wait. I argued that I'd come in of my own accord and couldn't be detained. Another nurse joined her, and they went about trying to convince me together.

I'm stubborn and willful, and in the end they had me sign some form saying I'd left the hospital against medical advice. I signed without a second thought. The only hitch came when they insisted that I list a next of kin. Though many suicide attempts are interpreted as pleas for attention, I wanted no one, *no one* to know about this brief lapse of judgment, this temporary insanity of mine. But they wouldn't let me leave unless I filled out the form; it became the lesser of two evils. The only name I could conceive of putting down was Bob's. I listed a false reference.

The nurses continued to talk about my safety and well-being, repeating that it would be highly advisable for me to stay. They bargained for twenty-four hours, then for twelve, but I was firm.

"Mrs. Tucker, are you sure? You really don't look well."

I may have looked like hell, but I was feeling better than I had in a long time. I'd salvaged my will to live, and though it was a thin and weak will, it was gaining strength.

When you're at the bottom, there is no way to go but up. I was ready for that climb. I was ready to face both my divorce and my deafness—for the sake of my children if not myself.

THE FEEL OF SILENCE

Of the hundreds of deaf people I have met in the past seventeen years, I know of only two marriages between a deaf woman and a hearing man that did not end in divorce and that could be termed relatively successful. Frequently, a marriage between a deaf woman and a hearing man ends because the hearing man cannot put up with the inconveniences and annoyances of being married to someone who is deaf. While hearing men and hearing women face the same problems and the same inconveniences when married to a deaf spouse, hearing women have a greater tolerance for, and a greater ability to cope with, the problems that arise. They have more compassion. (A cynic might also note that in many cases older divorced women have less choice in the marriage market than do older divorced men, whose second marriages are often to much younger women.)

The *Silent News*, the largest newspaper serving deaf people, reported a few years ago that almost all of the prominent, well-educated deaf men in the United States are married to hearing women. Yet, of the approximately twenty prominent deaf women the paper investigated (names of members of both sexes were provided), not one was married to a hearing man. Frequently the hearing women married to deaf men are tremendously helpful to their husbands' careers. Henry Kisor, for example, book editor of the *Chicago Sun-Times*, wrote vividly in *What's That Pig Outdoors?* about the hours his wife, Debbie, spent typing tapes of interviews that he could not hear, or taking notes during his interviews of authors. The president of Gallaudet College (the only university in the United States for deaf people), I. King Jordan, who became deaf at about twenty-one, frequently thanks his wife for her support and assistance. She often interprets for him when they meet with hearing people. I have never seen or heard a similar story told by a deaf woman of her hearing husband. Indeed, the wives in the two purportedly successful marriages I know of between deaf women and hearing men are both homemakers who have never aspired to other careers.

This syndrome is not unique to deafness. While I am sure that I will be accused of making stereotypical judgments and placing men and women in stereotypical sexual roles, as a general rule, I believe, women are much more sympathetic and understanding than men and more willing to put up with other people's "differences," of whatever kind. When I worked as a respiratory therapist with quadriplegics paralyzed from the neck down, my patients were both men and women. The men patients almost invariably had wives or girlfriends who saw them through the therapy, remained married to them, and stayed with them. The women patients, however, rarely had the same advantage. Their husbands and boyfriends almost never stuck around to the bitter end.

The third life

LAWYER, LAW PROFESSOR,
AND GRANDMOTHER

Chapter
FOURTEEN

The climb back up from the depths involved a series of decisions. Before I could even think about my main challenge—finding a job and a means to support my family—there were many things to take care of in the sudden reorganization of our lives. The house had to be sold and smaller, less expensive housing found. The children had to be removed from private school and placed in public schools. And the larger animals had to be given away. (In every cloud there is a silver lining. I've always thought that one of the best things to come out of my divorce was that I never had to shovel horse shit again.) The small and large details of all this upheaval kept me from succumbing to my ongoing misery. It was the children who kept me on my feet.

Not knowing what to expect from the divorce settlement, I needed to ensure that I could put food on the table if it turned out I had to. I entered an on-the-job training program for respiratory therapy that included four months of classes and part-time work at the hospital. During my hospital rotation I stumbled into the job of working with newly injured quadriplegics.

People whose spinal cords are broken at the C-2 level are completely paralyzed from the neck down. The only part of their bodies they can move is the head. Newly injured C-2 patients cannot breathe for themselves, because their diaphragms and all other breathing apparatus are essentially paralyzed. Instead, they are hooked up to a respirator via a hole in the neck—a tracheostomy. Because the tracheostomy tube interferes with their vocal cords, patients are unable to speak.

Put yourself in that position. Suppose you are a hearty, athletic individual who has broken your neck while diving, jumping on a trampoline, or riding a motorcycle—some accident arising as a result of your very active life. Suddenly you are lying flat on a hospital bed, wires and tubes sticking out all over your body, completely unable to move. To top it all off, you are unable to speak. You cannot ask the hundred and one questions you want answered, because no one can understand you. This is your worst nightmare come true, a nightmare from which you will not wake up.

Those are the patients I saw when I began my rotation at the rehabilitation center of the hospital where I was being trained. At first, because I don't hear, I had no way of realizing that the patients couldn't use their vocal cords. So I walked up to one fellow, a big guy who looked like he might've been a football player, and asked him a question.

"How did you sleep?"

"Better," he said. There was a gentleness in his eyes that was moving. In spite of the obvious shock at his recent accident and the resulting paralysis, he managed to emanate warmth.

"That's good to hear," I said. I checked his tracheostomy tube, part of the daily routine on this ward. "Are you comfortable?" It was a question we asked even though these patients were anything but comfortable. Everything had been taken from them except consciousness and the capacity to think.

The man smiled, then winked at me. "I can't feel a thing," he said.

I laughed at his sense of humor, rare under the circumstances. But no sooner had I laughed than the man began to cry.

"What is it?" I said, immediately sorry. Perhaps he hadn't wanted me to find his joke funny.

"Is this a dream?" he asked.

"No," I said, "I'm afraid not."

"I mean a good dream. Can you really understand me?"

"Of course," I said. "Why shouldn't I?"

"How? Do you read lips or something?"

I nodded. And then it dawned on me. These patients couldn't talk. The tube interfered with the vocal cords. I was the only human being on the ward who had understood this man in all the days he'd been here. I wiped the tears from the side of his face.

"Don't cry," I said.

"You're a miracle," he said.

I am not the kind of person who cries easily in public, but this genuine gratitude was about to get the best of me.

"I have a million questions to ask you," the man said. "You'll be sorry you let me know you lip-read."

"Not at all," I said. "Shoot."

"Okay," he said. I could see his brain working to prioritize. "This is a big one."

"Go ahead," I said.

"What's going to happen to my sex life?"

I thought for a minute. Truth was, I had no idea. So I answered honestly. "I don't know, but I'll find out." And I did. I spoke to the doctors, and I relayed their answers. He felt better having gotten an answer; I felt suddenly purposeful. Never before had my deafness been an asset, but in this world, a lip-reader was a valuable commodity.

And so it was decided. I would work at that hospital with the C-2 patients. It was a memorable time. The patients helped me as much as I helped them. Every time I was tempted to give in to my own misery, I thought about theirs and felt ashamed.

Among my many patients, one stands out in my mind. For eight or nine months I worked with an undercover police agent from California who had been thrown into a truck by security policemen on a college campus when he was making a drug bust. Their misjudgment left John paralyzed from the neck down.

John was a big, hearty man with a lovely family. He had been brought to our hospital in Phoenix (I had flown with a pilot in a small prop plane to pick him up) because of our reputation for working with patients with spinal cord injuries. His wife, Shirley, and their two young daughters moved to Phoenix to be near him. Shirley was devoted to John and spent every weekday in the hospital while the girls were in school. On weekends the girls spent their days in John's room with Shirley. Inevitably, Shirley and I became good friends.

Due to a series of complications, John ultimately lapsed into a coma, a state he remained in for several months until he died. During this time I decided that I had no choice but to leave respiratory therapy. As much as I loved the work and felt needed there, the job didn't pay enough. The welfare of my family took priority. The decision had been a hard one to break to Shirley.

While John's death was devastating to his family, when it occurred it had been expected for some time. After John's funeral, Shirley returned to Phoenix with the girls to pack their belongings and move back to California. Before they left, Shirley and her girls and my son Scott and I went to the Grand Canyon for three days, primarily to give the girls some happy hours. One night during our visit, the five of us went on a hayride and barbecue organized by the lodge where we were staying. After a pleasant cookout, laughing and joking, everyone got back on the hay wagon to return to the lodge. In the midst of our ride home dusk fell, and as the sun went down I lost the conversation. As we pulled up to the front of the lodge and parked under the bright lights, I was shocked to see that everyone in the wagon was crying.

"What happened?" I asked, frightened.

Shirley, it seemed, had told our fellow guests that her husband had just died, and that I had been his "nurse." She had shared with those strangers her distress that I had chosen to leave the field of "nursing," because I was the only person at the hospital who could understand patients like John. At the end of her story there wasn't a dry eye in the wagon.

I worked at that job for a year after completing my training. If the hospital had paid a living wage I might still be a respiratory therapist today.

But a family could starve to death on a respiratory therapist's annual salary of about $13,000 to $15,000. It had become evident that I would have to find a job that would allow me to send my children to college. I still didn't know what my divorce settlement would bring, but Bob's attitude made it increasingly obvious that it wouldn't be much. At any rate, I wanted to be able to depend on myself.

The decision to move on to another field was difficult, and I felt guilty, especially after that tear-jerker hayride. Although no one is indispensable, I felt as if I were abandoning patients who could turn to no one else to make their needs understood.

After much reflection, I decided that law school was the best bet. Not just as an alternative to respiratory therapy, but because my experience when Bob obtained our divorce led me to believe there was a great need for legal reform. My initiation into our system of justice in the United States had been a real eye opener.

For starters, I couldn't find an attorney to represent me. Most of the big divorce lawyers in town wanted a retainer of at least $5,000 (and this was back in 1977). I didn't have a penny. And the ones who didn't want a fortune up front were friends of either Bob or his partner. The only respected divorce lawyer who would have taken my case I refused to hire; he insisted that the only way he would represent me was to fight for lifetime alimony based on my deafness. The very idea was anathema to me. Eventually I wound up with an attorney who finally admitted he knew nothing about divorce law and requested permission to hire a "specialist" to work with him. Attorney number two turned out to be more inept than attorney number one. (I was not surprised to read several years later that attorney number two, the "specialist," was suspended from the Arizona bar.)

To say that my attorneys lacked a feel for their case is an understatement. That they never got a handle on *my* feelings was glaringly obvious. After a long day in court, during which Bob had testified for over an hour about how he wanted the divorce because I was deaf and how frustrating it was to live with a deaf person, attorney number one and I went to a restaurant to discuss the case. In the midst of his second beer, he looked at me and asked, with a puzzled look, "Why did Bob marry someone who was deaf, anyway? He must be a masochist."

(His comment reminded me of a remark made by a friend whose family had taken many vacations with ours. Upon learning that Bob wanted a divorce because I was deaf, Mary exclaimed, "How can he do that? Doesn't he realize that your deafness makes *him* look good?")

Aside from the impossibility of finding a good attorney without any money, the divorce trial was a farce from my point of view. With the exception of questions posed directly to me when I was on the stand (when the lawyers stood facing me and spoke clearly), I wasn't able to understand two-thirds of what was said. When the attorneys questioned another person on the stand, they faced the witness; their backs, rather than their mouths, faced me. And for the most part the witnesses were blocked from my view by the attorneys. Even when the witnesses were not blocked from my view, they and the judge were too far away to lip-read from where I sat.

It troubled no one but me that a party to the action before the court was unable to understand the proceedings. That divorce trial was really a trial. It was reminiscent of those early cheerleading tryouts, and the dreadful interview with the man from Cornell. The judge's face blended with all of theirs as I sat, unable to follow what was happening in my own life. It was one of the worst violations I'd endured yet.

To top it all off, I got caught in the cross fire between the feminists and the courts. In the mid- to late 1970s, women were demanding the right to work and to take their equal place in society. The old-fashioned view of women as housewives and appendages of their husbands must be discarded, argued the feminists, not incorrectly. And their vocal arguments were making headway.

The "ability of women to work" issue was so prominent in Arizona's judicial and legal circles that the judge who presided over our divorce hearing decided our case from that perspective, at least in part. (He had to be pulled from a remote area on the outskirts of the Native American reservation in northern Arizona, since all the Phoenix judges disqualified themselves because they knew Bob.)

Despite our marriage of almost seventeen years and our three children, despite my not having worked for most of those years because we mutually decided that I should stay home and raise our family, and despite our family's living on Bob's earnings of more than $80,000 a year for several years, the judge awarded me approximately $25,000 per year in combined alimony and child support for two of our three children for only three years. Most of it was called "alimony," so that I would have to pay the taxes on it, and it would be deductible for Bob. (Kevin, who was fifteen and had a good relationship with Bob, stemming in large part from their mutual interest in baseball, opted to stay with his father. When Bob moved to Switzerland shortly thereafter, however, Kevin moved back in with me. Ronale, however, did join Bob in Switzerland for a few months.) For the next two years the judge awarded me a combined total of alimony and child support of $800 per month. After that, the decree stated that I was to receive $300 a month child support until Ronale and Scott reached age eighteen. Indeed, our divorce decree did not even require Bob to pay for the children's college educations. As a "young" woman, to quote the judge (I was thirty-seven), I was fully capable of earning a living.

Women were insisting they were able to work, and our judge appeared happy to agree with them. (Indeed, many Arizona judges handling divorce cases were focusing on the ability of women to work. I had a fifty-five-year-old friend whose sixty-year-old lawyer husband demanded a divorce so he could marry a twenty year old. The judge awarded my friend a relatively small amount of alimony since she had a nursing degree and was capable of working, despite her not having worked as a nurse for many years and not exactly being in great shape for nursing. My friend questioned whether the judges were just going to bat for their fellow—male—lawyers.)

You may not believe this, but the judge's ruling that I was capable of earning my own living was okay with me. I didn't want to depend on Bob any longer than I had to.

What *wasn't* okay with me, however, was the judge's comment after the hearing was over. The kindly looking, mild mannered man asked Bob and me to come into his chambers. There, as he looked directly at me with an intense expression, the judge remarked, "I know I awarded you a fairly small amount of money. But I did that for two reasons. First because you are capable of earning your own money. But second because you are a young, attractive woman, and I don't want to give you so much alimony that it would foreclose you from remarrying. You'll remarry much faster this way."

He had to be kidding. Where was that judge when Bob discussed the miseries of being married to a deaf woman? Asleep? And who gave him the right to manage my life for me—to decide that I should remarry?

Any lingering question that Bob did, indeed, obtain a divorce because I was deaf was dispelled a few years ago when I gave the commencement speech at Clarke School for the Deaf in Northampton, Massachusetts. One of the graduating students happened to be the son of one of Bob's Hamilton fraternity brothers and his wife, Dan and Sue. During one of several discussions between Sue and me, Sue mentioned that she had recently met Bob for the first time at a Hamilton reunion. When Sue and Dan told Bob that their son was deaf, Bob replied that his wife had also been deaf. Subsequently he volunteered the information that he had obtained a divorce because of my deafness. When Sue, somewhat startled, asked why, Bob responded that deafness created too many hassles. By way of illustration, Bob explained, "I couldn't buy an expensive stereo—I didn't feel comfortable purchasing one when Bonnie couldn't hear it." (This was news to me. We had a stereo. I had no idea Bob craved a better system, nor would I have objected to his purchasing one.) That Bob continued to claim, eight or nine years after the fact, that my deafness was the reason for our divorce was the clincher. All nagging (hopeful?) doubts that my deafness was not the real reason for our divorce disappeared.

Would any woman in her right mind subject herself to that kind of rejection again? Not me. I could fight other women. I could fight other interests. I could even fight disinterest. But my deafness I can't fight. Remarriage was—and is—the furthest thing from my mind. Never again would I depend on someone else to be my link to the hearing world; I would build that link on my own, and this time it would be a lasting one.

I decided that anything Bob could do, I could do. Or could I? Bob was not deaf. Could a deaf person make it through law school? Apprehensively, I penned a letter to the only deaf lawyer I had heard of, a man who had become deaf as an adult and practiced law for a corporation in Chicago. I knew of this lawyer because he had represented a deaf man in a well-known case that was reported in a book and movie called *Dummy.*

"What do you think?" I asked him. "Should I go to law school?"

"No." His response was emphatic. "It's near impossible to get in and if you *do* get in, being deaf you'll *never* make it through," he wrote. "And if by some luck you *squeak* through," he continued, "you'll *never* get a job. No one will hire a deaf lawyer."

That was all it took to make me determined to apply to law school. In a sense I'd said "I can't" during the seventeen years of my marriage. "I can't be myself—a deaf person." Henceforth, I resolved, the word *can't* would not be part of my vocabulary. The only thing I can't do is hear. I wasn't going to let someone tell me there was more I couldn't do.

I didn't have to be married to a lawyer; I could be one. Yes, I decided, I would do what Bob did and do it at least as well, if not better.

THE FEEL OF SILENCE

I can't hear you with my eyes closed. Ergo, you can't hear me when my eyes are closed. A perfect example of an imperfect hypothesis, I know. The conclusion doesn't follow from the facts. Nevertheless, that's how my mind sees it. So when my eyes are closed I can't talk. At the stroke of dusk I become silent. In the dark I don't exist.

Eye contact is the name of my game. When the person I am conversing with looks away from me or walks around the room while I am speaking, I stop talking. And I'm reluctant to turn my eyes away from someone who is speaking to me, even if I don't want to know what that person is saying. It's rude. Just as hearing people listen and think of other things, I watch and think of other things. I let it go in one eye and out the other.

I had been exploring the possibility of having a cochlear implant—a surgical procedure whereby an electrical device is implanted in the cochlea to which electrodes are attached that generate mechanical sounds—the modern-day improvement on the hearing aid. I discussed the future possibilities of that miraculous invention with a deaf friend.

My initial reaction was one of optimism. Should I prove to be a likely candidate for the implant, and should it appear probable that I would receive benefit from the implant, I would leap at the chance. And that's what I told my friend.

"Bonnie," he replied, "I've been a deaf person all of my life. I'm not ready to be a hearing person."

I understood my friend's concerns. If a miracle occurred, and modern science provided me with hearing (even if only an artificial form of hearing), would the real Bonnie Poitras Tucker disappear?

What will I be if I can hear? More to the point, who will I be if I can hear? Will you recognize me? Will I recognize me?

Later, I spoke with a prominent authority in the field of deafness. "Bonnie," he asked, "what would an implant do for you? You speak and lip-read better than any deaf person I've ever met."

"The difference between us, Bill," I responded, "is that you compare me to other deaf people. I, however, compare myself to hearing people."

Chapter
FIFTEEN

I applied and was accepted to Arizona State University College of Law and entered in August 1977. Getting in was the easiest step for me. Classes were huge—more than 120 students in most of them—the mere numbers were enough to intimidate. Then, as my lawyer acquaintance had warned, classes were taught completely by the Socratic method (full discussion between professor and students and among the students themselves), which meant that I couldn't comprehend a word that was said. The classes were simply too big, and the discussion so fast and furious that most of the time I couldn't even figure out who was speaking. And with the classrooms structured so that the students sat on each side of the professor, I never saw the professor full face.

I realized early on that my attendance in classes was purely for appearance's sake. I could've been anywhere else and learned about as much—more if I had a book to read! But I was determined not to rock the boat; if only for political reasons I would be physically present at each class. I informed each of my professors that I was hearing impaired and could not participate in class discussions that were impossible for me to follow. They were gracious, for the most part, and agreed not to call upon me to respond to questions that were (to me) unintelligible.

In all of my schooling up to this point, I'd managed to do quite well without following what transpired in class. It was clear that this was not to be the case with law school. Grades were determined solely on the basis of a single exam taken at the end of each course. No quizzes, no papers, no way to impress these professors except by acing the test, which came straight from the class discussions. I panicked. How was I going to acquire this information if not in class?

My first savior came in the form of Bob's former law partner, Art. (Bob had not only divorced me; he had "divorced" his law firm as well and moved to Switzerland temporarily.) Art made an incredibly generous offer. Handing me a gift of an expensive, compact tape recorder, Art suggested that I tape the classes and give the tapes to his secretary to transcribe on a weekly basis. I was overwhelmed by his thoughtfulness, thankfully accepted his offer, and felt temporarily saved.

This salvation lasted two short weeks. Each tape, containing an hour or an hour and a half of spirited class discussion, took at least four hours to transcribe. At fifteen tapes a week, that meant that Art would have to hire one and a half full-time secretaries just to transcribe my classes. This clearly went above and beyond anyone's idea of generosity.

So I went to the state department of vocational rehabilitation, and they agreed to fund student note takers to assist me. The first year I hired three third-year law students, who I figured by this time knew how to separate the wheat from the chaff in law school discussions, to attend my classes (one per class) and take notes. Under this system, instead of thirty or forty pages of transcribed notes, I now received three to four pages of handwritten, condensed notes. But, because the note takers were paid for an hour of work for each fifty-minute class hour, I had between thirty minutes and an hour at the end of each week saved up to ask the note takers to explain any portions of their notes that were too abbreviated for me to understand. This proved to be a workable, successful solution, and I started to relax as much as is possible in the stressful world of "one L," as novelist and lawyer Scott Turow appropriately labeled the first year of law school.

While the notes did enable me to understand what my professors were focusing on, they could not reflect every aspect of lengthy class discussions. To fill in the gaps, I spent several hours a day reading legal treatises, hornbooks, law review articles and additional legal cases to better understand the concepts being explored.

The first year of law school is an indescribable experience for all law students. The method of teaching seems bizarre. The professors, much to the frustration of the students, ask questions rather than provide answers to questions. Moreover, many of the questions they ask have no right or wrong answers, but merely logical or illogical arguments to support suggested answers. The law is learned through the study of legal cases, from which the untutored, unskilled law student, who has never before confronted such a seemingly irrational and disorganized method of learning, is expected to glean the significant legal precepts upon which the case has been decided *and* the extent to which such legal precepts may or may not apply to similar or dissimilar situations. Only the fact that every other first-year law student is in the same boat as you are keeps you from going insane.

As a deaf law student I felt even more confused and overwhelmed. Unable to follow the rapid-fire discussion, I was terrified that I was missing too much and would never survive amidst the competition. All of law school involves a great deal of competition, and this was made painfully clear during first year. The pressure to be in the top 10 percent of the class is enormous, at least for students who hope to obtain reasonably well paying jobs upon graduation. The pressure to be one of the twenty or so students selected for Law Review (or Law Journal as some schools call it) is equally intense, since being on the Law Review is viewed by some employers, including most major law firms throughout the country, as a prerequisite to employment. In most law schools Law Review membership is granted to the top 10 percent of first-year students, plus a few students chosen as the result of a writing competition. You can make or break your law career in that first year.

I, like everyone else in my class, approached first semester finals with terror. Even today, many years after the fact, I can still taste that fear. While I had entered law school with great confidence, the reality of the first semester whittled that confidence down to nothing; I was a trembling mass of self-doubt.

I hardly slept during the weeks I studied for those all-important exams. How could a person rest? Because this was the first semester, I had no way of knowing how effective my strategies were at keeping me abreast of all the material I missed in class. I cursed my deafness now more than ever before. All I wanted was a fair shot at this. But what had possessed me to think I could do this without being able to hear? Had I gone truly mad?

As I entered the classroom on the day of my first final, I did not expect to fail, but I expected mediocrity—I would probably place somewhere in the inglorious middle of the class, at which time I imagined I'd have to give careful reconsideration to this whole insane endeavor. If I couldn't do well enough in school to get a *good* job, what was the point? I took my seat. Other people looked as scared as I was. Many people had circles under their eyes, and we looked a sick bunch, certainly no up-and-coming group of fresh, successful lawyers. I gave the man next to me a shaky smile, which he returned. This was it. Sink or swim. Papers were distributed, and I began.

I went somewhere else while I took those tests. In my mind, I had to block out the fear and doubt or I wouldn't have gotten past the first question. This took a sort of self-hypnosis that I was practiced at. It wasn't the first time I'd had to renounce the demons of low confidence. If I'd given in to my fears, I would've walked right out of that room and never returned.

As I finished the first test, then the second, third, fourth and fifth, I left the classrooms in a serious fog. Where had the time gone? What about that one ridiculous question? Had I done as well as I could? Had I done at least as well as some of my peers?

It was mid-December and cold even in Phoenix. Inside me was a cold I hadn't experienced before. I was plagued with anxiety about my performance. Nothing I did could thaw the fear, a glacier gaining mass inside me, filling all available space. Why had I ever thought I could do this?

I went through the pre-Christmas motions, played Santa, and braved the malls. But there was nothing remotely merry about my mood. It would be weeks until I learned the results of my tests, and my whole future hung in the balance.

It was Ronale who suggested we get the heck out of Phoenix and go where there was snow. I needed something to distract me, and this seemed a good prescription. We loaded up the old Datsun station wagon and took off for Colorado. Skiing, as much as I enjoy it, did not erase my worry, but at least the kids were having fun and I was spending uninterrupted, quality time with them. On the long drive home, my anxiety returned, full force. I had plenty of time to think about it all.

I knew the final exams were graded anonymously. Each student was given an exam number for a specific course and the professor would give a grade to each number, with no idea as to the identity of the student. The results would then be posted on the bulletin board, each class listed separately, exam numbers and grades side by side. This system, I knew, was totally unbiased and fair. And the anonymity was something I was grateful for; I would not have to endure the embarrassment of having my mediocre grades posted next to my name. Knowing that there would be no public humiliation, it still took me three weeks to go anywhere near that law school. The thought of it could take away my appetite.

On the morning of New Year's Day 1978, I made a resolution that before the day was over I would check my grades. However poorly I'd done, I would resolve right then and there to work harder the following semester, to raise my ranking in the class of 160. There had to be a way to succeed. I would accept no less of myself.

All day I put off going over there. So much was resting on those grades. How low would my ranking have to be before I would give up, wave a yellow flag that said in capital letters "DEAF . . . EXCUSE ME FOR TRYING." And if I couldn't be a lawyer, then what?

I spent the evening answering some letters I'd received in Christmas cards. I wanted to share with these friends, some of whom I only communicate with at Christmastime, what I'd been doing with my life, but I didn't dare mention law school. It all felt tenuous, uncertain. Eventually the kids turned off the TV and went to bed. It was after ten.

I made a cup of tea and drank it in such haste that I burned my tongue. I could not relax. I wrote another letter, drank another cup of tea, and tried to read. No dice. When I can't read, something is wrong with me. I put down the book, looked at the clock—11:35. I had twenty-five minutes exactly to fulfill my New Year's resolution, and if I couldn't stick to my guns on January 1, what kind of year was I in for?

I checked on the kids, set the thermostat at sixty-eight degrees, and put on my coat. As I backed the car out of the driveway, I said a prayer, and

I am not religious. But I was ready to invoke the help of any god, genuine or idol.

It was almost midnight when I parked the car. In keeping with my resolution, I jogged the short distance from the parking lot to the building. The least I could do was get there before midnight—I'd had the whole damn day to get this over with. I fingered the five slips of paper in my pocket, each containing the number of the exam booklet I'd used for that course. My number for the first exam—contracts—was 138, and I remembered when it was first given to me, randomly, that I'd considered it lucky—I was thirty-eight years old.

As I entered the building the heat was a noticeable change from the air outside, but I remained numb. I marched right over to the glass-encased bulletin board where the rosters of numbers were tacked in a perfect horizontal row, as precise as the futures they dictated for us. I looked at the contracts scores first, hoping my lucky number really had been lucky. And then I froze, too paralyzed by disbelief to breathe. Was I hallucinating? I was not. There, the first of 130 students in that contracts class, was my lucky number—138. 138. That was me. I let it sink in, began slowly to breathe again. I looked at the other four grades. All As. First, second, or third in each course. I would place among the top three in our class of about 160.

When I was finally able to take my eyes off that roster, I glanced around me. The lobby of the law school—chairs, couches, decent art on the walls, a couple of stray newspapers left from before break. Everything was silent. And standing there, alone for the first time, I felt a new affection for the place, a new affection for myself. I would be spending a lot of time behind these walls, and I was confident for the first time since August that with enough hard work I was going to be a lawyer, and a good one. And, yes, a deaf one. Me, Bonnie Poitras Tucker.

THE FEEL OF SILENCE

Sometimes I mind being different more than I mind not being able to hear. I yearn to blend into the crowd, to be the same as everyone else, to hear simply for the sake of becoming one anonymous face among many, not for the sake of hearing.

Women in the legal profession frequently discuss a bias against members of our sex. When asked if I've experienced that bias, I've honestly replied that I have not. "How can that be?" ask my questioners. Why don't I experience the frustrations of my female colleagues? I think I know how, and why.

All of my energy is expended on minimizing the differences of deafness, of surviving despite those differences. That's my big picture. I have no energy left for the "differentness" of being a woman. In the same way that puberty was nothing compared to the difficulty of being deaf, being a female lawyer is nothing compared to the difficulty of being a deaf one.

Being different has shaped my life. In some respects the resulting shape has been positive. But I'm weary of being different. I'm ready for a breather.

Several friends of mine are in therapy, and they all think it's great. One friend recently said to me, "I don't know how I got to the age of forty without being in therapy." They're in therapy for a variety of reasons. A few are going through divorces and experiencing differing degrees of stress; a few are exploring their inability to sustain long-term relationships; one seeks help coping with the inability (we hope temporary) to have children; one spends too much time working to the exclusion of a personal life; one simply wants to understand herself better.

I would benefit from therapy geared toward helping me to cope with my anger and frustration at being deaf in this hearing world. But there's a catch. All of my friends who speak so highly of their therapy say that their therapists "really understand" their problems. Either the therapist has "been there before," on a personal level, or he or she has a wealth of experience in dealing with similar problems. To really help me cope with being deaf a therapist would have to understand what it means to be deaf in the totally hearing professional environment in which I live. I know of no such animal.

Only once did I seek the assistance of a therapist—when trying to cope with my husband's wanting a divorce because I was deaf. I tried to explain to the therapist—a clinical psychologist with a Ph.D. who came with good credentials—why I was so devastated, why I felt that my whole being, my whole existence, was threatened. He simply could not understand the problem. "You're making a mountain out of a molehill," he said. "You hardly have a major problem. You are sitting here communicating with me perfectly. What's the big deal? Your husband may have a problem, but it's not your problem."

Because I was able to communicate easily one-to-one with that doctor, to his mind no problem existed. Having no frame of reference from which to analyze my alleged problem, he could not see my deafness as a problem at all.

I was reminded of that incident years later, when, after I began teaching law, I was a finalist for a White House fellowship. Coincidentally, the year I was a finalist another of the finalists was deaf. That highly intelligent deaf man (I'll call him Mr. Z) communicated via sign language rather than speech. He attended all of the interviews with a sign language interpreter, who signed the interviewers' questions for the deaf man and voiced the deaf man's responses for the interviewers. I, on the other hand, did not use an interpreter during the interviews (although I did have an oral interpreter present for group meetings and standing at the ready in case one of the interviewers, like the man from Cornell, was not lip-readable). I was able to communicate easily with each of the interviewers.

During one of my interviews, the interviewer asked me: "How would you like to live your life with the dreadful burden that Mr. Z has to live with? Can you imagine being deaf like that, and having to face so many frustrations on a daily basis?" Although I had stated in my personal statement that I was deaf, and although I had an oral interpreter present at all meetings, that interviewer clearly did not understand that I was every bit as deaf as Mr. Z and shared many of the same limitations and frustrations. He simply asked me the question that I later learned he had asked at least one other finalist. I was so nonplussed that I said I was unable to respond to the question at that time.

Chapter
SIXTEEN

Although I was relieved to learn that the extra reading I was doing was compensating for what I missed in my law school classes, my excitement about my ranking was short-lived. Two days after we returned to school from Christmas break, I was approached by two classmates, Ann and Laura. I'd often seen them studying together and knew that they were friends. Something about the way they walked up to me in the lobby let me know that the encounter might leave a sour taste in my mouth.

I was eating a bag of corn chips between classes—since starting law school nutrition had gone down the same drain my time had—and I was also glancing at the headlines of an abandoned newspaper when they walked up.

Ann did most of the talking. "Bonnie," she said, careful to look at me as she spoke, "do you have a minute?"

Since my mouth was full, I didn't speak but nodded.

"We've been thinking, and it seems it's not really fair that you have the help of note takers."

"Why?" I asked. "I don't hear the discussions that you hear, nor do I hear the professors."

"Well, it's really an unfair advantage," she said, "considering that we have to participate in class discussions and can't possibly take the kind of verbatim notes you're getting."

"My note takers don't take verbatim notes," I said.

"Well, the point is they have to take better notes than we're able to, while we're getting called on and all that."

Laura took a stab at it. "Yeah, it really isn't fair, when you think about it."

This conversation couldn't be happening. I didn't know what to say in my own defense, but they were standing there, waiting for me to say something. My books were right next to me—evidence. I grabbed one of my notebooks, then another, and started opening them to last semester's notes taken by my note takers, laid them out for Ann and Laura to inspect.

"Let's see yours," I said.

They each flipped open a notebook, though they were already looking hesitant after seeing how brief my notes actually were. We compared one day's notes, then another, then another. In every case, their notes were much more extensive, more comprehensive, than mine. They began to look sheepish.

"Still," Ann said, "it's not the same. You don't go through the same stress we do every day in class, knowing we can get called on at any time."

"Have you read Williston on contracts?" I asked them.

They look puzzled. "No. Why?"

"What about LeFave's book on criminal law?"

They shook their heads no.

I took out my list of supplemental reading, treatises, hornbooks, law review articles, and extra cases I had read, reread, and taken my own copious notes on.

"Have you read any of these?" I asked.

They couldn't lie. They both said no.

"But what does this have to do with—"

I cut Ann off. "I spend every minute that I'm not in class, sleeping, or with my children, in the law library. I read everything I can get my hands on because I can't follow what is said in class." With that I popped the last corn chip into my mouth, brushed my hands against each other, and collected my things.

"And now if you'll excuse me," I said, "I need to get home to my children." They moved out of the way and let me pass.

I wasn't sure if I had pacified them, but frankly I didn't care. Maybe I did have one advantage—that I didn't have to sit on the edge of my seat at all times, fearing I'd be called on. On the other hand, the students who heard the class discussions and lectures had a distinct advantage that I lacked. Some of my friends who discussed the cases and heard the subjects in class seemed to retain the information better than I did; through discussion it had become more applicable. I don't have a photographic memory. I remember what I "hear" (lip-read) and talk about far better than I remember what I read. But comparisons like this are useless. We all do the best we can with what we have. I was fully aware that to remain in the top 10 percent of my class I would have to continue doing the additional reading and studying that my classmates were not required to do. It was imperative that I graduate in the top 10 percent. For any lawyer, finding a good job was hard. As a deaf lawyer I was going to find it even harder. I needed all the pluses I could get.

That whole first year of law school at Arizona State University (ASU) I felt comfortable staying in Phoenix. I did not have to worry about running into Bob or dealing with Bob, because he was out of town, first in

Switzerland and later in Tucson. But by the end of first year, I learned that Bob planned to return to Phoenix that summer or early fall. The divorce, which had become final in December, was something I could ignore for the most part; I was busy enough that, had I had a husband, I might not have known it. But if I were to run into Bob on any sort of regular basis, in the flesh, I was sure it would rattle me. I couldn't afford to lose the momentum I'd established in school, or my fragile equilibrium. It seemed there was only one thing to do if Bob was coming back to Phoenix—leave. Even though it meant giving up the coveted spot I'd earned on the Law Review at ASU, I arranged to transfer to the University of Colorado School of Law in Boulder (CU). They assured me that I would be permitted to enter a writing competition to get on the Law Journal there. More confident of my writing ability than of my ability to interpret unfamiliar legal precepts, I decided to take the chance.

M oving is never easy, but our move to Colorado was especially trying. Physically, moving myself and the children was exhausting, but emotionally it was worse. Packing up and leaving the city Bob and I had moved to together when our older children were toddlers, and in which our youngest child was born made me see in some way that I hadn't before that Bob was really gone, out of our picture; I was a struggling single mom. Divorced and deaf. Divorced *because* I was deaf.

Kevin opted to stay in Phoenix to finish his last two years of high school. So Ronale, Scott, and I had to say goodbye to him, knowing we might not see him for months. Our once normal family was dissolving before my eyes. And it seemed that none of it was within my control anymore.

That is why, when we whittled down our belongings to move only the essentials, I stood fast about my piano. Everyone tried to talk me out of taking it to Boulder. It was big and bulky and would take up valuable room in the moving truck. It was in such bad shape it might not weather a move. It was going to cost $500 to have it transported from Arizona to Colorado; it had only cost $200 and was hardly worth that now. Friends, neighbors, and family looked at me as if I were nuts.

As far as I was concerned, the piano was irreplaceable. I'd looked at dozens before I finally found one old enough (and perhaps out of tune enough) to let me *feel* its base chords. The piano I'd had as a young girl *was* my music. Music, back then, was my connection to the hearing world. This was the piano I had searched for as a replacement when on some level I'd anticipated the dissolution of my marriage. I wasn't giving it up. I didn't care who wanted to differ with me. Some things are more important than money.

Our new home in Boulder was a small, inexpensive townhome, three stories high and very narrow. There was a basement, a ground floor with a tiny living/dining room and kitchen, and a second floor with one bathroom and three of the smallest excuses for bedrooms I'd ever seen. My plan was to put the piano in the basement.

When the movers arrived, I brought them inside to show them where I wanted it. They took one look at the staircase to the basement and looked at me as though I were crazy.

Was I completely ignorant of the laws of nature and physics? Couldn't I see that short of removing half the first floor there was no way that piano would go down the stairs to the basement? Ronale and Scott were starting to give me funny looks, too, as was my father, who had come with us to Boulder to help us move.

I looked, I thought about it, and there was no denying they were absolutely right. So I reorganized my plans. Since the piano would not go up the stairs to the top floor any more than it would go down the stairs to the basement, it would have to go in the tiny living/dining room. No matter that it would take up virtually the entire room; we'd use the basement as a living room if we had to. A small price to pay for my piano, I thought.

Even that price was not enough. When the movers got that heavy piano to the front door, we discovered that it wouldn't go into the house at all. Even if we removed the front door entirely, it wouldn't fit through the open space. The movers were tired and wanted to give up.

"That's it, ma'am," said the taller man. "It's not gonna make it."

"There's another door," I said, "in the back."

"Same size as this one," the shorter guy said. He took out a bandanna and wiped sweat from his upper lip.

"How do you know?" I asked.

"We measured it already, before."

"They did, Mom," Scott said, and Ronale nodded agreement.

"Well it looks bigger to me," I said.

"It ain't any bigger, ma'am," the tall mover said, less tolerant than the small sweaty one.

"Well, I'm the one who's paying you, and I'd like you to try the back door," I said. I watched the bigger one roll his eyes and put his cap back on. "Bring the piano around," I continued, "and I'll meet you at the back."

Rather than argue with me (they must have assumed by now I was beyond reason), they lugged that old piano around the townhome to the back entrance and tried again to squeeze it in. They were right. It wouldn't fit. I sat down on the back stoop afraid I might cry. The movers, out of patience, were about to take off, leaving me with a piano in my back yard. I composed myself and got an idea. Opening the door to the single-car detached garage that came with the house, I asked the movers to place the piano against the far wall. They complied, glad to be seeing the last of me. We didn't need the garage for the car; there was plenty of room for park-

ing on the street. And we hadn't brought any extras with us so we would-
n't need the garage for storage. The piano would work there just fine.

The next morning there was a note in my mailbox: "Hi. I heard you're
deaf. So am I. Would like to meet you. I live right across the driveway. Please come say hello."

I didn't want to go. I had no desire to meet this deaf person, certainly
not because we were both deaf. My deafness was still something I tried to
get away from. But I was new in the neighborhood, and she'd been kind
enough to make the effort. It was common courtesy to go.

She answered the door in a panic. I started to extend my hand and say
my name, but she was in too big a hurry. Signing and speaking at the same
time she said, "I'm sorry. I can't talk now. I've flooded my kitchen."

From the door I could see into her kitchen, where the floor was like a
Slip 'n' Slide. She was very pregnant, I guessed about seven months; I was
afraid to let her go skating into that mess. "Let me help," I said. "You'll
hurt yourself."

"I'm so damned forgetful!" she said. "I've done this so many times—
I leave the water running and then . . . this happens."

"You should know how many times it's happened to me," I confessed.

She looked amazed, relieved. "Seriously?" she said. "Honest?"

I nodded. "Where's the mop?"

"Thank God. I was sure I was the only person in the world stupid
enough to let this happen time and time again."

"Well, you're not," I said. "It happens to me all the time."

"Betty Ann," she said, holding out a wet hand.

"Bonnie," I said. We shook hands. "Now where's the mop, and I'll
help you clean this up." As we both surveyed the damage, the dishes in the
sink, and the soapy water having run over, gallons' worth, we started to
laugh. I had found a soul mate, and she was deaf. Fancy that.

Several days a week Betty Ann and I would get together for an hour or
so when I got home from school—for coffee or a glass of wine. Though she
signs and I don't, and she's prosigning and "Deaf culture" and I'm not, we
got along wonderfully. We simply agreed not to talk about that subject. She
was able to lip-read me, and her lips were very easy to read—she moved
them perfectly without even trying. Betty Ann was the warmest welcome
I could ever have hoped for in Boulder. Instantly a friend.

Besides Betty Ann, I made few attempts to socialize in Boulder. We'd
moved early enough in the summer to get settled in before we all started
school again. Part of the reason for settling in early was so that I could meet
some people before I got too busy with second year. In an attempt to do
this, I decided to visit a duplicate bridge club in town. I liked to play
bridge, and it seemed a good way to meet people. When I arrived at the

club, I learned that one was expected to bring her own bridge partner. Since I didn't have a partner, I couldn't play. But just as I was about to leave, a couple came in with a visiting brother-in-law. Learning that I was alone, the brother-in-law suggested we be partners. I agreed. The people at that club, I quickly learned, played bridge for blood.

One of the men at the first table to which my partner and I were assigned had such an enormous beard and mustache that his lips were entirely covered by hair. Indeed, his whole face was covered by hair. Not only was it impossible for me to tell what he was saying, it was impossible for me to tell when he was saying it. In desperation I explained that I was a lip-reader and couldn't read his lips. I asked my partner to repeat the bearded man's bid. He complied. The bearded man immediately raised his hand, and the arbitrator appeared at our table. A brief conversation ensued. With a stoic face the arbitrator informed my partner and me that he had no choice but to grant the bearded man's request that we forfeit the hand. We forfeited.

Next round I told the bearded man that I would ask him if he had bid the various suits and he could nod his head one way or the other. So began an inane conversation. "Did you bid clubs?" Shake, no. "Diamonds?" Shake, no. "Hearts?" Shake, yes. "One heart?" Up went the hand. The arbitrator reappeared. To this day I do not know why.

The evening went downhill from there. I became so flustered that any bridge-playing skill I might otherwise have exhibited disappeared. My partner and I wound up in last place. I decided that perhaps the duplicate bridge club was not the best place for me to meet people. But soon enough school started, and I was too busy to consider socializing. And there was always Betty Ann.

Summer turned to fall, October to November, and snow fell. The first morning with temperatures below freezing, my old Datsun wouldn't start. I tried and tried, but it seemed permanently frozen, as if it had never run before and never planned to again. Betty Ann gave me a ride to school, and by afternoon the sun was out and the car started like a charm.

The next morning, same thing. I turned the key of a dead beast. Nothing. Hibernating. Betty Ann peeked out her window and motioned for me to come inside.

"Just let me throw something on," she said, "and I'll take you."

I refused, not wanting to impose on her two days in a row. There was a city bus I could take easily enough.

"You sure?" she said.

"I'm sure. But what am I going to do about this car?" I asked. "It works later in the day when I don't need it to."

"You need to keep it in the garage, Bonnie. Outside is just too cold. In the garage it should start okay even in the mornings."

Of course what she said made perfect sense. Why did I not want to hear it? Because the garage was my piano house, and not big enough for a car and a piano.

I had no choice but to move the piano out and the Datsun in and to put my piano up for sale. An undergraduate student at CU bought it for $100. I watched out the window for his truck that Saturday morning. When he and a friend parked in front of our house, you would've thought they'd come to take away one of my children. I started to cry.

It took no time at all for them to load the piano onto a dolly and roll it down the icy driveway to the waiting truck. I cried the whole time. When the student came up to give me five twenty-dollar bills, he was shocked to see the state I was in.

"I'm sorry," he said. "Is this a bad time to do this?"

"There's no good time," I said, continuing to sniff and wipe at my eyes.

"If you've reconsidered . . ." he began.

"No. I haven't," I said. "Don't mind me. Just take it away."

He must've felt like a criminal as he shut the back of the pickup and got into the cab. He and his friend both waved to me, concern on their faces, as they pulled away. I stood on the front step until the piano, bobbing in the back of that truck, disappeared from view. Then I sat down on the step and sobbed.

Throughout most of the divorce I hadn't cried. Through all the financial woes, all the frustrations of first year of law school, all the difficulty that came with leaving Phoenix, my ex-husband, my oldest son. As I watched that piano moving away from me, I cried for all those things. It was going to be a bitter winter.

THE FEEL OF SILENCE

I flush the toilet, exit the stall in the restaurant's ladies' room, and begin washing my hands at the adjacent sink. A woman exits the stall next to the one I just vacated. As I watch from the mirror, she peers into "my" stall, then forcefully slams the stall door. Hands on hips, she marches toward me, glaring. "That was really vicious of you," she says menacingly. "There are two rolls of toilet paper in the stall you were in, you could easily have passed me one—or at least a few pieces."

Before I can gather my wits sufficiently to reply that I never heard her request she storms out of the rest room. I can see the muscles on the sides of her neck moving fast as she walks. It doesn't take much imagination to figure out what she must be saying to me while her back is turned.

It's probably a blessing I can't lip-read her.

When dancing was really dancing, and people danced in couples with the man leading, I was a good dancer. I have an innate sense of rhythm, and I can follow anyone. When dancing became an individual sport in which each person dances around the floor alone while a "partner" dances several feet away (this is a partner?), I stopped dancing. I didn't feel comfortable about dancing alone when I couldn't hear the music.

One night a friend convinced me to join him on the dance floor at a cowboy bar in a small town in Arizona where we were attending a conference. "It's no big deal if you can't hear the music," he said persuasively. "Everyone is doing their own thing anyway; you can't do anything weirder than some of these people." After watching the dancers for a few minutes I saw the logic of his argument. So we danced.

It took me a few minutes, but finally I began to get comfortable. Having picked up the rhythm of the music from watching him I began dancing in earnest. "This is fun," I remarked. "I guess I don't need a partner to dance after all—what do I need you for?"

After a while we happened to be almost the only people on the dance floor—everyone else had apparently taken a beer break. I stopped watching my partner and paid attention to my dancing. Suddenly I looked around and saw that my partner had stopped dancing, as had the few remaining people on the floor. I was dancing alone without music.

"Now I know what I need you for," I said sheepishly. "I need you to tell me when the music has stopped."

I like my steak rare. Very rare. But the word "rare" begins with an *r*. the bane of my lip-reading existence. So when I order my steak "rare," nine times out of ten I get it cooked "well." Despite my best efforts, somehow my *r* sounds like a *w*, and thus when I say "rare" it comes out sounding like "well."

I've got a new trick. Now I order my steak "rare" and continue by saying, "That means bloody—almost walking." Usually it works. But last night I still got my steak "well." I was *most* annoyed.

"For heaven's sake," I snapped at the waiter, "I told you bloody and walking, I don't know how much clearer I could be."

He blanched. "I thought you were being sarcastic," he stammered. "After all, you ordered your steak cooked 'well' and *then* said 'bloody and almost walking.'"

Chapter SEVENTEEN

CU law school was every bit as challenging and time consuming as ASU had been. Luckily, I continued to do well. I eventually became editor-in-chief of the Law Journal. While at CU I gave up going to classes just for the check in the attendance book. Between the extra reading I did and my work on the Law Journal, I had no time to waste twiddling my thumbs in class, the way I had since kindergarten, when I couldn't hear a word that was said. Finally, after all those years, I was willing to rock the boat.

But I did attend one class at CU, the one on water law. There were insufficient legal resources available on that topic for me to do the additional reading that I did in other courses. Since the class was relatively small (about forty students) and followed a lecture format more than the usual Socratic format, and since the professor expressed his willingness to help, I thought I would give it a try.

I wasn't the only one who had to give it a try. Everyone in that class did. Professor Corbin spent a great deal of time talking to us while facing the board and drawing diagrams of plots of land, water lines on those plots, breaks in the water lines, and surrounding houses and scenery. Although I sat in the very front row of the class, directly in front of Professor Corbin, that was of no help when he faced the board. While Professor Corbin really wanted me to understand him, he kept forgetting that in order for me to read his lips he had to face front and center when he spoke.

He was as conscientious as he was forgetful. Every time he finished talking to the blackboard he would turn around to confront the blank look on my face. With a sheepish smile, the professor would apologize and repeat everything he had said while his back was turned to the class. For a while the students put up with hearing everything Professor Corbin said twice. Pretty soon, however, they got bored with that. So every time he began to talk while facing the board, they would shout in unison, "Turn around so Bonnie can see you!" And, with a smile, Professor Corbin would turn around.

This system actually worked pretty well for a few weeks. I even got over my embarrassment about the whole situation. And then one night

Professor Corbin decided to go roller skating. I guess the good professor was not a very good skater, or maybe he was being punished for past sins, because somehow while skating he broke his arm. Two days later he appeared at our water law class with his arm in a cast and the cast in a sling that rested at an angle completely obscuring the lower half of his face, including his mouth. I strained to peer above and below the professor's sling to lip-read him, while the people sitting on either side of me in class took copious notes in an effort to provide me with the information I missed. I a rather heroic team effort, we muddled through. While I appreciated everyone's efforts, I wouldn't want to go through all that again. Nor, I am sure, would Professor Corbin or my classmates.

For the most part I was able to fully understand the subject matter of all of my classes by studying on my own. On a few occasions, I was confronted with issues that I was not sure I grasped completely. Certain aspects of my courses on the Uniform Commercial Code and on the federal courts seemed especially confusing, the latter because the notes I received from my note takers showed that our professor disagreed with the positions taken in the legal treatises and articles I was reading. In both of those courses, I went to discuss the issues with the professors, whom I found to be enormously helpful. In one course the professor let me read her classroom lecture notes for the few classes in which that particular topic was discussed. I was pleasantly surprised by the faculty's willingness to help.

But at CU I again confronted someone who thought that I might be obtaining an unfair advantage by not having to participate in class discussions. This time it was a professor, who felt that I should compensate for the "privilege" of not having to come to class by writing a specially assigned paper. He handed me a list of topics from which to choose and told me that the paper would be due any time before the final exam. I received the assignment with mixed feelings.

On the one hand I recognized that I did not have the nervous anxiety (if second- and third-year law students still had that anxiety) of having to respond to questions in class. On the other hand, I felt that being unable to attend class was much more a disadvantage than an advantage, and I was already trying to compensate for that by doing extensive additional reading. Some of my friends thought the professor was unfair, and suggested that I discuss the matter with administration. I chose not to do so and spent my Thanksgiving vacation, the only free time I had, writing the paper.

My philosophy was that, like it or not, we deaf people have to do extra work to succeed in this hearing world. If that's what the professor required, I'd respect his right to set the rules, even if I didn't agree with them.

I've thought about that instance several times since I wrote that paper.

I still believe that deaf people have to comply with the rules of society, even if those rules sometimes affect us in a manner that seems unfair. But I don't believe that society's rules should unfairly exclude deaf people from doing things that they would otherwise be fully capable of doing. Writing one extra paper certainly didn't prevent me from completing law school. And I accomplished something from writing that paper; I learned something. But if all of my professors had made similar demands I'd have been forced out of law school. It would have been physically impossible for me to write a paper for every class and still keep up with the required classroom reading, much less do the extra reading I needed to do and edit the Law Journal. At the point where the additional demands became unduly burdensome to me, I would have had to protest.

Perhaps it was my growing awareness of imponderables such as when to conclude that additional demands become unduly burdensome, or perhaps it was a growing acceptance of my own deafness, that led me to take my first real venture into the deaf world. (My one-day foray to Gallaudet while in college hardly counted.) Up to this point I had met only three deaf people: Jack (that student leader at Gallaudet), my friend Betty Ann, and a young man, a Harvard graduate student, who had contacted me when I was in college at Syracuse and whose efforts to establish a friendship I summarily rejected. Since I had always refused to view myself as a deaf person, I wanted no part of organizations dealing with deaf people or of other deaf people themselves (which is what I told the young man from Harvard). Indeed, whenever possible I went out of my way to prevent others from knowing that I was deaf. Perhaps I can make the extent of my near phobia on that subject more clear if I recount an incident that happened when I was an undergraduate at Syracuse.

At that time, Syracuse had an excellent speech and hearing program headed by an eminent authority in the field, Dr. Louis DeCarlo. Dr. DeCarlo ran a program for graduate students who planned to work with deaf children. As part of that program Dr. DeCarlo ran a speech clinic—staffed in part by graduate students—for children in the community, most of whom were hearing impaired. I learned of that clinic through a sorority sister who was in the program, and I was persuaded to volunteer to help out on Saturday mornings. During those stints at the clinic I came to know, like, and respect Dr. DeCarlo.

One day he approached me. "Bonnie," he said, "can you come into my office for a minute?"

I followed him in. Something was up. I could tell by the look in his eyes.

"I'm making a film," he said, "and I'd be very grateful for your help."

"Oh, I know nothing about filmmaking," I answered.

"That's all taken care of, actually. What I really need you for is to be in the film, to show how you speak and lip-read, to tell a little bit about your story."

"What is this film about?" I was confused and immediately opposed to whatever it was he was considering.

"It's an educational film about teaching deaf children to speak. It's something I've wanted to do for a long time. Your ability to function and your attitude toward your deafness are special, and I'd love to document this in the film."

"No." I was adamant. It was very hard for me to say no to a man I so revered, but what he was suggesting was out of the question.

"Don't answer now," he said quickly. "I want you to think about it. It's a real opportunity for you to help other people in your situation. Your communication skills are like none I've ever seen. I want you to consider this carefully, Bonnie."

"But . . ." I stammered.

Dr. DeCarlo held his hand up toward me. "Stop," he said. "Please give it some careful thought, and we'll talk again tomorrow."

I left the speech clinic that day under a lot of stress. I didn't mind volunteering with the kids, enjoyed it really. But to be put in a movie like a freak? No, thank you. Very few people at Syracuse knew about my hearing problem; for what he was suggesting I might as well post flyers of myself all over campus with the caption: DEAF. No, as much as I admired him, I couldn't do what Dr. DeCarlo was asking. I would tell him that firmly tomorrow.

The next day when I arrived, Dr. DeCarlo was so excited he could hardly wait to talk to me privately. He took me immediately into his office. I knew I had to speak fast, or I was going to lose my nerve.

"Dr. DeCarlo," I began. "I'm honored that you asked for my help, but I've decided against it."

"Bonnie," he said, "you must reconsider. You have a responsibility to others in your same circumstances. It's for educational purposes, an excellent cause. What are your reservations?"

"My deafness is something I'd rather not advertise," I said. "I've spent a good part of my life trying to lessen the difference between myself and the hearing world. Putting myself on film just emphasizes that difference. I can't do it. I'm very sorry."

"So it's the publicity factor you're concerned about," he said.

"Well, yes. I assume this film is going to be shown, that's the idea, isn't it? You don't make a film to be kept in the closet, right?"

"Right. But what are the chances of your knowing the people who view the film? Syracuse University is a big place. And the film will be shown all over—not just here."

"I know a lot of people here," I said. "The chance that I might know someone and that someone might see me in a movie because I am deaf . . . I can't risk that."

"Okay," he said. This was a man who was not going to give up until he got what he wanted. A man as stubborn as I was. "What if I were to promise not to show the film here at Syracuse until you graduate?"

I thought about this. He was wearing me down. He was someone I admired; his approval was something I sought. If he showed the film after I left, the chances were slim that I'd know anyone who saw it.

"You would swear to that?" I asked.

"I would swear," he said. "In blood if need be." And then he smiled, and it was the smile I could not refuse.

"Okay." I finally said. "But never never never, until I graduate, right?"

"You're the boss," he said.

And so we made the film. It was quick and relatively painless, and then I put it out of my mind. I never even saw it. In fact, to this day I haven't seen it.

A few months later I was hurrying across the Syracuse campus, late for a class, when a guy stopped me. He actually grabbed the sleeve of my jacket to halt me.

"Aren't you the gal I saw in that film in my speech class?" he asked.

"I don't know what you're talking about," I said. I was horrified.

"You're deaf, right? And you were in that movie with Dr. DeCarlo?"

My horror began to blend with anger. I was livid.

"Where did you see the movie?" I asked.

"Speech class."

"In what building?"

He pointed. "Why?" he asked.

"I have to go," I said. "I'm late for class." I left him standing there, puzzled.

I skipped class, marched directly to Dr. DeCarlo's office, and announced to his secretary that I needed to see him right away.

"He's out of town," she said. "He'll be back Monday."

This *was* Monday. I couldn't wait a whole week. I gave her the necessary history about the film, about Dr. DeCarlo's oath in blood, and told her I wanted all showings of the film on this campus stopped *immediately.*

"Honey," she said, "I have no authority to do that. You'll just have to wait till Dr. DeCarlo gets back."

I was not open to negotiating. Our discussion got heated. The secretary thought I was out of line. I thought she was insensitive and unresponsive. If she couldn't take care of a serious matter like this in his absence, what the hell was her purpose? I persisted. She persisted.

"You'll have to leave," she said forcefully. "There's nothing I can do to help you."

"I'm not budging from this office until you order the showings stopped or call Dr. DeCarlo and get his okay to do so."

"I can't do that. I told you."

At that point she decided to really ignore me and took out a nail file and started grinding.

"Fine," I said, forcefully calm. "I'll just sit here and wait and watch you, until you contact Dr. DeCarlo."

She didn't look up.

A half hour later, however, when it became apparent that I was not going to leave and she obviously wanted to do her own thing without being scrutinized, she capitulated.

She called Dr. DeCarlo, and the film was banned.

Given my intense desire to keep my deafness as much under the table as possible, it is not surprising that I had not participated in any organizations of or for deaf people, and that I had not associated with other deaf people. While a law student, however, I agreed to attend the international conference of the Alexander Graham Bell Association of the Deaf (AGB) with an acquaintance who was a teacher of the deaf. It was becoming more and more clear to me that, like it or not (and I did not), I *was* deaf, and I would have to learn to deal with that fact in a professional environment. Perhaps I could learn something from the members of AGB. (You will, I'm sure, recall my lifelong fondness for Mr. Bell.)

My experience at that AGB conference was a real eye-opener. For the first time I met a group of deaf people who, although deaf for all or most of their lives, like me communicated via speech and lip-reading and were fully integrated into the hearing world. It was a relief to know that I was not a freak, not one of a kind. It was a special relief to spend time talking with other deaf people about the unique problems of being the only deaf person in a hearing environment. I made some friends at that conference who are good friends to this day, and who I think will always be.

In addition to meeting some people that I could relate to, I gleaned invaluable information from that AGB conference. It was there that I learned about flashing light systems for the doorbell. I was quick to purchase such a system, which meant that I no longer had to leave my door unlocked and allow any and all visitors to walk in on me and catch me unaware and unprepared. Now I, like everyone else, was able to lock my door if I wished and respond to a doorbell. (I also learned, too late to be of help to me, about flashing "baby-cry" systems, which inform deaf parents via flashing lights that their baby is crying.) And I learned about the phenomenon of "oral interpreting," whereby a hearing person mouths the words of a non-lip-readable speaker for the benefit of a deaf listener, who lip-reads the interpreter. It didn't take much thought to realize that an oral interpreter would solve many of the problems that would confront me as a deaf lawyer. With an oral interpreter, for example, I would be able to converse on the telephone.

That AGB conference provided other benefits, both tangible and intangible. I became part of a network of deaf people, and of people who worked with or provided services for deaf people, who shared information about new devices, coping strategies, and the like. Through that network I learned about the newly developed telecommunication devices for the deaf—TTYs—that allow deaf people to use the telephone by typing back and forth with others who have TTYs. And later it was through that network that I learned about closed-captioning decoders that print the spoken word on the television or VCR screen for the benefit of hearing-impaired viewers. Those two technological devices literally opened up my world.

When I first got my TTY I thought it was a miraculous invention. Now I would be able to use the telephone. The problem was, who would I talk to? I could only communicate via TTY with another person who also had a TTY. No one I knew except the few deaf friends I had made at the AGB convention had TTYs. So I purchased several more machines, for my parents and my brothers, and for my children as they grew older and went to live on their own. (This has been a very expensive process, since TTYs range in price from $200 to $600.) Just being able to use the telephone with family members and a few deaf friends, however, was an enormous improvement over the previous state of affairs.

But the advent of the TTY brought its own frustrations. For in order to be able to answer the telephone when someone called on the TTY, I had to set up a light system that would indicate when the phone was ringing. No problem, you say? Well, setting up the light system was no problem; the same companies that sell flashing light systems for doorbells also sell flashing light systems for the telephone. But the flashing light can't discriminate between TTY calls and non-TTY calls. So nine times out of ten when the phone rings I put the receiver on the TTY only to find that the caller is not calling on a TTY. And then I spend hours worrying about who was calling and whether the call was important. Particularly nerve-racking are the middle-of-the-night calls. Was a hospital calling to tell me a family member or friend was injured? Were the police calling to tell me about an accident? To this day when I receive non-TTY calls late at night or in the middle of the night I lie awake all night long, worrying.

Because TTY users can only communicate with other TTY users, and because most hearing people do not have TTYs, in the late 1980s some states began implementing telephone relay services. Hearing relay operators act as go-betweens for TTY and non-TTY telephone users. The TTY user calls the relay service, and a relay operator answers via TTY and places the call to the non-TTY user (or vice versa). The operator then relays messages back and forth by typing messages for the TTY user and speaking messages for the non-TTY user.

Though a boon to deaf people, the original relay services brought a host of new frustrations. Most only operated for a few hours a day. If the relay service closed at 5:00 P.M. and a deaf person had to make a call at 5:15 P.M., he or she was out of luck. Virtually none of the relay services operated in the late night or early morning hours (not to mention the middle of the night), and many didn't operate on weekends or holidays. Since the original relay services were staffed by a small number of volunteers, thirty-minute or hour-long busy signals were common. And callers were at the mercy of the operator's whims. Operators sometimes refused to translate a message because they took offense at its tone, its language, or even, in some cases, its substance.

As of July 26, 1993, however, the Americans with Disabilities Act requires all telephone companies to provide twenty-four-hour inter- and intrastate relay services for hearing- and speech-impaired people. As a result, deaf people have much greater access to the telephone.

The decoder is even more simple than the TTY. Written captions setting forth the audio portions of a TV show or video tape become visible when people who have purchased a special decoder (for approximately $200) turn it on. Again, I thought that was a miraculous invention.

I was one of the first to buy a decoder when they came on the market. It was 1980, and I was clerking for the Honorable William Doyle, a judge on the Tenth Circuit, U.S. Court of Appeals. *Barney Miller* was the rage, and the two law clerks and the secretaries I worked with often laughed about the previous night's episode. When I learned that *Barney Miller* was to be one of the first shows to be closed-captioned, I rushed right out to buy my decoder.

I managed to get the decoder hooked up on a Thursday afternoon, just in time for that evening's *Barney Miller* show. A man I was dating was coming over, and I planned to watch the show with him. All went according to plan . . . almost. The show was really funny; the dialogue was great. As my friend laughed at the dry humor, however, silent tears ran down my cheeks. To be able to enjoy such a simple pleasure as a television show— it was overwhelming.

For deaf people the cancellation of a popular show that has been closed-captioned can be a disaster. Because the decision to closed-caption a TV show or a video is left to the discretion of the television station owner/manager or the producer of the video, and many of them refuse to spend the money, there is no guarantee that a canceled show will be replaced by an equally good closed-captioned one. When *Barney Miller* went off the air, one of the next shows to be captioned was *Dynasty*. What a disappointing trade-off!

As with TTYs, decoders brought their own frustrations for deaf people. I am sometimes driven to the brink of despair by my inability to watch shows that I desperately want to watch or feel a need to watch for professional reasons, such as the initial congressional hearings of Supreme Court nominee Judge Clarence Thomas. (Although I begged and pleaded with PBS and wrote letters to everyone I could think of, the station refused to spend the money to caption the hearings.) I am equally frustrated at my inability to watch certain videos (I could care less about watching *Superman*, which is captioned, but would like to watch *Mr. and Mrs. Bridge*, which is not).

To date, deaf people have been unsuccessful in their efforts to pass a law requiring that all TV programs and videos be closed-captioned. In 1990, however, Congress passed the Television Decoder Circuitry Act, which requires all television sets having picture screens of at least thirteen inches to be equipped with built-in decoder circuitry designed to display closed-captioned television transmissions. This will allow deaf people who cannot afford to pay $200 for a special decoder to watch TV. It will also allow deaf people to watch TV in such places as hotels, hospitals, and the homes of hearing friends. It is hoped that if all TV sets are equipped with built-in decoders (allowing the display of captions at the option of the viewer), television stations will voluntarily increase the number of closed-captioned TV programs.

The magic of closed captioning sometimes turns hilarious when shows are captioned live rather than on tape. See if you can decipher some phrases that I copied during a half-hour discussion by a prominent TV newscaster following the 1990 elections:

"What will he do about the budget Deaf set?"
"He seems to lack pay shuns."
"This is a grand ad ven clur."
"He is just leaving his sweet."
"I have those wal tees."
"He is entering the haul."
"According to conventionalwise dumb"
"There has been opposition to the in come been see."
"What will be the fiscal paul tease?"
"According to our perfect sep shun"
"This is in ex applicable."

Give up? Here are the translations from an expert (that's me; after several years of translating I've qualified myself as an expert): deficit, patience, adventure, suite, qualities, hall, conventional wisdom, incumbency, fiscal policies, perception, inexplicable.

The people I met at my first AGB conference introduced me to the technology available at that time for deaf people. Since then I've become a part of that network and have actively lobbied for the development of technology and the promulgation of laws to allow deaf people to become part of mainstream society. One of the intangible benefits of that AGB conference was that I became an active participant in this process.

Another intangible benefit of my first AGB conference was that, to a certain extent, I became involved in matters related to deafness. I served for many years, for example, as chairperson of the Arizona Council for the Hearing Impaired. Through the lobbying of our agency, Arizona became one of the first states in the nation to have a twenty-four-hour intrastate relay service. I served for four years as a member of the National Advisory Group to the National Technical Institute for the Deaf at Rochester Institute of Technology (NTID), and for four years as a member of the board of directors of the Arizona Schools for the Deaf and Blind. The bulk of my activities related to deaf people, however, has been on behalf of organizations that promote the oral education of deaf children, and the full integration of deaf people into the mainstream. To further those ends I remain an active member of the board of directors of AGB and of the board of trustees of the Clarke School for the Deaf in Northampton, Massachusetts. I also serve on the advisory council for National Deafness and Other Communications Disorders, part of the National Institutes of Health.

Working with those organizations has brought its own anxieties. In some respects I found it more irritating to be around hearing people who worked in the field of deafness, and who supposedly understood deafness, than to be around hearing people who knew nothing about deafness. The professionals had preconceived notions of what deafness should be all about, and I didn't (and don't) fit into any of their cleverly constructed boxes. One of the most common preconceived notions, of course, is that *all deaf people must sign.* By not using sign language, I failed to comply with the very first rule of the game.

The first meeting I attended of the National Advisory Group to NTID began with a cocktail party and dinner at the (hearing) president's home. One of the first people to come up and talk to me was the (hearing) provost and dean, a very nice fellow I'll call Tom. Since at that time most of the members of the National Advisory Group were hearing, Tom had no reason to know that I was deaf. While sipping our glasses of wine, Tom and I had a very entertaining conversation about a variety of things unrelated to NTID, including skiing, tennis, books, and the like. After about a half hour, the conversation turned to the purpose of our meeting: NTID. Tom naturally asked me, "What brings you to this board? How do you happen to be interested in NTID and deafness?" I responded, "Well, I've been deaf all my life and thought it was time to get involved with helping other deaf people."

Tom seemed flabbergasted. "You are deaf?" he exclaimed. "I had no idea." And then Tom began signing to me.

Gently, I interrupted Tom's signs. "I'm sorry, Tom," I stated. "I don't know how to sign. Could we just go back to talking?"

Tom looked at me askance. "You don't sign? Then how do you communicate with deaf people?"

With a smile I explained that I had spent almost no time with other deaf people and thus had had no opportunity or reason to learn to sign.

Tom was aghast. "But if you don't sign, and you don't spend time with deaf people," he exclaimed, "who do you socialize with?"

It took some effort on my part not to lose my temper. "Why, Tom," I replied, "I socialize with hearing people, of course, and we communicate just as easily as you and I did before I told you I was deaf."

Not every professional who works with deaf people thinks that all deaf people must sign, of course. Those professionals who work with organizations promoting oralism do not. But initially I was uncomfortable with those people, too. Many of them insisted upon speaking s-l-o-w-l-y to me, and exaggerating the movements of their lips, under the mistaken belief that they were making it easier for me to understand them. Actually, the reverse is true. Having spent all of my life with fast-talking hearing people, I lip-read best when people speak quickly and normally. Overly exaggerated speech seems distorted to me, and I find it difficult to understand. And when someone speaks v-e-r-y s-l-o-w-l-y, I find it just about impossible to lip-read, because I lose my train of thought and become impatient.

A (hearing) British educator of the deaf once told me a poignant story. One of the children in her school was mildly retarded and profoundly deaf. His teacher spoke slowly and distinctly to him, thinking to make it easier for him to lip-read. With a smile, the child said to his teacher, "Please, speak *fast*, like you normally do. That way I get an eyeful to lip-read."

I can't say it any better.

As I have spent more and more time with organizations of or for deaf people, I have come to know many of the professionals well. And most of them have come to speak normally to me. There are still some diehards, however, who insist on signing to all deaf people, including me, despite my repeated efforts to explain that it is very difficult to lip-read someone who is signing at the same time.

The signs are distracting. It's hard to concentrate intently on someone's lips when they're waving their hands around in front of their face. And when they sign and speak at the same time, their speech becomes distorted. Many words of the English language have no corresponding sign. Those words, therefore, must be finger spelled, which means that rather than making a single sign for that word, the signer has to make a different sign for each letter of that word. If the word is to be spoken at the same time it is signed, the spoken word must be dragged out to correspond with the lengthy sign. My name, when signed and spoken simultaneously, must be spoken "Booonnnnnie," so that the speaker has time to sign all six letters. Even an expert lip-reader has a hard time lip-reading words that are so distorted. Further, people who sign and speak simultaneously sometimes do not speak some of the words that they sign. There are some single signs that are intended to convey a whole sentence of words, such as the sign that says "Think yourself," which means "It's up to you, it's your decision." The signer will sign that word with great gusto but not speak the lengthy sentence that the single sign reflects. In that type of situation I am left hanging in midsentence. (It is for these reasons that I, and many others, do not believe that the communication system known as "total communication"—which encompasses the simultaneous use of speech and signs—is a viable means of teaching deaf children to speak and lip-read. It is also for these reasons that many proponents of sign language are strongly opposed to "total communication" but believe that people should *only* sign rather than attempt the near impossible task of signing and speaking properly at the same time.)

Of all the petty annoyances involved in working with so-called professionals, however, the one I find the most irritating is the one for which there appears to be no one to blame and no solution.

Sometimes when I attend board meetings of organizations pertaining to deafness, such as AGB, I feel like a black person forced to sit in the back of the bus. I don't like that feeling. About twenty-five people attend AGB board meetings, of whom about five are deaf. An interpreter is present to orally interpret for the deaf participants. For practical reasons, the five of us are relegated to one section of the long conference table across from the interpreter. We must sit together, and we are viewed as a group. I don't know how my deaf colleagues feel, but I feel isolated—and segregated—even if I really am not.

One annoyance that is not petty, however, is the inherent, generally unconscious attitude of some hearing parents of deaf children, and of some educators and professionals in the field of deafness, toward people who are deaf. While on the surface deaf and hearing people are treated alike at meetings and gatherings of members of organizations pertaining to deafness, at times an undercurrent, sometimes strong, sometimes subtle, suggests that hearing people are perceived as having greater value or worth, at least intellectually.

This unintentional attitude is so intangible that it is almost impossible to describe, and some deaf people who have tried to do so have been accused of imagining things or being paranoid. Perhaps this unconscious attitude on the part of some parents and professionals is unavoidable, and learning to live with it comes with the territory of being deaf—a territory in which people who are deaf are frequently placed, because of our communication limitations, in a position subservient to people who can hear.

The greatest benefit of participating in the deaf world has been my growing acceptance of myself as a deaf person. That acceptance has had a lot to do with the manner in which I have conducted my professional life since entering law school.

THE FEEL OF SILENCE

My life is a kaleidoscope of lights.

A remote control device is hooked up to a lamp in every room in my house save the bathrooms, which don't have room for a lamp. When the phone rings, every one of those lamps flashes in harmony with the rings, slowly . . . rinnnggg, rinnnggg, rinnnggg. When the doorbell rings, the lights flash in a different pattern in conjunction with the bell, sharp and snappy . . . beep, beep, beep, beep—a dozen times in a row.

My bedside alarm clock has a built-in strobe light, the brightest light I have ever seen. When the alarm goes off the strobe flashes, flashes, flashes. It's enough to wake the dead. I know, because in desperation I used it to wake up my teenage son.

I keep the blinds on my windows open. In fact, many of my windows don't have blinds. I like the sunlight and the feel of open spaces. That, of course, means that all my flashing lights are visible to the world. A paper carrier came to my door one evening. He must have been about eleven or twelve years old. "Oh, ma'am," he exclaimed breathlessly as I opened the door, "something is terribly wrong. Lights are flashing all over your house. Should I call the fire department? The police?"

I went to visit a friend the other day. He lives in one of those big apartment buildings with an intercom system. You know how it works. If you want to visit Tommy Smith in apartment 6B, you push button 6B, and, if he's home and not hiding from visitors, Tommy answers on the intercom and says, "Who's there, please?" Whereupon proper etiquette requires you to identify yourself by saying, "Hi, Tommy, this is Sally Smart, come to visit you." Tommy then has two basic choices. He can tell you to get lost, or he can say, "Great to see you, Sally, I'll push the beeper and when you hear it ring you push the door open." Try doing that one as a deaf person!

But at least I was only a visitor. Imagine how it would be if Tommy was the deaf one. Only deaf hermits can live in high-rise apartment buildings with intercom systems. Deaf people who want visitors had better find other accommodations, which is exactly what I was forced to do when I wanted to buy a house in an area that has a security guard system. Again, you know the kind. We have lots of them in the West. To get into the housing complex, visitors have to go through a guard station. As you stop your car, the guard politely asks who you are and whom you are visiting. You respond by saying, "I'm Howdy Doody, and I'm here to visit Buffalo Bill." Whereupon the guard picks up the telephone and calls Buffalo Bill to inquire whether Mr. Bill wishes him to allow Mr. Doody to proceed to Mr. Bill's residence.

After discussing the matter with the security people at the housing development in which I wished to purchase a relatively modest townhome, we realized it simply would not work. I could not live in that development and receive visitors, as no security guard could leave his post (gasp) and come notify me in person (via my light system) that I had a visitor. Nor could I waive my right to security, because some robber might use my name (gasp again) to get into the complex and rob one of my neighbors. I would have to find other housing. And so I did.

What a world we live in.

Technological advances seem to bring deaf people two steps forward yet one step backward. Some of my favorite backward steps include drive-in bank tellers and restaurants. It's often necessary for me to use drive-in bank tellers, because the real banks are never open during the hours I can get to them. Unfortunately, the tellers are invariably too far away from the drive-up machine to be visible from my car, and often they try to talk to me, shouting louder all the time through the microphone, until someone in my line of vision at the adjacent machine finally shouts to me, "Lady, give the poor teller a break and answer her, will you?" Then I explain to the teller that I'm deaf and a lip-reader and she'll have to write me a note. That takes forever. And it seems to make everyone mad, especially the people on line behind me.

Drive-in restaurants aren't really necessities, but they sure are convenient sometimes. When it's broiling outside in the Arizona summer and I'd love to stay in my air-conditioned car and pull into the drive-in window of a fast-food restaurant and order dinner rather than brave the heat, I can't. A couple of times when there was no line at a McDonald's or a Wendy's, I drove right up to the window and tried to place my order. No luck. The kids that work at those windows haven't been programmed to take orders in person; they can only do their jobs by following rigid programs, and those programs call for food to be ordered only by the speaker phone.

Another of my favorite steps backward involves talking trains. Have you had to change planes at the airport in Atlanta, Georgia? You get on the train to go from Terminal A to Terminal D, and the train makes a dozen stops before it reaches your destination. At every stop a robot talks to the riders in the train, telling us where we are and under what circumstances we should get off. I know this, of course, only because someone told me so after I failed to get off at the right stop and missed my connecting flight.

I once moved into a new townhouse. It came with a built-in burglar alarm as a standard fixture. When you wanted to set the alarm, you pushed certain numbers; you pushed different numbers (which no one but you was allowed to know) to turn the alarm off. When triggered by a door or window being opened, after thirty seconds the alarm made a hell of a lot of racket—for a hell of a long time.

Upon learning that I was deaf, the man in charge of the alarm systems installed a light in the living room and the master bedroom of my unit. If the system was on and someone broke into my house while I was home, those lights would flash in a strobelike pattern and alert me to the intruder's presence, even if I was sleeping. (Then what was I to do? Jump out the second-story window?)

One day I finally convinced myself that I might as well turn the alarm on at night and make use of it. No burglars or would-be rapists arrived. At seven o'clock the next morning, I pushed the magic buttons to turn the alarm off so I could open the door and go to work. Everything seemed to work fine. I got into my car and began pulling out of the driveway. An old man who lived and worked at the still unsold model house came running up to the car saying, "Your alarm is going, your alarm is going; go turn off your alarm."

I could picture the neighbors standing in front of their bedroom windows watching me calmly drive out of the garage and down the street, leaving my alarm blasting away. What a way to make new friends.

I open the bag of microwave popcorn. "Microwave on high until bag is expanded and popping slows to 2–3 seconds between pops," the instructions read. I put the bag in the microwave and watch carefully. I see the bag expand. I see it popping furiously. It stops. I take the bag out and open it. Damn, I didn't leave it in long enough; half the corn hasn't popped. I unpack another bag and put it in the microwave. Again I watch carefully. Again it pops furiously and stops. Aha, I smirk, it hasn't really stopped, it's just popping slowly so I can't see it. I wait another minute and a half. Too late. The popcorn burns. I try one more time and burn another bag of corn. My last bag.

Anyone for pretzels?

Chapter
EIGHTEEN

I guess you could say that my professional life began the summer between my second and third years of law school, when I clerked for a law firm. Because I was at the top of my law school class and editor-in-chief of the Law Journal, I didn't have any trouble getting a summer clerkship with a large, major law firm in Denver. When I interviewed for the job I told the hiring partner that I would need my own secretary, whom I would train to orally interpret for me on the telephone, at large meetings, and so forth. That seemed reasonable to him, and so we left it at that. What I didn't tell the hiring partner was that I had never worked with an oral interpreter and had no idea whether that experiment would be successful. I kept my anxieties and insecurities to myself.

On my first day on the job I arrived with another law clerk, Ramon, promptly at 8:30 A.M. to meet with Joe, the lawyer in charge of all the summer clerks. (Actually, we were called "summer associates," which sounded much more important.) Joe was one of the lawyers who had interviewed me for the job, and I remembered him as being easily lip-readable. As soon as he began to speak that morning, however, I realized that his mustache had grown a full quarter of an inch since I had last seen him and now covered his upper lip. Not wanting to begin the summer by calling attention to my need to lip-read, I bluffed for a while. But I must have said yes too many times when I should have said no, or vice versa, because Joe voluntarily retired to the men's room with his desk scissors and returned with a half-visible upper lip. My stomach returned to its normal place.

Then the real work began. Ramon and I were taken on a tour to meet all of the firm's hundred and more lawyers that we could find. Our tour guide, an associate in the firm named Barbara, led the way as we trailed behind. I do not know how long Barbara had been talking to us, while walking in front of me with her back to my face, before I realized that I was supposed to be responding to her comments. Subsequently, at my request Barbara and I walked side by side while Ramon followed behind.

During the course of that day, with only an hour's break for lunch, Barbara, Ramon, and I visited about two-thirds of the firm's lawyers. Sixty-five to seventy different sets of lips. I began to see what I was in for. As each lawyer made casual chitchat with us for an average of five to ten minutes, I found myself straining to keep up. There simply wasn't enough time to get used to one set of lip movements before we moved on to the next set. Already I was faced with a dilemma. Should I try to bluff? Or should I call attention to my deafness on the very first day of work?

Bluffing . . . I've spent a good chunk of my life doing that. During my elementary and secondary school years I pretended to hear what was said in the classroom, because if it were known I couldn't hear I would have been banished from school. During social situations as a teenager and an adult I continued to bluff, laughing when others laughed, clapping when others clapped, and nodding sagely when it seemed appropriate. As a lawyer, however, it was obviously going to be much more difficult to bluff. A mistake on my part could have grave consequences. Nevertheless, I couldn't eliminate bluffing entirely. In some situations it would have to remain the name of the game.

The real task lies in knowing when to bluff and when not to. We deaf people simply can't go around saying What? every time we don't understand something, or we'll drive the hearing people around us crazy. So every now and then I have a decision to make: Shall I pretend I've understood, and let it go, or might what I've missed be sufficiently important that it's worth irritating a hearing person for? Any success I've achieved in this hearing world I attribute to my ability to make this decision correctly about 80 percent of the time.

But now, for the first time, I was confronted with this dilemma as a "lawyer." What to do?

I decided to bluff. Clearly the conversations at issue were casual and relatively unimportant. No one that we met that day was discussing legal matters with Ramon and me. I only made an ass of myself twice that I knew of. I was grateful, however, that we would not have to repeat that experience during the course of the summer.

And then I was taken to my office and introduced to my secretary. In one respect I was lucky. I was given a permanent office for the summer. The rest of the summer associates rotated offices each week and thus had a different secretary each week. Since I obviously couldn't train a new interpreter each week, and since my office needed to be equipped with a speaker phone for interpreting purposes, it was not feasible for me to move.

My secretary, Joan, was eager to learn how to interpret. I really didn't know much more than she did about oral interpreting, but I figured we'd make up the rules as we went along. I told Joan there were two basic ground rules that would never change. First, she was to repeat what a speaker was saying to me without using *any* voice or sound. Second, she was to try to keep up with the speaker, so that she mouthed the words at most three words behind the speaker. The trick was not to think about what the speaker was saying, much less to try to understand it. Just take garbage in and spew garbage out. Finally, I told Joan, she would have to walk into my office and tell me if I had a phone call or a visitor, even if the door was shut, since I wouldn't hear her knock.

"But I can't do that," Joan blurted. "That's rude."

I laughed.

Joan and I tried out our interpreting system with the speaker phone and found that it worked reasonably well. Joan would listen to the speaker phone and silently repeat what the person on the other end of the line said at the same time the speaker was talking, and I spoke for myself. Over the course of the summer, however, I came to realize that a speaker phone was not the best kind of setup. First, there is too much static on a speaker phone. Second, speaker phones seem to distort voices; my voice becomes harder to understand. Finally, the speaker phone picks up noises at both ends of the conversation other than the voices of the people conversing.

As a result of that summer experiment, a deaf friend, Richard (whom I met at that first AGB conference), made me a more efficient telephone setup. He cleverly installed a double jack at the spot on the side of my telephone where the receiver cord plugs in, to allow two receivers, rather than just one, to be plugged into the phone. Richard took the second receiver and literally sawed it in half with a hacksaw, being careful to saw only the receiver itself and not the wires inside. He then discarded the bottom half of the receiver, which contains the mouthpiece, and shoved all the wires into the top half of the receiver, which contains the earpiece. He sealed the bottom of the earpiece half with "shoe goop," a substance for patching shoes. That half receiver is for my secretary/interpreter to listen with. I use the full receiver to speak into. The advantage of this system is that it eliminates the problem of the speaker phone and allows me to speak directly into the mouthpiece. And since the interpreter's receiver has no mouthpiece, the interpreter *cannot* speak to the person with whom I am conversing. If the interpreter misses something, he or she tells me, "I missed that," and I ask the speaker to repeat. My new system, developed after that first experimental summer, has proven so effective that few people realize when they talk to me on the phone that I am deaf.

It was during this summer as a law clerk that I was introduced to the pitfalls of being a deaf lawyer and attempted to find means of avoiding them. It wasn't going to be as easy as I had hoped.

Lawyers are busy and impatient people. They don't like to be interrupted unnecessarily, and they understandably resent any intrusion into their lives that wastes time. If I thought before that being deaf was like walking through a mine field, I hadn't seen nothin' yet. As usual, it was the little things that took the most getting used to.

Minor problem number one: names. When I went into an attorney's office for an assignment, and the attorney would talk at length about the case I was to be working on, it was imperative that I know the name of the case, as well as the names of all the parties and any significant participants in that case. Since names aren't lip-readable, I finally got enough courage to hand the attorneys a pad of paper and ask them to write down all relevant names. More than one attorney found that procedure an irritating waste of time. Although ultimately they all complied, I got the feeling that my work had better be damned good to warrant this extra step on their part.

Minor problem number two: unwittingly intruding. I stand before the closed office door of an attorney I must talk to about a project I've been assigned to do for him. I knock gently and pause. Is he saying "Come in," or "Please come back later"? I open the door despite my uncertainty. Maybe he's not even in the office. But he is. He's on the phone and annoyed at my interruption. "I *said* I was on the phone," he snaps.

Minor problem number three: pacing attorneys. There seems to be a correlation between successful attorneys and the amount of time they spend pacing their offices while brainstorming about important cases. Making every effort to keep up with the discussion, I would gamely pace back and forth side by side with the big boss. This was *not* an effective solution. Not only would the attorney face front rather than look at me, he would often look at the floor with his chin sunk into his chest, presumably muttering pearls of wisdom the entire time that I, in a state of near panic, was missing.

Minor problem number four: client meetings. Every now and then some attorney I was working for during the summer would decide that I should attend at least one meeting with the client, so that I could hear the client and his attorney discuss the case and ask appropriate questions. Another dilemma. Since it would be difficult for me to follow the conversation between attorney and client (try moving your head back and forth like a spectator at a tennis match and see how much you miss), should I bring my secretary/interpreter to the meeting? Or would it make both attorney and client uncomfortable to have an extra person in the room listening to this very confidential discussion and visibly mouthing the words for the benefit of a lowly summer clerk? Would it be better to miss part of the discussion—thereby defeating the purpose of my presence—or to risk offending the big boss or (worse yet) the client? A no-win situation.

Minor problem number five: informal meetings. Frequently several summer clerks and associate lawyers of the firm would be working on one big case, with each of us concentrating on a particular aspect of it. We would often find ourselves seated side by side in the library during the working day, and sometimes during the evenings and weekends. Not infrequently the lawyers and clerks would get involved in lengthy, informal discussions about the case, sharing ideas and theories that ultimately proved to be helpful to everyone—except me. I found it particularly aggravating to be unable to participate in those informal meetings or discussions. At night I would lie awake in bed, wondering if I had missed something that everyone but me would focus on in their memos or brief sections.

That rough sampling of the minor hassles of a deaf summer associate proved an accurate foretaste of the minor hassles that would plague me as an attorney, at least until I developed enough clout to set my own rules. Overall I found the summer quite productive. I learned a little bit about what the real practice of law as all about, and I learned that despite the aggravations I still wanted to be a lawyer. I also made a few friends.

I made one friend in an unusual manner. The lights went out in our office building one day that summer. I was in the library, which had no windows. It was so dark it was like a cave, and I froze in fear. To be unable to see or hear is terrifying. Ramon, the clerk had toured the firm with me the first day, was aware of my fear. He quietly came to my side, took my hand, and led me to an office with windows. He then stayed with me until the lights went on. He had made a friend for life. To this day we keep in touch.

When I went back to law school for my final year, I had my systems down and was able to graduate among the top ten (top 5 percent) of my class.

The summer after graduation I did what most of my classmates were doing—studied around the clock for the Colorado bar exam. My fellow graduates all signed up to take the bar review course, which was given via a series of lectures to several hundred aspiring lawyers four or five nights a week for two to three hours, lasting about five weeks. Obviously I was not a candidate for this method of review, since I wouldn't be able to hear the lectures. Somewhat panic-stricken, I offered to pay the fee for the course for a CU classmate if he would take notes of the lectures for me. He agreed, and we both passed and became members of the Colorado bar. (I was later to pass the Arizona and California bar exams without any participation in the bar review courses. In those instances I didn't know anyone to ask to take notes for me, so I had no choice but to study on my own.)

I already had a job arranged for the first year after graduation. I had been offered the honor of clerking for the Honorable William Doyle, a judge on the U.S. Court of Appeals, Tenth Circuit, in Denver. During the year of my clerkship (1980–81) the Tenth Circuit decided a number of significant cases. I probably learned more about the law and our legal system during that year than I had learned in all of law school.

For a deaf attorney, serving as law clerk for an appellate court judge proved to be a lot less frustrating than working as a summer associate in a large law firm. For the most part I worked with a small group of people: Judge Doyle, his two additional law clerks, and two secretaries. While we three law clerks also had dealings with other Tenth Circuit judges and their law clerks, the bulk of our time was spent among ourselves. Oh, the luxury of getting to know the lips you will read the whole year, and knowing that for the most part the lips won't change.

Because Judge Doyle required his clerks to attend all oral arguments of the cases he was assigned to, I hired an oral interpreter who lived in Denver to come to court on those days and hours to interpret. Other than that, I was able to manage on my own. While the judge was sometimes difficult to lip-read, he was quite good about repeating when necessary. We often had lengthy debates—sometimes arguments—about issues relating to the cases. When the judge got too mad (he had quite a temper), and I was afraid to ask him to repeat, one of the other law clerks would gladly fill me in. I enjoyed the stimulating working atmosphere and found the whole process fascinating. I still keep in touch occasionally with my fellow law clerks.

I remember particularly a time I attended oral arguments before the court in preparation for writing a draft opinion. I "listened" to the attorneys argue. Intently I watched my oral interpreter as she silently mouthed the attorneys' words and the judges' questions. "Is that legal or legal?" the interpreter appeared to mouth as she parroted the attorney's rhetorical question. Or was that "Is that illegal or illegal?" Must have been "Is that legal or illegal?" I deduced.

"Clearly, your honors, that's legal," the attorney answered his own question. Or was that "illegal"? "No," responded one of the judges, "that's clearly illegal." Or was that "legal"? In desperation I wrote a hasty note to the interpreter: "The 'ill' isn't visible on the lips. Please say 'legal' or 'not legal.' "

Another memorable incident from that time was a visit I had from a deaf friend I'd met at that first AGB convention, Mickey, who came to Denver for a dental conference. Mickey met another deaf dentist, John, at the conference and the two of them walked over to my office at lunchtime so that Mickey could introduce me to John. While Mickey and I were talking, John became extremely agitated about something that had occurred during the conference. He began talking in a very loud voice, and neither Mickey nor I was able to calm him down. Fortunately, Judge Doyle was out to lunch. But the other law clerks and the secretaries were not out to lunch, and they were outraged that John was speaking so loudly in the chambers of a U.S. Court of Appeals judge. After Mickey and John left, my co-workers came into my office and expressed their outrage.

I tried to explain that since John was deaf the sound of his voice was unknown to him, and he hadn't realized that he was speaking so loudly (nor had I). No amount of explanation would satisfy my co-workers. They felt that it was John's responsibility to either ensure that his voice did not exceed normal levels or refrain from entering such places as a judge's private chambers. I felt torn between the two positions. Of course my co-workers were right. John's loud voice was totally inappropriate in that setting. On the other hand, John really had no way to monitor his voice. Should John's autonomy be restricted in that type of situation?

Shortly thereafter I was attending a conference in San Francisco and went out to a bar for drinks and then to a restaurant for dinner with three other people—one deaf and two hearing. The bar was very noisy, and my deaf friend, whom we'll call Sam, and I had to speak very loudly so our hearing friends could hear us. After the bar, we went to a restaurant. One of the hearing men, Joe, told me to speak softly since the restaurant was very quiet. I thanked him and lowered my voice accordingly. When Sam began speaking loudly, Joe made the same soft remark to him. Sam blew up. He raged at Joe that he didn't give a damn about the other people in the restaurant, he'd never see them again, and he would not, under any circumstances, allow anyone to criticize him for his deafness. I sat quietly throughout Sam's tirade. I sympathized with both Joe and Sam and could find no fault with either of their positions.

The next day Sam and another deaf friend drove me to the airport to catch my flight home. My plane was late, so we sat in the airport bar to have a drink. It was obvious that Sam was again speaking too loudly, since people at other tables were staring at him—and us. I knew to keep quiet; this was obviously a big issue with Sam. But it was worse even than the day before, because Sam began telling an off-color story that the whole place became privy to. Apparently, he'd once traveled on a boat in Europe and was assigned to a sleeper that was none too clean. Later he discovered that he had caught the "crabs" from the mattress. The poor people in the bar were eating and drinking—one man was actually munching on a different sort of crab at that moment. He put it down, disgusted. As people at the tables around us made faces and stared at us, I wished I could evaporate. But I couldn't decide whether I should politely ask Sam to quiet down or just grin and bear it and say nothing. I chose to keep quiet. I still don't know if I made the right decision.

THE FEEL OF SILENCE

It's like eating potato chips. You can't eat just one, you want more, and more, and more. That's what happens to us deaf people. With progress comes danger, and a bad case of the "I wants."

With the advent of closed-captioned TV shows I lost my benevolent acceptance of being unable to watch television and began wanting more. If I can watch ten TV shows, I want to watch them all—or at least the ones I want to watch. I thought my fury at being unable to watch the initial congressional hearings of Supreme Court nominee Judge Thomas was unsurpassable. But I felt even greater fury when PBS responded to pressure and began captioning the second round of hearings relating to the Judge Thomas/Anita Hill controversy but inexplicably ceased captioning at approximately nine o'clock Sunday evening in the middle of a sentence. A curt typed announcement appeared stating that "captions will resume at 10 A.M. Tuesday morning," although the hearings would continue for several hours on Sunday night and were scheduled to continue all day Monday. We deaf people were sent to bed like children in the middle of a murder mystery, left in suspense.

With the advent of captioned videos I lost my benevolent acceptance of being unable to understand movies and began wanting more. I want them to caption all movies.

With the advent of TTYs I lost my benevolent acceptance of the inability to use the telephone and began wanting more. I want everyone, everyplace, to have a TTY, so that I can talk to anyone I want to on the telephone.

This is very dangerous.

On a river rafting trip I took with several other deaf women we were part of a group of about twenty-five. We had no interpreter with us, but two hearing friends did their best to informally interpret when the guides gave formal presentations. Because of their inexperience, our friends were not able to keep up much of the time. And, of course, no one interpreted the informal conversation and instruction that took place most days.

Of the seven deaf women on the trip, only one lives in a primarily deaf environment. That women, whom I'll call Ms. Y, lives in a community where she and her husband both work at a program for deaf college students. Although Ms. Y is an excellent lip-reader who grew up in a primarily hearing environment, for the past fifteen years or so she has been part of a community where an interpreter is present at all classes, functions, meetings, and events, and where almost everyone knows how to use sign language. At one point during our rafting trip Ms. Y burst into tears from frustration. Unable to control her tears, she explained her feelings to the rest of us. Simply stated, she could not stand the frustration of missing so much of what was said. "I'm spoiled," she said honestly. "I've gotten so used to having an interpreter whenever I want or need one that I can't tolerate being without one in this type of situation."

All of us could sympathize with Ms. Y. And most of us had missed just as much as Ms. Y had missed. But, unlike Ms. Y, we don't live in a primarily deaf environment where easy communication is a part of life and where interpreters are available on command. Thus, we are still able to tolerate being unable to understand.

That's one reason I have chosen not to learn sign language or to spend a lot of time with deaf people. I don't want to lose my ability to tolerate the frustrations inherent in living in a hearing world. I don't want a greater case of the "I wants" than I already have.

That raft trip was an eye-opener in another way. Having lived all my life among hearing people, I treated my deaf companions exactly as I treat my hearing companions. When a deaf friend was in front of me in the boat, on the trail, or in the campsite, I called ahead to her, to no avail. When necessary I made comments to my deaf friends in the dark, again to no avail. I talked with my mouth full of food and through laughter and then had to repeat my words when I had swallowed my food or finished laughing. When I was in a position on the raft to be able to see the guide's lips and a deaf friend was not, I interpreted what the guide was saying. This took some doing. I had to think before I spoke, and sometimes I got frustrated. I guess turnabout is fair play.

There must be a special hell for deaf people. A totally dark hell. No burning fires that would allow us to lip-read by their bright glow. The most severe form of punishment for a deaf person is to be plunged into eerie darkness.

I hate the darkness. I fear the darkness. At dusk I give an involuntary shudder. I feel helpless and vulnerable. I *am* helpless and vulnerable.

Traditionally, romance and candlelight go hand in hand. Dinner by candlelight is not romantic for a lip-reader; it is torture. After I was divorced, I wondered how I'd ever have enough nerve to go to bed with someone. I'd never be able to hear a word he said. For a time I had quite a few offers. While I'd like to say it was my ultrapure morals that made me turn them all down, in reality there were a few offers I might have accepted but for my terror of talking in the darkness. One man was sensitive enough to figure that out. He offered a candle (for a "slight light") along with his proposition. So cameth my fall from grace.

Like Cinderella we deaf people leave the ball early. Instead of fleeing at midnight we leave at the stroke of dusk. It always seems that the picnic, barbecue, hayride, or patio party is just beginning to be a lot of fun when the sun goes down, and faces turn dark and take their words into the night. The party is over for me. I haven't made my life easier by living in Phoenix, where life is conducted primarily outdoors during eight months of the year.

Darkness often comes upon us when we least expect it. I was once traveling in Europe on a Eurail pass and was having a great conversation on the train with an interesting group of people. Suddenly the train went through the longest, blackest tunnel I have ever seen. For more than five minutes our conversation ceased. When the lights came on, I tried to explain to my newfound friends what had happened. Try as they might to understand, we lost our easy rapport and our conversation came to a standstill.

I hate the darkness.

Walking while lip-reading a companion at the same time often has perilous results. I've tripped up or down a curb and bumped into people or objects on more than one occasion while watching my companion's lips rather than the path in front of me. Hiking brings its own travails. The hikes I take in the magnificent Southwest are usually on narrow trails meandering through the mountains. For the most part there is room for only one person on the path. So we hike in single file, making conversation impossible for me. Biking is something else. Riding a bicycle while lip-reading a companion sometimes requires real heroism on my part. And riding in a car with me as a driver may require heroism on the part of my passengers. I drive sideways, one eye on the road and one eye on the passenger sitting next to me to allow me to lip-read. This sometimes makes my passenger a little nervous, maybe even very nervous.

Chapter NINETEEN

Although I planned to stay in Denver for a year to clerk for Judge Doyle, I had to decide if after that year I should practice law in Colorado or Arizona. Ultimately I decided to return to Phoenix. My parents were now living in that city, and my eldest son was there, as were many friends. Scott had been begging to go back, and it seemed time to return to the place that had been our home for thirteen years. Having made that decision, during my last year of law school I interviewed for jobs with the major Phoenix law firms. After several offers, I opted to go with Brown and Bain, which turned out to be a wise decision.

I took the two-and-a-half-day Arizona bar exam in July, while I was still clerking for Judge Doyle. Of the old school, the judge had informed his clerks that we would not be entitled to any time off during our one-year clerkships. I had tried to study from seven to midnight nightly for a month before the exam, and I arrived in Phoenix at ten o'clock the night before the exam, having worked until six.

I joined Brown and Bain in the fall of 1981. This was the real thing. At forty-one I was to become a litigation attorney. A lawyer friend once commented that as a litigation attorney I had to rely on an interpreter in the courtroom. "Being a litigation attorney is so frustrating in itself," he remarked, "I don't think I could handle one more complication. How—and why—do you do it?"

How do I do it? By ignoring the frustrations of using an interpreter. Why do I do it? Why climb a mountain? Because it's there. And it feels good when you get to the top. And the scenery is unbeatable. Why raft a river? Because it's there. And it's exciting to go through the rapids. And the scenery again. Nonsensical answers. I don't know why I do it.

Of the many frustrations that come with being a deaf lawyer, the worst are a product of my dependence on interpreters. I should thank the powers that be for the invaluable assistance of my interpreters, and for not requiring the use of an interpreter more frequently. Instead, I complain about and strongly resent having to use interpreters at all. Because while I can't live without 'em, I often feel I can't live with 'em, either.

The perfect interpreter would be a robot—someone who never thinks an independent thought, someone who is available the minute my need arises. Unfortunately (for both me and my interpreter), interpreters are human beings who have private lives, hearts, opinions, and days off. I resent having a third person privy to my most intimate telephone conversations and thoughts. I resent having a third person interject their personality into my telephone conversations. I'll be making a phone call, for example, and once in a while an interpreter might say to me, "Just say so and so." Invariably I explode when that happens. And I resent having interpreters express their opinions about my telephone conversations—silently, but with unmistakable facial distortions. A raised eyebrow is as vocal as the loudest comment. In short, I resent having to rely on a third person at all. And since no one has invented the robot interpreter, mine continue to be human beings.

It was at Brown and Bain that I first had to rely on an interpreter every day.

I've always trained my secretaries to serve as interpreters. The first secretary/interpreter I trained at Brown and Bain, Sue, had worked at the firm for some time. She was very competent. Unfortunately for me, Sue graduated from college and moved on. But we struck up a friendship that has lasted to this day. The next secretary I trained was a young woman who, upon retrieving my mail from my mailbox as she did daily, saw a memo scheduling a major meeting on a case I was working on. The meeting was set for a day when she had planned to be out of the office and would be unavailable to interpret. She called the senior partner on the case and requested that he reschedule the meeting because "Bonnie would not have an interpreter." I was livid. I explained to her, through gritted teeth, that the appropriate procedure was to inform me of her planned absence and let me handle the matter as I saw fit. (I would have found a replacement interpreter or would have missed the meeting. Under no circumstance would I have requested that a major meeting involving several attorneys and clients be rescheduled due to my lack of an interpreter.)

Another time, when a temporary interpreter was filling in for my ill secretary, my ex-husband happened to telephone, a rare occurrence that was inevitably awkward. We had few pleasant words to say to one another.

The temporary's name was Gayle. She'd been instructed to do what all my interpreters do: Pick up the phone when it rings and, without using any voice, repeat verbatim everything the caller says, complete with "uhs" and "uh-huhs." The interpreter is also supposed to convey any attitude or feeling on the part of the caller. If the caller sounds angry or happy, the interpreter should relay those emotions through facial expression. If the caller laughs, the interpreter must laugh; if the caller should cough or sneeze, the interpreter must do the same.

So the phone rang and Gayle picked it up, listening while I said hello. I watched her lips for the first piece of conversation to appear. "Bonnie, this is Bob," she mouthed. I stiffened as I always did when he called. As soon as I knew it was Bob, I felt defensive. "Hello," I returned, barely cordial.

"I was wondering," the temp mouthed, "how you were doing."

This wasn't like Bob, to start a conversation with pleasantries. "I'm okay," I said. "Why?"

The temp was looking flustered, but I attributed this to her never having interpreted before.

"Just . . ." She paused. "Just wondering . . . you know . . ."

I knew Bob well enough to know that he *never* called to see how I was doing. Not in all the years we were married and certainly not after the divorce. There had to be something on his mind. What was his hidden agenda? I didn't know how to respond.

"What is it, Bob?" I said finally. "I'm really busy." At this point I saw the temporary start to look shocked, and her lips froze, silent. She sat like that for awhile, then without even mouthing goodbye she set down her part of my phone.

"What happened?" I said.

"Oh, he had to go," she said.

"Did he say that?" I asked. "Because your job is to say everything he says, word for word."

"Oh, I forgot," she said. "He said he had to go suddenly and would call you back another time."

Frustrated by the lack of closure and by the useless interruption, I went back to what I'd been doing before the call. I couldn't get it off my mind though. What had possessed Bob to sound almost sweet? So nice? And why had he ended the call so abruptly?

Gayle excused herself and went off to the ladies' room. Eventually I got the whole encounter off my mind.

Until the next day, when my regular secretary returned, and I ran into the office manager, Dorothy, in the elevator.

"I have to tell you a funny story," Dorothy said. "Yesterday, when Gayle left, she mentioned that she felt she'd been put in a very compromising position."

"How so?" I asked.

"Well, from what she says your ex-husband called and was being quite unpleasant. So much so that she didn't feel she could repeat what he was saying."

"And?" I was becoming more angry by the second.

"Well, she didn't want to say these things that she felt would insult you, Bonnie, so she made something up, and then ended the call as soon as she could."

I couldn't even see by this time, I was so furious. That a person could censor my calls, decide what I could and could not hear, infuriated me. And the worst part was that I had been fairly civil to Bob, thinking he was being pleasant, while all the while he was probably hurling profanities at me. Someone had chosen to protect me, against my will and against my instruction, and there wasn't a damn thing I could do about it. Even today, I tell this story to any new interpreter I train, and I say, "If you *ever* do something like that, you will be history, do you understand?" Usually they do. And to my knowledge, that's never happened again. But the fact that it *could* happen again is enough to drive me crazy. To depend on someone else's ears, and someone else's version of a conversation, is a dependency I detest, yet one I will never get away from.

I never did find out what Bob said on the phone that day.

At Brown and Bain my secretary answered all my phone calls. She would answer the phone, get the caller's name, come into my office to tell me who was on the phone, and interpret for me if I wanted to take the call. If she was at the copy machine, in the library, in the ladies' room, on a coffee break, or elsewhere in the building, I would watch the little red light on my phone ring and ring and wonder who was calling. Sometimes the caller would leave a message with the switchboard, sometimes not. If the call was from one of the other in-house attorneys, the caller could not leave a message. My frustration mounted. Often the phone would ring before my secretary arrived in the morning or after she had gone home for the evening (we lawyers all worked much longer hours than our secretaries). I'd want to scream, "I'm here, who are you?"

When I was still a relatively new associate at the firm, an important visitor came to the office to see me when my secretary was at lunch. The visitor went to the reception desk on the eleventh floor and asked for me. The receptionist then called me at my office on the ninth floor. Since my secretary was at lunch, I could not answer the phone. The receptionist told the visitor I was not in my office and he left. Actually, I was sitting at my desk waiting for that visitor.

Someday someone is going to invent a mechanical interpreter, that never has a thought of its own, does not eat lunch, go to the bathroom, talk to friends in the hall, take vacations or days off, and, best of all, never minds my temper and never talks back. A deaf lawyer's dream.

As a litigation attorney I didn't ask my secretary to interpret only on the phone but at depositions, in court, and at meetings of more than four people. Occasionally I even asked my secretary to interpret in a one-to-one situation, if the speaker was for some reason non-lip-readable. But for the most part when I communicated on a one-to-one basis with up to four people I managed on my own. I'll do anything to understand what someone is saying. If I have to stand on my head to lip-read someone who is standing on *his* head, I will.

One of the partners at Brown and Bain has a mustache that hangs over his upper lip. When he was standing and I was sitting, I could manage to peer underneath his mustache and lip-read him, since he is considerably taller than I am. When he was seated, however, I could not get beneath his mustache to see his upper lip, even if I was also seated. So when I'd visit him at his office to discuss a case, and he would sit at his desk, I was stymied. But not for long. On my third visit to his office I simply knelt on the floor. It worked. From a kneeling position I could see under his mustache. He never asked me why I was kneeling on the floor, and I never explained. I was sure he thought I worshipped him. When I finally did mention it, he was genuinely surprised. "I just thought you were getting comfortable," he said.

Communication is the name of the game for lawyers. It is up to me, as a deaf attorney, to figure out ways to reduce the communication barriers as best I can. For the most part I was lucky to work with lawyers at Brown and Bain who were responsive to suggestions, and willing to cooperate. I exercised caution, however, not to focus excessively on my deafness. People are only people, after all, and too much of even a good thing becomes a bore, or worse.

A primary reason that the lawyers at Brown and Bain were willing to put up with my "difference," of course, is that they felt they were getting value for their money. I do not think I will exceed the bounds of reasonable modesty if I say that I quickly became known around the firm as a lawyer who would get the job done well, and in a timely fashion.

I can concentrate better and harder than anyone I know. Some people have surmised that this is so partly because I'm not distracted by sounds, either environmental or human, and partly because of the many years I've spent intently concentrating while lip-reading. I guess if there is any advantage to being deaf, this is it.

Due to my powers of concentration and ability to read and write at rapid speed, I generally produce twice as much work as anyone else in the same amount of time, sometimes three times as much. And I'm never frazzled when I have several projects that must be worked on at once. I quietly plod through them one at a time. Respecting my work and my capabilities, Brown and Bain put up with a few inconveniences, as long as I bore the major brunt of those inconveniences. I was happy to do so, and practiced at it.

B eing a career woman did not preclude domestic hassles. Not long after we moved back to Phoenix, the refrigerator went on the blink. It had been acting odd ever since the move, as if something had gone wrong during its transport. The kids told me it made a funny noise, but I couldn't hear it, and it was still making ice, so I figured it would hang on for awhile. It was early fall, but if you know Phoenix at all you'll know it was still quite hot—torturous even. When you live in a place like that, you thank God daily for your air conditioner and your refrigerator. You don't take these things lightly. Or you do only until they're taken away from you.

I drove home one day through a bad traffic jam after a stressful day at the firm. I was hot and tired and wanted nothing more than an ice-cold Pepsi. I went straight to the refrigerator and knew the second I opened it that something was wrong. Everything was covered with condensation, and the ice that collects on the bottom of the freezer section was dripping like a spigot. A pool of water had formed at the bottom and now began spilling onto the floor. The Pepsi was barely cool. No problem, I'd add several ice cubes. Right. The ice trays offered little cubicles of water. In the freezer, two weeks' worth of meat was thawing prematurely. It was too late to call a repairman, even if I'd had a way to call; I'd have to make do until the next day. I went out for ice, filled the ice chest, and put as much of the refrigerator's contents into the chest as would fit. I've done my share of camping, so I was sort of used to this kind of thing.

The next morning at work I called the repair place through my interpreter. They'd get to me when they got to me, couldn't predict when and someone would have to be there at the house to let the repairman in. Having no choice, I agreed to take the day off and go home and wait, even though that was horribly inconvenient for me—I didn't have an hour to spare on that job, much less a whole day.

I was careful to speak clearly. "Please inform the repairman," I said, "that I'm deaf. He should not, under any circumstances, try to call me to confirm that I am there, because I won't be able to answer the phone."

"I understand," the woman said.

"It's very important. I will be there, I promise, but that can't be confirmed over the phone."

"I'm sorry, ma'am," the woman said. The interpreter conveyed a confused look. "If you're calling me now, how come we can't call you to make sure you're home. It's policy."

"Yes, I understand," I said. I'd been through this so many times with plumbers, electricians, delivery people, but I was trying to be patient. "I'm using the phone now with the help of an interpreter. I'm at work. When I go home to wait for the repairman, I'll be alone," I said.

"Oh, I see. I'm sorry. I'll make sure he understands."

"You're sure?" I said. I'd gotten promises before and still the plan had been foiled. I wanted two things at this point. A working fridge and to get back to work. The woman assured me everything would be taken care of. She would personally see to it that the repairman covering my part of the city would know to just go on to my house without calling. I went home to wait.

Shortly after noon my phone started to ring, which I knew by the lights that flashed in conjunction with the rings. I picked up the receiver and put it on the TTY. Not a TTY call. A half hour later the lights started flashing again, and I repeated this procedure. Nothing. I continued to await the repairman's visit. At four o'clock I drove back to the office, angry by this time. I hunted down my interpreter and placed the call. "Why didn't anyone show up to fix my refrigerator?" I asked. From my interpreter's expression, I easily deduced that the woman with whom I was speaking was quite put out with me. "The guy called your house," she said, "twice in fact, and no one was home."

I gritted my teeth. Should I try the same thing the next day and hope for better results? Or should I trust past experience and just go buy a new fridge? Truly it seemed easier to buy a new one.

Why didn't I pick up the ringing phone and say, "If this is the repairman, I am home and waiting for you, but I can't hear you on the phone so just come on over"? Because my phobia about the telephone was so great, I'd as soon have picked up a dead rat. I was terrified of it. I had no way of knowing whether the person on the other end would still be on the line when I spoke, would be listening to what I said rather than speaking at the same time, or would be able to understand what I said. It was beyond my ability to speak into that great void. It would feel like talking to a ghost.

As a litigation attorney at Brown and Bain, I primarily worked on very large cases for prominent corporate clients. By very large cases I do not refer only to the amount of money at stake (most cases involved claims in excess of a million dollars), but to the complexity of the issues and the number of parties embroiled in the controversy. It is not unusual in an antitrust, trade secret, or product liability action, to name just a few, to have several plaintiffs and several defendants, each represented by different counsel. When handling such cases I needed to have frequent contact with the attorneys for other parties, by both mail and the telephone. So I often had telephone conversations with lawyers from all over the country about discovery requests, scheduling of depositions, settlement negotiations, or the like. I, of course, handled those telephone conversations by having my secretary orally interpret via my special two-receiver telephone system.

Given this background, picture the following scene: After months of talking on the telephone with four attorneys for other parties in a case I've been handling, we all fly to the state in which the case is centered and appear at the appropriate courthouse for legal arguments on a significant motion, ready to argue on behalf of our clients. I arrange for an interpreter in the applicable city to meet me at the courthouse. The interpreter will mouth the arguments made by the other attorneys, who will be facing the judge or judges rather than me, and will mouth questions and remarks made by judges who may be too far away or too difficult for me to lip-read.

As we lawyers introduce ourselves to one another, I introduce the interpreter, announce that I am deaf, and explain the interpreter's function. Four faces smile and four hands extend to shake my interpreter's hand. Then, double takes! Four sets of eyes look at me in astonishment; four mouths open wide. "But," stammers one of the four, "you can't be deaf, we've talked on the phone a dozen times." "Yes," I reply, "with the assistance of my secretary/interpreter." Again, double takes.

Sometimes even the most well-intentioned people, who know I'm deaf, forget. I don't know how often the lawyers in my firm would stand in the doorway of my office and talk to me while I was busy writing or reading at my desk, blissfully unaware of their presence. My secretary would have to intervene. "Mr. Jones, she can't hear you. You have to walk into her office and stand in her line of vision." And once I played bridge with a few people from the firm, including a partner I often worked with. I mentioned that I was considering renting the vacant room in my house to someone who could use the telephone. My partner asked why in the world I would do that. "Well, it's really difficult to live without a phone," I responded. "Get a phone, then," he replied. "What's the problem?"

I guess I should take it as a compliment that people forget that I am deaf. Certainly I shouldn't be surprised when "outsiders" forget, since there are times when my own children do.

I was in Washington, D.C., to give a presentation and stopped in to visit my eldest son, Kevin, who, following in his parents' footsteps, was practicing law with the firm of Skadden, Arps, Slate, Meagher, and Slom. We arranged that I would come back to Kevin's office at seven that evening to take the subway with him to his house in Virginia. Kevin carefully explained that the Skadden, Arps offices were in a secured building that was locked after six. To get into the building I should pick up the telephone outside the door and call security. Kevin would advise security that I was coming, and, when I gave both our names, security would come and open the door for me.

I looked at Kevin blankly.

"What's the problem?" he asked.

"Well, Kevin," I responded. "You haven't told me how I'm supposed to use the phone to talk to the security people."

"Oh! Oh, yes," Kevin exclaimed. And we agreed that he would come to the door at seven and wait for me to arrive.

In addition to experiencing lapses of memory about my deafness, the lawyers I worked with were sometimes unable to understand exactly what that deafness really means. This, too, is not surprising, but it was sometimes a tad annoying. I remember having mock oral arguments for cases that several of us (including me) were going to argue in different courts. About twenty lawyers in the firm sat around a long conference table and played judge. I brought my secretary with me to interpret the questions of those lawyer/judges who were too far away to lip-read or who were simply un-lip-readable. When I spoke I was required to stand at the head of a long conference table. My secretary had to sit at my right, while the presiding judges sat to my right, to my left, and in front of me twenty feet away. (Under normal court conditions, however, my secretary sits in a chair in front of the podium at which I am standing, directly in front of the judge or judges before whom I am arguing.) I watched all of the judges as I spoke but kept my eye on the interpreter so I'd know when I was being interrupted with a question. During the barrage of questions, I watched the interpreter as she relayed each one, and I looked at the judge who had asked the question while answering it.

The performances of the arguing attorneys were all critiqued. When critiquing my performance, a senior partner remarked that I lacked sufficient eye contact with the judges. He noted that because of the interpreter I was going to have to work twice as hard as others to maintain eye contact and said that it was generally disconcerting to have me look at the interpreter when a question was being asked rather than at the judges. I tried to explain that in court, when a long conference table is not blocking my way, I have much better eye contact with the judges, since the interpreter is directly in front of them and I can look at the judges and the interpreter simultaneously. But I was unable to make that partner understand.

And then there were the times my fellow lawyers were just too preoccupied with the case at hand, too busy or too frazzled or too deep in thought, to have any excess energy to expend worrying about my communication difficulties. Those instances, too, were understandable, but picture it: I was still a fairly new associate in the firm, conducting arguments on an important case. I had written much of the briefs, but a senior partner argued in court, and two other partners came to court to observe the arguments. (I was pleased to watch the arguing attorney introduce the interpreter to the court just as I would have done.)

After the court's ruling, pursuant to which we won some points and lost others, we came back to the office to work on strategy. The senior partner did most of the talking at that meeting for about an hour. He covered his mouth with his hand, played with his mustache, and paced the room so that 50 percent of the time his back was facing me. My frequent attempts to position myself and pace alongside him, and my infrequent attempts to remind him that I had to see his lips, were to no avail. He was simply too worried about the case to have room for any other thoughts.

Fortunately, as I became more experienced and acquired seniority, those situations occurred less and less frequently. I began to do more and more of the talking during those strategy discussions, and the lawyers I was working with wanted my input. To get it, they had to ensure that I heard their comments so I could respond appropriately. Eventually, when I assumed major responsibility for cases, I was able to conduct all discussions in a manner that was easiest for me. Seniority pays.

As a practicing litigation attorney, I had to make some compromises. There were some things that I didn't feel comfortable doing. One of them was defending depositions in which numerous parties and their attorneys were present. Taking depositions was fine. If I was the one taking the deposition, I was in charge. I sat the deponent in front of me and placed my interpreter behind the deponent. That way I had constant eye contact with the deponent I was questioning but could see my interpreter at the same time. If an attorney for another party interjected a comment or an objection, I could see my interpreter's lips move even while I was addressing the deponent, and I would respond appropriately to that attorney's comment. If I was not the attorney taking the deposition, however, but was merely attending the deposition to represent the interests of my client, along with five or six other attorneys who were attending the deposition to represent the interests of their clients, I was not in charge, and I had no control of the manner in which the deposition was conducted.

As usual, the attorneys at Brown and Bain were quite willing to accommodate me with respect to this problem. Since the cases I handled or worked on for the firm were usually large ones, involving complex litigation and numerous parties, there were usually two or more lawyers assigned to a case. I would arrange for another lawyer to defend those large depositions, and in exchange I would assume another responsibility.

With very few exceptions, I was capable of handling every legal task that came my way. I even became inured to the tension that inevitably arose when I argued in court with the assistance of an interpreter. While every attorney is nervous when arguing in court, I faced a double pressure. Any worry about the substance of the argument itself was secondary; my primary anxiety was that I would be unable to lip-read a crucial question. As time went by I spent less and less time worrying about that problem. I did a modest amount of traveling to handle cases in other states and, with advance planning, was always able to locate someone to interpret in other cities when an interpreter was required. (We handled so many California cases that I ultimately took, and passed, the California bar exam.)

Traveling as a deaf attorney brought its own humorous incidents, and some not so humorous. I remember one especially embarrassing incident.

When handling a class action employment discrimination case filed by women scientists against a major business in New Mexico, I frequently brought associates or paralegals with me to help with document retrieval and review, witness interviews, and other housekeeping matters. Because the business is in a small town virtually in the middle of the desert, we usually stayed in nearby Santa Fe or Albuquerque. One time a young male associate, Dolph, who was a good friend, accompanied me on the trip. We were staying in Santa Fe but drove one evening to Albuquerque to have dinner with some New Mexico attorneys whom we planned to use as local counsel in the case. The two attorneys that we had dinner with happened to be friends of both of us. (One was my old friend Ramon from my summer associate days in Denver.) After our business was over we spent a couple of hours socializing with those old friends, and between the four of us we polished off a couple of bottles of wine.

When Dolph and I left the restaurant to make the one-hour drive back to Santa Fe, it was after midnight. We were driving very slowly and chatting about the dinner and other matters, which meant that Dolph, who was driving, had to turn on the ceiling light in the car so that I could read his lips. All of a sudden, as we were driving across the desert in the middle of nowhere, Dolph pulled the car over and parked on the side of the road.

"My God," I thought. I couldn't believe this was happening. Dolph, who'd been my friend and colleague for years, was going to make a pass at me. It had to be the alcohol; this just wasn't like him.

My stomach was suddenly nervous. I liked Dolph, but not in that way; we were friends. He pulled farther off the road and turned off the car, then the ceiling light, and I was prepared for the kiss.

"Dolph," I said. "Don't. You've been drinking and you don't know what you're doing."

"What?" He looked confused.

Right then a police officer appeared at Dolph's window. I'd never seen the lights and obviously hadn't heard the siren.

"Did you know," the police officer said, "that it's against the law to drive at night with the ceiling light on?"

Dolph carefully explained that I was deaf and the light was to allow me to lip-read. After several skeptical questions the officer finally believed us, gave us a warning, and let us go.

Dolph and I sat there for a minute, relieved, and then he turned to me and said, "Now *what* were you saying?" I was stunned and embarrassed, until I began laughing uncontrollably.

"What?" he kept saying, over and over, but I was laughing too hard too speak. Finally, between laughs, I managed to squeak out, "I thought . . . I thought . . . you were about . . . to make a pass at me." Then it was Dolph's turn to crack up. We finally composed ourselves enough to drive away before another police officer would have reason to stop us for unruly conduct.

The greatest problem I continue to confront when traveling and using an interpreter is the attitude of people who do not know me and are not familiar with my capabilities. Being deaf makes it difficult to assume a position of respect in meetings, particularly meetings with strangers, when an interpreter is required to sit next to me and mouth what everyone is saying. I often lack eye contact with the speaker, since I am watching the interpreter instead. And the gap between the time the speaker finishes speaking and the interpreter finishes interpreting—even if the interpreter is good and that lag time is minimal—makes it difficult to get a word in edgewise in a room full of lawyers who all want to speak all of the time.

A less significant issue, but an issue nonetheless, has been learning how to deal with the stereotypes that are so prevalent about deaf people. Stereotypes die hard. Some may even be impossible to kill. I was startled to learn, for example, that a judge before whom I had argued in court was telling people that I used a sign language interpreter during the proceedings. While attending a social gathering with one of my law partners, the judge remarked that I had done a good job of arguing in his court and opined that the sign language interpreting had gone smoothly. My partner corrected the judge. "No," my partner explained, "Bonnie doesn't know sign language; she uses an oral interpreter."

Despite the difficulties or annoyances presented by my deafness, I thoroughly enjoyed both the practice of law and working with Brown and Bain. Although my practice primarily involved corporate litigation, including antitrust, trade secrets, products liability, large contract disputes, securities fraud, and the like, I spent one memorable year handling the employment discrimination class action and two major Freedom of Information Act cases. But I was slowly developing an interest in the rights of people with disabilities, and laws dealing with those rights. I was interested not in practicing law in that area but in writing on the subject as a legal scholar.

Coincidentally, during this time I got a traffic ticket that I felt I didn't deserve and went to argue my case. I brought along my secretary to interpret in the courtroom. When we got to the municipal courthouse, I discovered that I would not be arguing my ticket but merely attempting to set a trial date to do so. This involved waiting in a series of lines, and talking to a variety of people. When my turn finally came to speak to the prosecutor, I brought my secretary along and explained that I was deaf and my secretary would orally interpret if necessary. The prosecutor thereafter spoke only to my interpreter. "What does she want to do?" he asked. "Has she paid her fine?" All of my explanations were useless.

Frustration piled on frustration when I was directed to the courtroom where I was to await my turn before the judge to receive a trial date. As my secretary and I sat down she began interpreting for my benefit what was said by the judge and the parties before him. The judge saw my secretary's lips moving and interrupted the whole show.

"We will await further proceedings," he said, "until those two ladies in the third row stop talking." I stood up and explained that I was deaf, that my secretary was orally interpreting without using her voice, and that we had not been speaking. The judge refused to understand. He wanted silence, and even though my secretary wasn't making any noise, he assumed she was because her lips were moving. He got up and announced to the courtroom at large, while looking pointedly at me, "This court is adjourned until all present agree to abide by the rules of the court." He and his bailiff then left the courtroom.

I entered the bailiff's office and asked, quite nicely, that she inform the judge that I was an attorney with Brown and Bain, that I always took an interpreter with me in court when I argued on behalf of a client, and that I was legally entitled to take an interpreter with me when I argued a simple traffic ticket on my own behalf. I returned to my seat and instructed my secretary to continue to interpret when proceedings resumed.

Shortly thereafter the judge reappeared and began calling people to the bench. My secretary continued to interpret until my name was called. When I approached the bench the judge apologized to me. "Under the circumstances," he said, "you are entitled to an interpreter in the courtroom."

To this day I wonder what a deaf person who was not an attorney would have been able to do in that situation. My interest in the rights of people with disabilities increased.

After practicing law with Brown and Bain for four years, and doing a little writing in the area of disability rights, I was invited to teach a course on that subject at ASU College of Law as an adjunct professor. The law firm graciously allowed me to use a great deal of my time one semester to do that.

I found that I enjoyed teaching. I also found it virtually impossible to write the legal articles I wanted to write about disability rights while practicing law full-time. On the other hand, I really loved Brown and Bain, and enjoyed the practice of law. When I was elected a partner (member) of Brown and Bain and offered a full-time job as a professor of law at ASU during the same year, I had an extremely difficult decision to make. Complicating the decision was my longtime desire to be an appellate judge.

Ultimately, I compromised. After practicing law with Brown and Bain for six years, I took an indefinite leave of absence from the firm to accept a tenure-track position as an associate professor of law at ASU. My partners at Brown and Bain, who did not want me to leave, assured me that the door was always open for me. We all believed I'd return to the firm in a couple of years, unless I became an appellate judge.

I left with mixed feelings. I'd had a satisfying tenure with Brown and Bain and had learned a great deal. But I looked forward to the opportunity to develop expertise in other areas of the law, which would assist me if I became a court of appeals judge. I also looked forward to the kind of time I imagined a professor would have for outside study. I very much wanted to become an expert on the rights of people with disabilities. For someone who'd denied her own disability for the better part of her life, I'd come a long way, baby.

THE FEEL OF SILENCE

For a deaf person, travel has its own delights.

Returning home once from a three-day conference, I was seated on the airplane next to a rather nice looking man in a business suit. My briefcase sat on the floor underneath my feet, while I busily made notes about the conference in preparation for a report I would have to write. My seatmate watched me out of the corner of his eye. An intriguing looking man, I thought. After we had been airborne about fifteen minutes, I felt his light touch on my arm.

"Excuse me, ma'am," he said in a soft voice, "but don't you think you should do something about that noise coming from your briefcase?"

What noise? I wondered, somewhat panic-stricken.

"Oh, of course," I managed to reply in what I hoped was a nonchalant manner, and I reached for the briefcase. It trembled in my hand, as if it had a life of its own. My vibrator alarm clock was still vibrating madly, as it must have been for the two hours since the time it had been set to go off.

I often get my room-service breakfasts served in style—by waiters accompanied by gun-toting security guards. Yes, really. I give a lot of talks on the law at various conferences and conventions. I'm an early riser and usually spend about an hour running through my talk for the day at about six in my hotel room. I like to have breakfast while I'm preparing. In many of the hotels at which legal conferences and conventions are held, a card is placed on the door of each guest room, asking guests to check various blanks and return the card to the doorknob if they wish to have breakfast served in their rooms.

You've seen those cards, I'm sure. You check which foods you want and the half-hour period during which you would like them served (6:30–

7:00 A.M., 7:00–7:30 A.M., etc.). I do one more thing. After checking all the appropriate blanks, I write a note at the top of the card explaining that I am deaf and will not hear the waiter knock on the door, thus I will prop the door open at the appointed hour and the waiter should walk in.

Unfortunately, most hotels won't allow their room-service waiters to walk into a guest's room, even if the guest has indicated in writing that the waiter is to do so. So, despite the fact that I awaken fifteen minutes before the appointed half hour arrives and place a wastebasket in the door to my hotel room to keep it slightly ajar to allow the waiter to enter, the waiter frequently arrives accompanied by a security guard decked out in all of his or her finery, including gun.

I'm used to it now. But the first time a gun-toting security guard entered my room unexpected and unannounced at six-thirty in the morning I thought I was being arrested. That sure woke me up for the day!

On one of my trips from Phoenix to Washington, D.C., via Chicago, the plane landed almost a half hour early on the first leg of the trip, a pleasant and welcome aberration. The tail winds must have been good, I thought. I got off the plane and began walking to the proper gate to take my second flight. The gate wasn't there. I looked around. This wasn't O'Hare Airport in Chicago! Where the hell was I? I went back to the ticket counter at the gate where I had exited the plane and saw the stewardess from my flight standing behind the counter.

"What's going on?" I asked.

"This is Indianapolis," she replied. "Our plane was unable to land in Chicago due to bad weather. How could you have missed the announcements and instructions? I woke up everyone who was sleeping."

We were driving to Colorado to ski one Christmas week. There were four of us—Ronale and Mike, Scott and I. We took two cars because Scott had to leave for home earlier than the rest of us to return to his part-time job. Ronale rode in my car with me while Mike rode in Scott's car with him. Along the way we hit bad weather. The men wanted to talk to Ronale and me about stopping to put on chains, so Mike rolled down his window and began shouting at Ronale, at the same time pantomiming to let her know he wanted her to roll down *her* car window. It was freezing outside. "We don't need the windows open," Ronale shouted to Mike through an open crack in her window. "Mom can read your lips." Now you see? I knew there was an advantage to traveling with a deaf companion!

I punched a security guard at the airport recently. Three times. I am five foot four inches tall and weigh 125 pounds (when I'm not fighting ten pounds of fat) and—to the best of my recollection—have not punched anyone since I hit Jennifer Adams on the playground when we were in first grade. That was more than forty-five years ago.

The security guard did not punch me back. I wish he had. It would have been less insulting, and much less painful, than what he did do, which was to continue to deliberately prevent me from lip-reading.

Here's the background. I travel a lot, and lately more than 50 percent of my travels have been completed without benefit of luggage. Not because I like wearing the same grubby blue jeans (my travel costume) for two or three days, but because frequently when the airlines fly me west (or north) they fly my luggage east (or south). So recently I decided to beat the airlines at their own game. I bought a weekender suitcase, big enough to hold everything the well-dressed businessperson needs for three days, yet small enough to carry on an airplane. It was very expensive. It was also very heavy when packed (I missed the class on how to travel light). I even squeezed into it my portable TTY and vibrator alarm clock. I lugged the bag from my car to the shuttle, from the shuttle to plane number one, and from plane number one for what seemed like miles at the Dallas airport to plane number two, headed for Washington, D.C. By the time I got on the second plane I must have looked as tired as I felt, because a ground steward greeting passengers on the plane took the bag from me and kindly said, "There's no need for you to lug this heavy bag all the way to your seat in the back of the plane, let me put it up front for you." Gratefully I complied and proceeded to my seat to await takeoff.

The plane did not take off. We sat on the runway for two and a half hours. After twenty minutes I began to wonder about the delay. So I pried a stewardess away from her engrossing conversation with a good-looking male passenger, explained that I am deaf, and asked her to relay to me in person any announcements made over the loudspeaker. She charmingly assured me that she would do so. Another hour passed, sans messages. The stewardess, however, had completed her conversation with the good-looking male passenger and was now engrossed in conversation with a second, slightly less good-looking male passenger. Being no fool, I tracked down another stewardess and made the same request. She, too, promised to relay any broadcasted messages (both stewardesses had clearly attended the same charm school). Another messageless hour passed before the plane took off.

As I prepared to leave the plane at Washington National Airport—finally—I opened the front cupboard to retrieve my bag. I don't know why I was so shocked when it was not there. Overhearing my query to the stewardess about the whereabouts of my bag, the pilot replied, "I put it off the plane, of course; it was in the space reserved for *my* bag." Gritting my teeth, I asked the pilot why he hadn't simply moved my bag to another location on the plane. He replied, "That's *your* responsibility. I got your name from the label on the bag and called you over the loudspeaker several times and told you to come move your bag. You ignored me."

It was now three-thirty in the morning, and once again I had arrived at my destination sans luggage. I was tired and frustrated. And *angry*. Between strangled gasps I asked the pilot how I could get my luggage, without even a claim check. He finally reluctantly agreed to provide me with a note to serve as proof that I did, indeed, have a "missing bag," once we were both off the plane.

Upon entering the airport, however, the pilot changed his mind. "Lady," he said, "I'm a *pilot*. I don't even have to *talk* to passengers, much less give you a note." I must have squealed loudly in protest, because a nearby security guard, seeking to protect this innocent six-foot-two, 190-pound pilot from a vicious female passenger almost half his size immediately moved to stand between us. As graciously as I could, I asked the security guard to move, explaining that I was a lip-reader and he was blocking my view of the pilot's lips. He refused. I moved left—the security guard followed. I moved right—the security guard followed. We must have looked like Abbot and Costello. Meanwhile, the pilot was talking, but his words were unreadable. I totally lost my cool. The unflappable security guard, however, simply ducked my punches until I ran out of steam. How could I fight someone who wouldn't fight back?

The airline didn't locate my luggage until almost twenty hours later, after they finally reached the pilot at his home to find out where he had stashed it—which was in the pouring rain. The bag and its entire contents were soaked.

Southwest Airlines doesn't assign seats. Instead, as you check in you are given a numbered boarding pass. Those with lower numbers board first and get first choice of seats on the plane. With all the recent air crashes and scares, I now try to sit in the front, in an aisle seat, so that in the event of an emergency I can lip-read the flight attendant giving life-saving instructions. This necessitates my getting to the airport very early, to ensure a number lower than twenty. Although I checked in at the flight desk forty-five minutes before a recent flight to San Diego, my boarding number was forty-eight. Too high! I explained to the ticket lady that I was totally deaf and a lip-reader and needed to sit in a front aisle seat so that I could lip-read the flight attendant in the event of an emergency.

"No problem," said the ticket lady. "Just listen for the preboarding announcement and tell the agent you are deaf and wish to preboard."

I sat in the back.

Chapter TWENTY

Any beliefs I ever held about the nice, easy life of a law professor were immediately and rudely dispelled when I joined the ASU law faculty. I worked harder than ever before, as I prepared to teach subjects that I knew little about. I teach courses in disability law, criminal law, wills and trusts, and judicial remedies. While I had a working knowledge of all of these subjects, I was not an expert in any except disability law, and in the beginning I was not really an expert on that either.

No one forced me to teach those courses; I chose to. Criminal law interested me because I aspired to be a court of appeals judge, and I needed a good knowledge of both criminal and civil law to serve effectively. What better way to acquire a good knowledge of a subject than to teach it? I chose wills and trusts because my entry at the College of Law coincided with the retirement of the professor who taught that subject—and who was a nationally recognized expert in that field. I agreed to "volunteer" to teach wills and trusts because, again, it would give me the opportunity to develop expertise in that subject. ASU College of Law, like most law schools, follows the belief that a good lawyer and teacher can learn to teach any legal subject and do a good job of it. Judicial remedies just happened, I'm not sure how.

In addition to becoming an expert on four unrelated subjects, immediately upon beginning my apprenticeship at ASU I began writing on the subject of disability rights. That was, after all, one of the primary reasons I had chosen to teach. Moreover, if I was going to seek tenure, I would have to publish. But for a brief period of time, my quest for a court of appeals judgeship took priority.

I'd wanted to be an appellate judge since my early years of law school. Analyzing and writing about the law are my strengths, and that's what appellate judges do. They carefully analyze the law and write concise, clear opinions explaining their analysis. My clerkship with Judge Doyle reinforced this desire. In fact, the judge strongly suggested to me on more than one occasion that I should become an appellate judge. Everything I'd done in law up to this point had been in preparation for this goal. I chose to practice as a litigator because an appellate judge should have litigation experience. I chose to practice general civil law, rather than to specialize in any one area of law, to gain a working knowledge of as many aspects of the law as possible, something else that I believe a good appellate judge should have. And I chose to teach about areas of the law in which I had not practiced to broaden my knowledge and experience.

After teaching at ASU for a year and publishing some significant articles, I began focusing on my pursuit of an appellate judgeship. Encouraged by dozens of lawyers and judges, for about a year and a half I went through the political appointment process to be a judge on the Arizona Court of Appeals. I should have paid attention to my initial skepticism about the appointment process for the court of appeals that arose when the trial judge who handled my divorce was appointed to that court. If I'm ashamed of anything in my life, it is that I subjected myself to the abuses of the Arizona political system.

I don't know what arrogance made me think that I, a deaf person, could survive in a political system that produced Evan Mecham (Arizona's impeached governor), the Keating scandal (involving financier Charles Keating's alleged questionable dealings with certain senators), AzSCAM (a political investigation during which several members of the Arizona legislature resigned or were dismissed due to charges of bribery, fraud, or both), the repeated rejection of a Martin Luther King Day (though sanity did finally prevail), and several other episodes that I won't mention for fear they won't let me back in Arizona after this book is published. Given the state's political climate, it should have come as no surprise to me that some of the powers that be that select judges in Arizona harbored outspoken and inflexible prejudices about deaf people. But I was not only surprised, I was crushed. I blew it. I let the so-called powers grind me down.

The details are not fit to be published. The general flavor of the process is clearly reflected in the words of two members of the Arizona political inner circle. "A deaf person couldn't possibly be qualified to be an appellate judge," said both a member of the appellate court appointments committee and a member of the governor's staff, despite the committee and the governor's office having received numbers of glowing recommendations attesting to the contrary. Indeed, according to the political grapevine (which I and my partners at Brown and Bain, unfortunately, were not privy to until after the fact, when it was too late to address the issue) some members of the committee insisted that I was named a partner at Brown and Bain only on the condition that I would immediately leave to teach at ASU. (That had to be so, didn't it? What firm would elect a deaf partner and really mean it?) Nothing could have been further from the truth. The partners at Brown and Bain were genuinely surprised that I left to teach, and several of the senior partners tried to persuade me not to leave.

The world of politics as I experienced it was so reprehensible that I re-assessed my career goals. Since under no circumstance would I be willing to subject myself to that political process again, it was time to decide whether I wished to pursue a life in academia or return to Brown and Bain. After much reflection, I opted to remain in academia. More and more I wanted to become a legal scholar in the area of disability rights. And so I opted to go through the tenure process at ASU.

Since my application for tenure followed too closely for comfort on the heels of my political fiasco, I was concerned. I knew my deafness did not in any way compromise my teaching. My secretary/interpreter sits in the front row of my classes of up to 130 students and mouths the student com-ments, which come fast and furious. I alternately watch the student who is speaking and the interpreter. When my students make side comments to one another, or comments under their breath, I can often lip-read them. When I ask a question of the class and someone silently answers that ques-tion to himself, I often respond by saying, "I see that you think such and such, Mr. Jones, why is that so?" The students are constantly amazed that I have caught what they've said and sometimes are not happy about it, es-pecially if they've said something they would have preferred I not hear. They can't get away with much in my classes.

I'm also as proficient as any of my colleagues—and more proficient than some—in the areas of writing and public speaking. But, as the sole deaf law professor among scores of hearing professors I do have one disad-vantage. Law school faculty pride themselves on their collegiality, which may be somewhat ironic, since my in-depth observation of several law school faculties and tales told to me by members of others reveal that law professors are at each other's throats as much or more than any other group of human beings on the face of this earth. (I think my fellow law professors will not take offense at this but will agree.) Nevertheless, collegiality is supposedly the cornerstone of the good life as a law professor.

Law professors sit around and exchange lofty views about highly the-oretical, abstract propositions of law that I suspect sometimes make little sense even to those of us discussing the subject. Such obtuse conversa-tions, carried on in rapid, somewhat staccato fashion among several law professors, all of whom want to speak interminably at the same time, are impossible for even the most expert lip-reader to follow. I rarely set foot in the faculty lounge of the law school, and rarely communicate beyond po-lite, mundane conversation with my colleagues. This is not because I do not like and respect them—I do—but because I can't follow their conver-sations. My deafness precludes me from taking part in the collegial process.

When I decided to apply for tenure at the law school, I was concerned that my purported lack of collegiality would have detrimental effects on my tenure application. Like it or not, we deaf people cannot usually rely on popularity contests to make our way in this hearing world because we are too restricted in our dealings with others. So I did what I've done my whole life: played the compensation game. If I wasn't collegial, I would have to be everything else, without question. I would publish twice as many articles as required, I would give several national presentations, and I would write (and eventually publish) a treatise on the legal rights of people with disabilities (and later a Nutshell and other books). I was good at this game by now, and, after four years of teaching at ASU, I became a tenured full professor at the College of Law.

I don't mean to say my colleagues and I are not friendly with one another—we are. But we sometimes fail to connect, and sometimes the result is funny. For example, recently I was planning to teach in Australia; I was pretty excited about it, and told one of my colleagues who has been to Australia many times.

"You must go to the opera in Sydney," he said. "It's magnificent. The best opera in the world."

"I think I'll pass on that one," I said, laughing.

He shrugged his shoulders, thinking perhaps that I didn't respect his opinion. I waited. He was halfway down the hall before he realized, turned around, and laughed. I laughed, too.

For now, my intent is to remain in academia, although in some ways the daily hassles are greater than those I endured as a practicing attorney at Brown and Bain. The interpreting situation is far more frustrating. ASU's secretaries are grossly underpaid and cannot, under state law, be paid overtime for working longer than a forty-hour week. Instead, they receive compensatory time. The more responsibility I assume—local and national presentations, visiting professorships, university and other committee meetings, board meetings, book and article publications, and so on—and the more phone calls I make and receive, the more frustrating the interpreting situation grows.

At ASU I have become acutely aware that I live at the mercy of my interpreters. And they have whims and moods and schedules and obligations like all the rest of us. When those moods and whims and schedules interfere with my autonomy I'm afraid I don't usually have much sympathy. Sometimes I get downright angry—at my own powerlessness rather than at others.

In this bureaucratic state entity in which I now work, I follow the rules rather than make them. The rules with respect to my interpreting situation during the first four years I taught at ASU stated that my secretary, whom

I shared with other professors, served as my interpreter, and when my secretary was on break, at lunch, on vacation, or sick, or when she had chosen to work on a nine-day-on, one-day-off schedule and was taking her tenth day off, a backup secretary (call her Ann) performed the interpreting function.

Understandably, my interpreting needs were not of primary concern to Ann, who is already underpaid and has obligations to the professors for whom she normally works. Never was that more apparent than the day I received a long distance phone call at 4:00 P.M. when my secretary was out of the office. A third secretary in the law school's secretarial pool (call her Carol) answered the phone and came into my office to tell me about the call. I badly needed to speak to the caller—we'd been playing telephone tag for several days. I asked that the call be interpreted by Ann, in her capacity as backup interpreter. When after a few minutes Ann did not come into my office to interpret, I was puzzled. I walked into the secretarial office to see what the problem was. Apologetically, Carol explained that Ann was getting ready to leave at 4:15 and since the call might carry over past the time her ride would be waiting for her, she wouldn't interpret the call. Telephone tag would have to resume.

At first I was furious at Ann. She didn't have to leave for another fifteen minutes, after all. But that soon passed. Ann is a nice person, and my phone calls *do* sometimes last more than fifteen minutes. My greater fury, the lasting fury, was at myself, at my own powerlessness, helplessness. I hate being at the mercy of other people's schedules or whims when I need to do something as essential as answer a phone call.

Now I have my own secretary/interpreter, and an answering machine that takes messages when she's away from her desk. Better, but still frustrating, because when she's not there I still watch the phone ring without being able to answer it. There's no solution for that one. (I'm fortunate, however, that the staff at ASU is quite gracious about helping out in any way they can. Someone is always willing to listen to my phone messages for me.)

THE FEEL OF SILENCE

Anger lives within me. It festers and festers, but only rarely do I let it erupt. When I do, it erupts at inconsequential things. Never at the thing that lies at the red heat of my anger. Never at my deafness.

At some point in our adult lives, most deaf people live with anger, whether justifiable or not. It is a never ending part of us. Some deaf people anger at sometimes sanctimonious hearing people who refuse to take the time to understand, who don't care to take the time to understand. Some deaf people anger at barriers placed in front of us by sometimes insensitive hearing people. I, however, anger at *myself*, at my own impotency in the midst of hearing society.

We deaf people live in houses without exists. When hearing people begin to develop knowledge and understanding of our deafness, a trail could meander out of the maze in which we live. If the trail doesn't fizzle out onto another dead-end path, as good intentions sometimes do, our anger should begin to fade. I'm ready and waiting for that to happen.

Chapter
TWENTY-ONE

I think I made the right choice in deciding to become a law professor. One thing teaching has done is to allow me the time to become a scholar on the rights of people with disabilities. I am becoming nationally known as an expert on that subject, and I give frequent talks around the country on the various federal laws and related matters. Not only do I enjoy this work immensely, but I feel it is important for people with disabilities everywhere, and for myself as one of them.

It has taken me a long time to accept myself as a member of that population—the "disabled." I have spent more of my life denying my deafness than acknowledging it. And even acknowledgment does not equal acceptance. One conference I attended as a guest speaker stands out as instrumental in that eventual acceptance.

I once gave a talk about the Americans with Disabilities Act at a conference for people involved in disability studies, and about a third of the attendees were disabled. Many were in wheelchairs—some were paraplegics or quadriplegics; a few were able to walk but had no use of their arms or hands. Some had no arms or had physical deformities resulting from cerebral palsy, other muscular diseases, or rheumatoid arthritis. Many were tiny, frail, thin people hooked up to oxygen tanks, struggling to breathe. Several had multiple disabilities. Sitting amidst a group of those people after the conference presentations had ended for the day, I was very uncomfortable. And I was careful to distinguish myself from them in my mind.

I was reminded of those early speech lessons, and the boy, Ethan, with cerebral palsy. He had so repulsed me as a child that I now felt ashamed. Sure, we grow up and our perceptions change, but we shouldn't fool ourselves into believing we really change. Even at this conference, as a professional woman just over fifty, I reassured myself, "You're not like *them*. You don't belong here, really, other than as a lawyer giving a presentation." As I told myself this, I felt better.

But then the conversation got lively. And those badly "disabled" people bantered back and forth, thoroughly enjoying what appeared to be a scintillating discussion. About what I do not know, because I, of course, was not able to follow the conversation.

Who's really the disabled person here? I wondered, as I tumbled down from my high horse.

O n more than one occasion I've found the struggle to assist people with disabilities overwhelming, never more than the time I agreed to help my friend Dolph—with whom I had worked at Brown and Bain—try a case involving a deaf child.

After I began teaching law full-time, I basically resigned from the active practice of law and went on inactive status with the various state bar associations of which I was a member (primarily to save on bar fees, which are quite high). While I get frequent calls from people asking me to handle cases, usually I limit my assistance to providing advice and informal help to individuals and their attorneys, filing amicus curiae (friend of the court) briefs, and the like. Shortly after Dolph took a position as head of a Native American advocacy project, however, he was asked to assist a Native American family who sought to compel the state of Arizona to educate their deaf son in his local school district with the assistance of necessary support services, including a sign language interpreter and sign language instruction. Since Dolph was not familiar with the law in this area, I initially agreed to assist him by providing advice and guidance and helping with research and the writing of briefs. When the federal judge ordered a full hearing in the case on less than twenty-four hours' notice, however, Dolph was desperate, and I had no choice but to join him as counsel of record and participate fully.

I updated my Arizona bar membership to active status and found myself in federal court, seated at the plaintiffs' table next to Dolph. At the defendants' table were our adversaries, lawyers for the state of Arizona and an Arizona school district. Seated right behind us were a gentle Native American couple and their son, a twelve-year-old boy with liquid brown eyes whom I shall call Tommy, who was the reason we were all in court to begin with.

The case was simple, really. The state of Arizona wanted Tommy's family to send him to live at the state school for the deaf and blind, almost four hundred miles away from his family and his Native American community. Tommy's family refused to institutionalize him and sought to exercise what they (and we) believed to be their constitutional and statutory rights (the latter under the Individuals with Disabilities Education Act, called the IDEA) to keep their child in their home on the reservation and to send him to the local school. Tommy's family felt that his family ties and Native American culture were of paramount importance.

Tommy was very close to his family; he hunted and fished with his father, uncles, and cousins; he watched his grandmother, a tribal court judge, perform her job; he had a close relationship with his mother. He did not want to leave either his family or his reservation. And Tommy's parents wanted to be the primary caregivers for Tommy; they did not want the state of Arizona to assume that obligation. They wanted to be the ones to tuck Tommy into bed each evening, to supervise his social and religious life, and so forth. The family thus refused to agree to send Tommy away from home. Consequently, Tommy's parents had no choice but to file a lawsuit asking the court to require the local school to educate Tommy.

On behalf of Tommy's family, we asked the court to order the state of Arizona to provide Tommy with an appropriate education in his local school district on the reservation. For Tommy an appropriate education would require provision of sign language instruction and a sign language interpreter, as well as tutorial assistance. We offered testimony of several educators who explained that they teach deaf children in their local school districts using sign language interpretation and other assistance, and who opined that the same method would be appropriate for Tommy. The state of Arizona offered testimony of Deaf culture representatives and officials from the state school for the deaf and blind, who stated that Tommy needs to be immersed in a completely Deaf environment until he is twenty-two years of age.

The court was obviously entranced with the issue of Deaf culture, and intrigued with the testimony of a Deaf witness who, through an American Sign Language interpreter, talked of the need for Tommy to be immersed in a Deaf world. When we tried to point out that many deaf people, like me, live successful lives in the mainstream, the court opined that I was an exception, and that other deaf people could not do the same. (I wondered how the hundreds of deaf people I know who live in a manner similar to mine would react to that statement and was sorry there was no opportunity to introduce the court to those people.) I spent many sleepless nights agonizing over the misperceptions the public, including that court, has about the capabilities of deaf people. (The court, for example, made the astonishing comment that deaf people cannot learn to read if they do not first learn to sign—my situation, again, was an exception. If given enough time I could have brought untold numbers of witnesses into the courtroom to testify to the contrary. The issue was irrelevant to our case, however, since everyone involved, including myself, strongly agreed that sign language was the proper communication mode for Tommy.)

The court ultimately ruled in favor of the state of Arizona and held that the state did not have to educate Tommy in his local school, but that the appropriate educational environment for Tommy is residential placement at the state school for the deaf and blind, four hundred miles from his family. At present, since Tommy's family cannot be forced to institutionalize him, Tommy is at home with his family, receiving only such education as his father is able to provide. (I can imagine how ostracized Tommy must feel being prohibited from attending the local school. His parents say he cries about not being able to go to school with his friends.)

This case is a real tragedy. It is a tragedy when parents are told that they may not choose to keep their child at home and have him be educated in the mainstream of society, but that, simply because their child is deaf, they must institutionalize him if they want him to receive the "free appropriate public education" to which he is entitled under the law (the IDEA). It makes me ashamed to be a part of our legal system. Justice does not always prevail.

THE FEEL OF SILENCE

During the past four years, when we have discussed what is known as the doctrine of "adequate provocation" in my criminal law class, I've learned a lot about the ability to empathize. The issue with respect to this doctrine is whether a defendant was provoked to kill. Legally, the question is whether a reasonable person in the circumstances would suffer extreme mental or emotional distress, and thus a momentary loss of judgment. In such cases, it is deemed appropriate to reduce the killer's crime from murder to manslaughter.

Examples of adequate provocation include situations in which one sees one's spouse making love with another person or one learns one's child has been harshly mistreated by an adult. While reasonable people in such situations would *not* kill, they might suffer extreme mental or emotional distress; they might be momentarily *tempted* to harm.

In my criminal law class we go through a series of hypotheticals designed to show the students how subjective this test is. I ask the students to pretend they are members of a jury, charged with responsibility to determine whether the defendant was adequately provoked in a given situation. Some students will say the defendant was adequately provoked in that situation; others will say the defendant was not. In most cases the vote is pretty evenly divided.

For the past four years I have given the class the following hypothetical:

> Suppose a deaf man is sitting in the park feeding the ducks in the lake. A woman comes up to him and asks why he has been rudely ignoring her. The woman has been sitting behind the man talking to him and he did not respond. He explains that he is deaf, and he

apologizes for not hearing her. The woman then goes off on a tirade about handicapped people and rages about how handicapped people should stay at home and not taint society. She makes several insulting remarks about handicapped people, including deaf and dumb people. The man pushes her in the lake and she drowns.

Was the man adequately provoked so as to give reason to reduce the crime of homicide for which the man is convicted? The issue in legal terms is: Would a reasonable person in this man's situation have been provoked (i.e., suffered extreme mental or emotional distress) under the circumstances? (Remember, the test is *not*, Would a reasonable man have killed?)

For the past four years an overwhelming majority of the students have said, "No, a reasonable person would not have been provoked—suffered extreme mental or emotional distress—in that situation."

As a deaf person, I would vote differently. I consider myself a reasonable person, but I might easily suffer extreme emotional distress in that situation. And all of the deaf people to whom I have posed the same hypothetical have said that they, too, would suffer extreme emotional distress in that situation.

Last year I asked my students why they had not found adequate provocation in that situation, although they *had* found adequate provocation in the hypothetical involving a man who had been taunted about having a sexual problem. They replied, "Oh, well, the deaf man just has to learn to shrug those things off," and "He should have been used to that kind of thing."

I guess empathy bears no relationship to intelligence.

In my judicial remedies class we discussed two cases in the casebook in which deaf children sued doctors for negligence for "wrongful life." In each case the doctor had negligently failed to inform the child's parents of facts that might cause the child to be born deaf. In one case the mother contracted German measles during the first trimester of her pregnancy. The doctor failed to inform the parents that, because of the German measles, it was likely their baby would be born with some disability, particularly deafness. In the second case the doctor performed an amniocentesis and gave the parents incorrect information. In both cases the parents maintained that, had the doctors warned them of the high risk that their children would be disabled, they would have aborted the pregnancies. Consequently, in both cases the children (through guardians) sued the doctors for damages for pain and suffering they would incur during a lifetime of deafness. The issue in both cases was whether the children had judicially cognizable claims.

It was interesting and frustrating to listen to the comments of my law students. Underlying those comments was a common theme: "What's the big deal? Deaf people live perfectly normal lives. What's so terrible about being deaf?"

My interpreter at that time had been a professional sign language interpreter before coming to work for me as an oral interpreter/secretary. Having had much experience with deafness, he was appalled. After the class he came into my office, very upset.

"How do you do it?" he whispered. "How do you stand it?"

He went on to say that he'd wanted to scream at those students, to rant and rave about how horribly frustrating deafness is, how every part of life is adversely affected. "The world is geared for hearing people, not deaf people; how can they be so ignorant?" he said.

I shared his feelings, of course. But my role was to serve as a law professor, to examine the cases from a judicial remedies viewpoint, not from my own point of view as a deaf person. It was not my place to educate the students about the frustrations of deafness.

What should I do in the following type of situation?

I was a featured speaker at a national conference attended by approximately seven hundred lawyers and educators who specialize in the education of children with disabilities. The conference was sponsored by the largest publisher of books relating to disability issues—who also publishes my legal treatise. The company had recently begun publishing a national disability rights legal reporter, and both my coauthor and I had agreed to be editors. The publisher, and the lead editor of the new reporter, arranged to take all the new editors out to dinner.

I was looking forward to that dinner. I wanted to meet the other editors, and also to talk to the publisher and the managing editor of the new reporter. The company picked a great restaurant—one of the nicest in Phoenix. But it was dark, with only dim candles to cast shadows on the tables. And the twelve of us were seated at a long table, six on one side, six on the other (there was no room for seats at the ends of the tables). I was seated at the very end of one side. Only two people were within lip-reading view—the person directly opposite me and the person immediately next to me. Given more light I could have lip-read those two people. Without it, however, even that was a hit-or-miss proposition. I smiled and said to one of the three company employees, "Oh, boy—this will be impossible." She responded, "I guess you are going to be our silent partner tonight, huh?" "I guess so," I answered politely.

My insides were churning. I was insulted and incensed at the thoughtlessness of these publishers of disability-related books. I silently pondered the situation. It had been a very long day. I'd given a lengthy presentation to two hundred people and had spent hours talking (via intense lipreading) with others. I was tired, and in no mood to sit there and fidget for three hours. As I saw it, I had four choices. (1) I could explain that the setting made it impossible for me to participate, say I looked forward to talking to all of them tomorrow, and leave politely. (2) I could feign illness and leave politely. (3) I could express my anger and leave impolitely. Or, (4) I could grin and bear it. (Requesting additional light would not have solved the problem. The restaurant was *dark*. Short of turning on the ceiling lights in the entire room and destroying the ambiance, no light could have helped.)

Put yourself in that seat in my place. What should I have done?

I stayed. Partly because I knew that if I left I would embarrass my coauthor and copresenter, who was also at the dinner as a new editor of the reporter, and I would embarrass the editor of our treatise, one of the three company employees at the dinner, who had become a friend of both of us. Members of the "Deaf rights" groups would have tarred and feathered me.

Did I do the right thing? I still can't decide. But I took a giant step. I actually *thought* about leaving. I've never consciously entertained that thought before. The times they are a-changin'! Are they changing in the right direction, or not?

When the public accommodation section of the Americans with Disabilities Act went into effect in January 1992, theater owners incurred an obligation to provide interpreters for deaf persons who wish to attend theater performances. I was thrilled at the idea of being able to attend and understand a play for the first time in my life. When Tommy Tune came to Tempe, Arizona, to star in *Bye-Bye, Birdie*, my opportunity arose.

I had given my mother two season tickets to the plays at a major theater in Tempe for her birthday. When Mother's guest had to cancel her date to see *Bye-Bye, Birdie*, I suggested that I join Mother at the play, providing the theater manager complied with my request to provide an oral interpreter. Mother thought it was a great idea. And the theater personnel were extremely cooperative. They not only agreed to provide the interpreter but, since this would be a first for both of us, requested that I come to the theater and help them figure where to seat the interpreter and how to place some light on the interpreter's mouth so that I could read her lips and yet others in the audience would not be disturbed. We worked out the logistics of the situation to everyone's satisfaction with no problem.

I told Mother about the extreme courtesy of the theater personnel and filled her in on the various possible arrangements for placing an interpreter in future shows. Suddenly, it became apparent to Mother that in some circumstances an interpreter would be taking a seat in the theater that could otherwise be used by a paying customer. She was appalled.

"You mean the theater would be required to give up a seat for free under that law?" she asked.

"Yes, if that was the only practical way to place the interpreter," I replied. (In my case, however, that was not the arrangement; the interpreter sat in an aisle.)

"But that's not a fair law," Mother exclaimed, shocked. "Why should the theater have to do that and lose the price of a seat?"

I struggled to respond. "Well, Mom," I began, "that's the basic premise of the law: that owners and operators of places of public accommodation should incur the expense of accommodating people with disabilities as part of the total cost of doing business." And then I stopped, frustrated. If someone with a deaf husband and two deaf children didn't understand, is it any wonder that the general public has a difficult time understanding?

Chapter
TWENTY-TWO

If anything has been the mainstay of my life, it has been my family. During my adulthood, I developed closer relationships with my brothers, Jim and Richard, and Jim's wife, Joyce. Jim lives in North Carolina, and Richard in Long Island, and with all the traveling I do, I manage to stop in and see each of them and their families infrequently. Jim and I play tennis, enjoy eating out (he reviews restaurants, sometimes for magazines, and is himself a gourmet cook), taking his boat out on a neighboring lake, or just sitting around taking it easy. Joyce and I are both craft buffs. We have twice spent three days driving around the Blue Ridge Mountains visiting craft boutiques and the remote homes of potters. Another time, Jim, Joyce and I, and my parents all vacationed in Vancouver. Jim travels a lot on business—he's the president of Integrated Silicon Systems—so he often stops in Phoenix, sometimes with Joyce, and we occasionally meet in other states.

With Richard and his children I have spent occasional long weekends. He doesn't fly, so I see him less often than I see Jim, but one of these winters Richard and I plan to spend a long skiing weekend together. Yep, I still ski, and I haven't caused a serious accident yet.

Three or four years ago I went with my parents to Montreal and Quebec. We visited my father's sister, my aunt Fernande, and her daughter, my cousin Carole—whose family speaks French at home. It was great fun and brought back memories of the summer I spent with my grandparents, and my inability to master French.

During the last few years I've also sustained friendships with a group of deaf women who live all over the country. Of the seven who took that memorable raft trip down the Colorado River and hiked out the Grand Canyon, four of us hiked Havasupai Canyon the next year with the addition of one of my hearing friends, Rosanne. We let Rosanne come along because she had written a beautiful and moving piece about Havasupai that had been the lead article in an issue of *Arizona Highways*. The following summer eight deaf women—some from the original group of seven plus a couple others—rented a houseboat on Lake Powell for five days. At night we all sat around with our wine and watched the sun set. Over dinner we talked about crazy topics. Do deaf men or hearing men make better lovers? We'd compare notes. We'll keep our findings to ourselves. (That reminds me, however, of some comments I received on early drafts of this book. More than one reviewer suggested I include some X-rated scenes. "If you want to sell this book, Bonnie, you've got to make it sexy. You need to include a chapter on the sex lives of deaf people." As if they were unique.)

I take frequent trips with hearing friends, as well. And on those trips, too, my deafness sometimes brings chagrin or amusement. Once, on a four-day trip with my hearing friend Sandy, the choice of entertainment at the remote cabin we stayed in one night on the outskirts of the Grand Canyon was basic Western: horseback riding, tossing horseshoes, or skeet shooting. I opted for the skeet shooting, since it was a sport I had never seen before.

I stood on the fringe of the crowd and watched as one person after another took a turn shooting. Finally there was no one left to try but me. Gamely I held the gun and waited for the skeet to be ejected into the air so I could shoot it. I waited. And waited. And waited. Nothing appeared for me to shoot. After an interminable time I looked at the crowd. Were they playing a joke on me?

As I stared at the crowd the crowd stared at me—and appeared to be shouting. What in God's name were they saying? It looked like "bull." I agreed—this was bull. But no, one woman was making a pulling motion with her hands. "He's waiting for you to shout 'pull' so he can eject the skeet," she yelled with an exasperated look.

Was she kidding? I decided it was worth a try.

"Pull," I yelled. And a skeet appeared in the air above me. I shot and missed. And yelled "Pull!" again. And shot and missed. I could not stop thinking about what an idiot I must have looked. How could I have watched a dozen or so people shooting skeet and not seen them yell "Pull"? I had looked at their bodies and not at their lips.

I usually take at least a couple of ski trips each winter and at least one trip in the summer with my hearing friends. A few summers ago my friend Brenda and I spent a couple of weeks in Scotland and Wales. This summer I plan to take a bicycle tour with another hearing friend, Sue. My friend Sandy and I (a different Sandy this time; I have three good hearing friends named Sandy) try to spend a long weekend in San Francisco every year; this year we also hope to get to Cabo San Lucas for a few days. And I have several women friends that I get together with for dinner or drinks or just to visit, especially Rosanne and Maxine. Life is full and busy.

Among all the people I spend time with, however, one of my best friends is my daughter, Ronale. Although she lives near San Diego, where she is managing editor of *Fitness Management* magazine and a graduate student in communications, we see each other frequently. She and I ski to-gether a couple of times a year and frequently spend weekends together. And, of course, we spend holidays together. Ronale and I talk on the TTY frequently.

My son Kevin eventually returned to Phoenix to practice law. Though he enjoyed working at Skadden Arps, he didn't like living in the D.C. area—he missed Arizona. So I now see him and his wife, Heidi, and their four children quite often. Often I take the children out for the day, or we all go on trips. Aubreigh is nine, Amber seven, Austin almost three, and Ashlyn a year old. I find my grandchildren immensely enjoyable, in the same way my own children were for me. I enjoy their laughter, their inno-cence, the freshness of their childish perspectives. We are good friends, and they, like my own children, accept my deafness as a matter of course. Though, since they don't live with me on a daily basis, they see it as more of a novelty sometimes.

My youngest son, Scott, recently graduated from college with a near perfect GPA (once he finally decided to do it—later than most people do—he did it quite well) and is in a master's program in international relations while working as an assistant to a professor (a sort of fellowship). He's in the process of applying to Ph.D. programs in foreign policy.

My children and I get together as a group sometimes. Two years ago Kevin and Heidi, Ronale and Mike and I spent three days hiking Havasu-pai Canyon, that incredibly beautiful land of the "people of the blue wa-ters" (to quote the title of the book by Flora Iliff). Mike's cousin Nancy and her husband joined us. Scott, unfortunately, was in Europe. Last year all of us except Heidi (who was seven months pregnant), including Scott and his girlfriend, hiked the Grand Canyon from rim to rim (twenty-six miles down the north rim and up the south rim) and stayed overnight at Phantom Ranch. This was the second time Scott and I have hiked the Grand Canyon. A few years ago the two of us rafted the bottom half of the Colorado River on small paddle boats—through the Class 10 rapids—with a group of other people.

My parents and I are good friends too, and often do things together. Two winters ago they, Ronale and Mike and I spent a week in Breckenridge, Col-orado, sharing a condo owned by my old Brown and Bain secretary, and now friend, Sue. We had a great time. Though my parents don't ski, we took them snowmobiling up to the Continental Divide, and we all went on a dogsled ride one day. This year we all spent time together in Victoria, British Columbia, where my parents go to escape the Arizona summers.

Over the years since my divorce I've dated a few men and even lived with one special man, Dan, for a year and a half while I was in Colorado. But, as I said before, marriage doesn't interest me. And in many respects I find the dating game unpleasant and very difficult as a deaf person. Darkness and the inability to use the telephone make it all so complicated. It no longer seems worth the effort. I don't feel there's anything missing in my life. I'm happy with things the way they are. Family and friends play a large part in my life. That's enough for me.

As for Bob, although I still find his response to my deafness callous, I've grown and learned myself and can sometimes see him in a more sympathetic light. I remember asking him once after we were divorced, "If you marry again, and your wife is in a terrible accident and becomes paralyzed, would you leave her?" "Yes," he said, without flinching, "definitely." He went on to explain: "Of course I'd feel badly for her, but it wouldn't be *my* disability, so there would be no reason for *me* to live with it." At the time I thought this terribly selfish.

Then, two summers ago I spent a lot of time with deaf people. I traveled with two different deaf people for two weeks at a time. I sometimes had to repeat what I said two or three times before either of those people understood. And sometimes they *thought* they'd understood and would respond to me, but the responses evidenced that they hadn't understood what I'd said. For example:

> Me: Where did you get the stamps?
> Deaf friend: Yes, I have some stamps.
> Me: Where did you *get* the stamps?
> Deaf friend: I have one extra.
> Me: No! Where did you *buy* the stamps?
> Deaf friend: Oh! I got them at the hotel desk.

I guess I occasionally make similar errors.

Due to the inherent difficulties of lip-reading and because their speech is sometimes hard for hearing people to decipher, some of my deaf friends have trouble at times communicating with the hearing people we come in contact with. On one trip with a deaf friend and a group of hearing people, the hearing people for the most part ignored me and my friend. One of the hearing women came up to me eventually and said, "We don't mean to be rude, but we find it almost impossible to communicate with your friend." At that woman's request I agreed to do my best to interpret my friend's speech. But it was frustrating for me to be in that role. It was even more frustrating when, after the trip, my friend expressed her resentment that I'd interpreted her speech for the hearing people who had asked me to. She felt that those hearing people should have tried harder to understand her. She also felt that I should not have interpreted her speech without first asking her permission to do so. In retrospect, I agree. I was wrong. At the time, however, my only concern was to facilitate communication. Excuses, excuses.

As much as I love my deaf friends and enjoy traveling with them, since I am used to being with hearing people I know it would take some patience on my part for me to be with them *all* the time. I imagine that some of Bob's frustrations were similar, though on a different scale. While I communicate fairly normally and do not have the typical "deaf speech," I still don't function well in a group setting, and I miss things when more than three people are present. Is it fair to blame Bob for not being able to live with that? I like to think I'm softening on this issue.

My own difficulties with deafness are put into perspective when I consider the frustrations that my brother Richard and my father have dealt with since they lost their hearing. Richard's hearing gradually deteriorated from the time he was first discovered to be severely hearing impaired at the age of thirteen, until he became almost as deaf as I am. And my father's hearing began deteriorating in his late forties or early fifties until he, too, became virtually deaf. This is, indeed, a genetic problem. (I remain hopeful, however, that the problem has ended. None of my children or grandchildren has hearing problems to date, nor does any of the children of either of my brothers.)

If I can consider any aspect of my own deafness fortunate, it might be that I never knew anything different. Rather than feeling I had something taken away from me, I never had it to begin with. I suspect that it was the gradual progression of the hearing losses of my father and brother that lay behind their refusal to "give in to their deafness." It took hours of battle on the part of my mother and me to convince both of them to use TTYs and decoders. I still have not managed to persuade either of them to acquire light systems for the doorbell and phone or to use the telephone relay services available in Arizona, where my father lives, and New York, where Richard lives. My father still refuses to use the TTY except to talk on rare instances with Richard or me; he prefers to have my mother make all phone calls. Richard reluctantly uses the TTY to call his former wife from his office and for other occasional conversations with my parents or me. He relies on his immediate family to make the bulk of his calls the same way my father relies on my mother.

I find this willingness of Richard and my father to let others take over baffling. I am such an independent soul I won't ask *anyone* to help me because of my deafness unless the situation is urgent and there is no way I can handle the matter alone. Many deaf people, to my surprise, do not feel the same way. I recall one recent incident when, during my visit with a deaf friend, she started off to a neighbor's house to ask the neighbor to call an electrician to repair a faulty light system. "Why do we need the neighbor?" I asked. "We can make the call ourselves via the relay service."

"Oh, it's so complicated," she replied. "It's easier to use a neighbor."

Not for me it wasn't. I'd die before I'd ask for help when there was a way I could handle the situation myself.

From the fights that went on around my parents' house when we tried to get my father to use the decoder that I gave him for Christmas one year, you'd have thought my mother and I were trying to murder him. It was a nightmare. "I don't need to watch TV," my father shouted at the top of his lungs as he stormed out of the house and slammed the door. This was the same willfulness I'd inherited from my father, though pointed in a different direction.

Eventually, however, he did begin to watch TV with the aid of the decoder. And once he became used to the decoder we went through the same battle all over again to convince him to rent captioned videos. Now, of course, he loves them. I've tried to show him how to use the relay service, since I worry about his inability to use the phone at all if an emergency should arise, but his reaction has been so violent I've backed down every time. I don't have the energy to go through all that again.

At first it was almost as difficult to explain to Richard that there are devices to assist him. Slowly, however, he began to make adjustments to his life-style. Knowing that he must be frustrated at his inability to use the phone in his position as a vice-president for Citibank, although he never acknowledged that frustration, on one of his rare visits to Arizona I managed to get him to my office at Brown and Bain on some pretext, where he "just happened" to watch my secretary interpret some calls for me. He didn't comment about the procedure, but a few months later I learned that he had adapted his telephone in a similar manner and had taught his secretary to interpret on the phone.

Luckily, Richard is also able to lip-read, although not quite as effectively as I do, perhaps because for so many years he relied on a combination of limited hearing and lip-reading. I remember once when Richard visited Bob and me and our three children. The children wanted to say something privately to Richard, and they spoke to him without voice, as they sometimes did to me (without my knowledge) when they didn't want to be overheard. Richard was ready to strangle them. "Hey," he exclaimed, "I'm not your mother. I can't lip-read like that. I need to hear you and lip-read you at the same time." Over the past fifteen years or so, during which time Richard has had virtually no hearing, his lip-reading skills have improved enormously.

Unfortunately, my father is not a lip-reader. His inability to hear is thus even more frustrating for him, and for the rest of us as well, especially my mother. Wearing two of the most powerful hearing aids available, my father is able to understand my mother and other family members when we are in a quiet room without any background noise to interfere and speak directly to him. Other than that, he is basically unable to understand what others are saying. In the past ten years I have watched my naturally gregarious father suffer from that exclusion. With a sad expression on his face my father said to me a few years ago, "Now I understand what you have had to go through all of your life."

Please God, I never wanted understanding at this price.

Watching my father endure this infringement of his autonomy for the past few years has not been a pretty scene. Unwittingly he sometimes talks at the top of his lungs—and his lungs have enormous power. "*Stop* shouting," my mother snaps. I can see him screaming even louder—the muscles in his neck are bulging. "If you say that to me once more I'm walking out," he bellows. The friction is so intense that normal conversation is now impossible. I see both sides. The problem is, they are both right. Or maybe, wrong.

If I have one hope for the future, it's that no one else in my family loses their hearing. We've had enough, thank you.

"Gramma," asked Aubreigh, at age four, "why didn't your ears work when you were born?"

"I don't know, honey," I replied with a shrug of my shoulders. "Fate, I guess."

"No, gramma, I know," stated Aubreigh, forcefully. "God must have made a mistake."

"A mistake?" I said.

"Of course, Gramma," said Aubreigh, in that scornful tone of voice that only a four-year-old female who knows the answer to her own question can muster. "God wouldn't have *meant* to do it, he wouldn't have *meant* to make you deaf."

Is Aubreigh right? Is there a God who just made a mistake? Is that the reason we have so many people with disabilities on this earth? Is that the reason for *all* the ills of humankind—that God made some mistakes?

Sometimes I do wonder, Why me? I am not a religious person. I don't believe in a supernatural power—a God, per se—for the very reason that a supernatural God could not make mistakes. Nor would that supernatural God deliberately make people live in some of the misery they suffer on this earth.

It has always been a puzzle to me why some of the most unhappy people, some of the people who have the greatest troubles, are often those who are the most religious, who have an unshakable belief in the power of a supreme being. How do they believe? Why do they believe? Is it because they *need* to believe in a supreme being? Because their lives on earth are so troubled that they need something to latch onto, something to give them hope—a lifeline of sorts?

How would such people answer questions like my granddaughter's?

Why didn't your ears work when you were born? Why didn't your eyes work when you were born? Why were you born to a family who lives in abysmal poverty and hopelessness? Why have several people in your family died of terrible diseases? Why do you have a hereditary disease in your family that causes the sons to be born with hemophilia? Why? Why? Why? How do they answer those questions? Do they ever ask such questions of their God? And if so, what does he answer?

THE FEEL OF SILENCE

With my grandchildren I've had to learn some lessons all over again.

When she was four, I took my eldest granddaughter to see the planetarium show at the Smithsonian Institution. We sat in complete darkness and watched the show unfold on the ceiling. Because the Smithsonian refused to caption the narrated show or to provide a script for hearing-impaired patrons, I have no idea what was said during the show, or what the show was really about. My granddaughter, however, found the show frightening. When Aubreigh told my son and daughter-in-law about the show that evening, she described this "very, very, scary, scary" show we had seen. I remarked that I couldn't see how it was scary. At that point Aubreigh turned to me with hands on hips and said very dramatically, "Well, Gramma, if *you* could have heard the words that were said, *you* would have thought it was very, very scary too."

It was Aubreigh's turn to bring something to "show and tell" at kindergarten. She chose to bring a picture of me and explain to the class that her Gramma Bonnie is "death." She told me very concisely how she explained to the class that she has to look at me when she talks. She also told the class that she wouldn't like to be "death." When I went to visit her she brought her friends home to show them her "Gramma who is death." She thinks we are both famous, and I guess at her class we are. It's nice to be famous, but must I be famous for being death? I wonder how many of those five-year-olds thought I was some kind of vampire?

My grandchildren have a whole bunch of new toys. And guess what? They all talk! Not that I've heard them talk myself, you understand. But my grandchildren assure me that the toys "reeaallly do talk, Gramma," and they faithfully try to repeat exactly what the toys say. I am overwhelmed. And while I guess I'm impressed on an intellectual level, on a more basic level I'm kind of disappointed.

Amber, at four years old, played for hours with a magic box that came with cardboard sheets, approximately eight by ten inches. One sheet dealt with science, another with math, one with animals, another with oceanography, and so forth. After inserting a chosen sheet into the box, Amber pushed a square containing the picture of her choice. The box asked a question about the picture, which apparently dealt with the subject matter of the chosen sheet. In response to the question, Amber pushed another square, and the box commented on her chosen answer.

Amber and the box had quite a conversation going. And throughout the entire conversation Amber made comments to me. "Is that right, Gramma?" "Why does it say that, Gramma?" "Isn't that funny, Gramma?" I had no idea what she was talking about. Gently I reminded her that I couldn't hear what the box said. "Oh, that's right," she nodded knowingly. And for a little while, instead of asking, she told me, very self-importantly, "It said thus and so, Gramma." Our roles were reversed, at least for a couple of minutes, until she forgot again.

Thank God I had my children before they invented talking toys! What do today's deaf mothers do?

I was babysitting for my two-year-old granddaughter one day. Sometime during the morning she kept covering her ears and saying, "Gramma, what's that loud noise?" I searched and searched and couldn't find anything that might have been making a loud noise. So I reassured her that all was well and spent the day distracting her. When Kevin came to pick up his daughter later in the day, his first words were, "My God, Mom, the smoke alarm is *blaring.*"

There's an old song about whistling when you're afraid. I used to play it on my piano. The refrain goes something like: "Make believe you're brave, / And the trick will take you far, / For you may be as brave / As you make believe you are." This make believing you're brave really works. I had a chance to try it a couple of years ago with two of my grandchildren.

We'd gone to the beach—me, Kevin, Heidi, Aubreigh, and Amber. After driving for several hours from their home in Virginia to the beach the kids were tired of the car. So Kevin and Heidi went grocery shopping, and the girls and I went out to have some dinner and walk around on the boardwalk. We had a great time for a couple of hours, and when it got dark we decided to go back to the room and use the bathroom before taking a nighttime walk along the beach with our feet in the water. We took the elevator up to our rooms on the top floor of the hotel and opened the door. We'd only been inside the rooms for about five minutes when all the lights went off in the hotel. We walked out on the balcony. The wind was blowing hard and there were no lights anywhere along the boardwalk in our line of vision. The world was pitch black.

Aubreigh and Amber were frightened. I could feel them questioning me, but it was too dark for me to see their lips. Trying to ignore my life-long terror of being deaf and blind in the darkness, I spoke as calmly as possible while reminding the girls that I couldn't hear them in the dark and reassuring them that all was okay. I was trembling, and the children could sense my fear. When I felt them begin to cry I pulled myself together. It could be hours before the lights came back on and would probably be at least another hour before Kevin and Heidi returned from having dinner after buying groceries. We couldn't sit in those dark hotel rooms with me unable to understand the kids.

I thought about having Aubreigh, who was six, call the front desk and ask for someone to come up and lead us down the stairs (having just arrived, we didn't even know where the door to the staircase was). But I couldn't see to read the instructions about how to call the front desk. More in an effort to give the children something to do than out of any real hope that we'd find the staircase, I told the children that we'd play a game. While holding hands we would try to find the staircase in the dark. No luck. But soon we came upon another balcony that, rather than overlooking the beach and pool as ours did, wound around the outside of the hotel overlooking the parking lot. Feeling like explorers, the children and I followed that balcony until we came upon an outside staircase, which we carefully climbed down until we reached the ground. In the moonlight we were able to walk around to the beach side of the hotel, where we saw that lights were shining brightly on the boardwalk about two blocks away. By then it was raining. Feeling as though we had just climbed the Matterhorn or conquered the enemy, we ran the two blocks in the pouring rain to the first ice cream parlor we hit.

"Oh boy, Gramma, that was *scary*," said Aubreigh as we sat, now in the glorious light, eating our ice cream cones. Amber solemnly nodded in agreement. "We couldn't talk to you, and that was the most scariest of all," said Amber. I laughed, but silently I agreed. And I resolved henceforth to always carry a flashlight when I was with my grandchildren, as I used to do when I was with my own children.

Chapter
TWENTY-THREE

In the spring of 1992 I gave a presentation at Cornell Law School, at a legal symposium on the Americans with Disabilities Act. During the course of my visit several of the professors and I discussed the possibility of my visiting Cornell to teach disability law. I mentioned that I liked Ithaca and Cornell, and that I would be honored to teach at the law school for a semester. Within a few weeks of my return to Phoenix I received a letter from the dean of Cornell Law School. It was an envelope I recognized; their letterhead hadn't changed much over the decades. As I opened it, I felt that same queasiness I'd felt at eighteen, when I knew to expect rejection.

"We are pleased to invite you," it began, "to join the Cornell Law School faculty as a Visiting Professor for the spring semester, 1993, to teach disability law and criminal law."

I could barely continue reading for the emotions welling up. I was going to Cornell after all. It may have taken me thirty-five years, a couple of careers, and a failed marriage to get there, but I was going to Cornell and nothing, certainly not my deafness, was going to stop me.

How glad I was that I'd chosen to live my life in the mainstream of society. There really was, as I'd known, a big world out there. And I was, as I'd planned, taking part in it.

Not that I expect the problems to disappear. If anything, they seem to multiply. Last semester I taught disability law as a visiting professor of law at Monash University College of Law in Melbourne, Australia. The Australian accents (not to mention the accents of students from other countries) were horrendous to lip-read. And the interpreting situation was fraught with frustration. My friend Maxine came to interpret, and she had her own problems understanding the Australian accents. But we worked it out, as most things get worked out, and the Australians, Maxine, and I got along famously in that breathtakingly beautiful country. In addition to teaching, I gave about twenty presentations throughout Australia and wrote several articles for legal publications and publications for parents of deaf children. And Maxine and I did a lot of traveling. All in all, it was a great adventure. I look forward to others like it.

epilogue

My life has been dominated by one burning desire—to fit into the hearing world. To learn to communicate as much like hearing people as physically possible. To endure whatever was required to enable me to live within the hearing world as an equal. I have succeeded in reaching that goal to some extent. I have always communicated easily, and well, with hearing people. By most measures I have been successful.

Indeed, I succeeded so well that everyone, including myself, expected me to be able to do everything that hearing people do, without noticeable limitation. And when I could not, people became angry or annoyed at me. I got angry and annoyed at me too, since, dammit, there was no room for "couldn'ts" in my game plan.

For thirty-six years I buried my deafness in a hole so deep no one ever found it, and I would not allow *myself* to find it. About seventeen years ago, at the time my marriage dissolved, I was forced to dig it up. During the past years I've faced the hard reality that, room or not in my game plan, the "couldn'ts" and "can'ts" are very much present. It was a tremendously difficult reality to accept. But once I accepted it, finally, I stopped getting angry and annoyed with myself when the "couldn'ts" and "can'ts" crept in.

And then the trouble began. For having acknowledged the "couldn'ts" and "can'ts" at last, I expected hearing people to follow my lead and give them the same recognition. I expected sensitivity, and a minimum of acceptance and understanding. It was not there. Perhaps it is not possible for it to be there, since the paradox is that I speak, lip-read, and function so well in the hearing world that the hearing people around me are sometimes incapable of understanding that there *are* limitations in my reality. And so when I don't know someone is speaking to me, and thus don't respond, I am "not paying attention." When I miss something in a group conversation, I have "ignored the speaker," or, worse yet, failed to ask for a "repeat" of what I missed, even when I don't *know* I have missed something. When I miss something in a one-to-one conversation, I am "stupid."

Paradoxically, life in the "deaf" community is even more frustrating and irritating for me. True, hearing people who work in the field of deafness have no artificial expectations of deaf people, but some of them have no expectations at all, or minimal expectations at best. I consider myself lucky when I meet a hearing professional who works with deaf people who will speak to me as, and treat me as, an *equal*. And I have little in common with members of the Deaf cultural community.

No, I am not a "Deaf person." I am deaf, yes. But I think, and communicate, like a hearing person. I am a hearing person with limitations. I have learned, however, that it is unrealistic to expect even hearing people who know me well to recognize those limitations. Thus the paradox.

Is it possible to succeed too well, to be so successful at attaining the goal you have set that you defeat the very purpose of that goal? After all is said and done, is that real success? Or is true success having the foresight to alter your goal before you reach it only to ensure your defeat? A catch-22 situation. How does one know that success will ensure defeat until one first achieves success?

In this self-created limbo in which I live, I cannot find the happy medium. Every path I take leads to an intolerable extreme. Are there other paths in the maze, or have I truly boxed myself into a house with no exits?

My hope is that this book will forge another path—to empathy. But I'm skeptical. I sent an early draft of this manuscript to an agent for her opinion and arranged to meet with that agent in New York City after she had read the draft. During the course of our meeting the agent made a phone call about the book in my presence. After speaking with the party she had called, the agent handed me the phone, saying, "Here, you should talk to him yourself."

"I'm sorry," I replied, "I can't do that."

The agent was exasperated. "What do you mean, you can't?"

"Well, I can speak, but I can't listen," I explained.

With a sigh the agent put the telephone to her ear. In an irritated fashion she remarked to the party on the other line, "She says she can talk but not listen."

Despite having read my entire book, for the agent the reality of my deafness had not sunk in. After speaking with me in a normal fashion for a half hour, she had completely forgotten that I was deaf. Of course, awareness came shortly thereafter, and she was embarrassed. I laughed away her apology. "It happens all the time," I said.